MĪMĀṂSĀ SŪTRAS OF JAIMINI

Mīmāṃsā Sūtras of Jaimini

Translated by

MOHAN LAL SANDAL

MOTILAL BANARSIDASS PUBLISHERS
PRIVATE LIMITED • DELHI

First Edition: Delhi, 1993
Reprint: Delhi, 1999

(Text and translation taken from the Allahabad edition of 1925 with minor correction and revision)

ISBN: 81-208-1129-1

MOTILAL BANARSIDASS
41 U.A. Bungalow Road, Jawahar Nagar, Delhi 110 007
8 Mahalaxmi Chamber, Warden Road, Mumbai 400 026
120 Royapettah High Road, Mylapore, Chennai 600 004
Sanas Plaza, 1302, Baji Rao Road, Pune 411 002
16 St. Mark's Road, Bangalore 560 001
8 Camac Street, Calcutta 700 017
Ashok Rajpath, Patna 800 004
Chowk, Varanasi 221 001

PRINTED IN INDIA
BY JAINENDRA PRAKASH JAIN AT SHRI JAINENDRA PRESS,
A-45 NARAINA INDUSTRIAL AREA, PHASE I, NEW DELHI 110 028
AND PUBLISHED BY NARENDRA PRAKASH JAIN FOR
MOTILAL BANARSIDASS PUBLISHERS PRIVATE LIMITED,
BUNGALOW ROAD, DELHI 110 007

DEDICATION

हे नाथ सर्वेश्वर सर्वपूज्य,
सर्वांतरात्मन्नरराजराज ।
गृहाण संसारपते मदीयं
पुष्पोपहारं रचितंत्वदर्थं ॥ १ ॥
शांडिल्यगोत्रोद्भवब्राह्मणेन,
हारीतवंशाब्जदिवाकरेण ।
नाम्ना प्रसिद्धेन च मोहनेन,
देवप्रसादाय कृतांजलिर्ते ॥ २ ॥
जैमिनीयस्य शास्त्रस्य टीका:वहूय: कृता: पुरा ।
तासांसारांशमुद्धृत्य मयाभाषांतरं कृतम् ॥ ३ ॥
क्षितिवसुनवचंद्रे विक्रमाब्दे च देशे
सकलभुवनपूज्ये तीर्थराजे प्रयागे ।
विदितमिहपुराणं जैमिनीयं प्रसिद्धं,
तवकरकमलेऽहं प्रहूया देव रामि ॥ ४ ॥
श्रीमद्दिवोदासपिता ममासीत्,
गंगा च माता सुरलोकपूज्या ।
तातप्रभावेन करोमियत्नं,
मीमांसितुंवादरिशिष्यशास्त्रं ॥ ५ ॥
पितामदीयो 'भवमोद' ग्रामे,
स्वजन्मना भूमिमलंचकार ।
तद्वंशजा: विष्णुमुपासमाना
स्सिंहावतारं सततं भजंते ॥ ६ ॥
तातस्य पुणयेन कृतिर्मदीया,
पूर्तिंगता क्लेशयुता विशाला ।
तस्यात्मजोऽहं वहुशास्त्रवेत्ता,
तत्पादपद्मौ शिरसा नमामि ॥ ७ ॥

TRANSLATOR

PREFACE

The translation of Jaimini's *Pūrva Mīmāṁsā* is now published and placed before the learned readers. The translator knows how difficult it was to understand the Mīmāṁsā in interpreting the Vedic rituals of the ancient Aryans and is still not sure whether he has correctly explained them. It is for the public to judge it.

The Vedic rituals which were once the be-all and end-all of the Aryans have fallen into desuetude and the study of the *Pūrva Mīmāṁsā* is completely neglected.

I my old age, I took to the study of the Hindu philosophy and I found solace in it. In the course of my study, I found the Mīmāṁsā system of philosophy to be the most difficult of all. I took Dr. Ganganath Jha's translation published in the series of the *Sacred Books of the Hindus*; but the translation stops short at the end of Chap. iii. Mr. Kunte who, I am informed by Major B.D. Basu, is the brother of Dr. Anna Moreswar Kunte, the demonstrator of Anatomy, Grant Medical College, Bombay, was one of the distinguished graduates of the Bombay University and belonged to the school of Ranade and Bhandarkar. He was a school master and undertook to publish the translation and annotation of the Sūtra works of the six schools of the Hindu philosophy at the end of seventies of the last century, in his well known periodical publication called *Ṣaḍdarśanacintanikā*. This useful publication to the students of Hindu Philosophy, came to an abrupt end by the premature death of Mr. Kunte in the early eighties. His translation of the Jaimini's *Mīmāṁsā* stops short at VI.6.10. It appears that a limited number of the journal was published from Poona from time to time and was distributed amongst the subscribers. Here only one copy of it was available in the valuable library of Major B.D. Basu. I must here frankly confess that I could not have placed this translation of the *Pūrva Mīmāṁsā* but for the help I got from Mr. Kunte in understanding it. I cannot discharge the debt due to him. I have got help from several other writers in this heavy and onerous undertaking.

I must thank Major B.D. Basu the learned editor of the series of the *Sacred Books of the Hindus* for rendering me help by placing his valuable library at my disposal and making important suggestions in order to enhance the utility of the book to the readers and the subscribers of this valuable series. In a word his was the head and mine was the hand in bringing out this big work before the public.

I must also thank Mr. Ram Nagina Pande of the Allahabad Collectorate for arranging the word meanings of the Sūtras from my manuscript from chapters vii to xii and the staff of the Panini Office for the help rendered in publishing the work.

I know what shortcomings and defects there can be in a big undertaking like this and, therefore, crave the indulgence of the learned readers.

ALLAHABAD
3. 3. 25

TRANSLATOR

CONTENTS

PŪRVAMĪMĀṂSĀ

ADHYĀYA I

PĀDA 1

अथातो धर्मजिज्ञासा ॥१॥

1. Now is the enquiry of duty (*dharma*)

चोदनालक्षणोऽर्थो धर्मः ॥२॥

2. The duty is an object distinguished by a command.

तस्य निमित्तपरीष्टिः ॥३॥

3. The examination of its cause.

सत्संप्रयोगे पुरुषस्येन्द्रियाणां बुद्धिजन्म तत्प्रत्यक्षमनिमित्तं विद्यमानोपलम्भनत्वात् ॥४॥

4. The perception is the knowledge which one has by the senses coming in contact with the soul. It is not the cause of duty by reason of acquiring knowledge of the thing existing.

औत्पत्तिकस्तु शब्दास्यार्थेनसम्बन्धस्तस्य ज्ञानमुपदेशोऽव्यतिरेकश्चार्थेऽनुपलब्धे तत्प्रमाणं बादरायणस्यानपेक्षत्वात् ॥५॥

5. Certainly there is eternal connection between the word and its meaning; its knowledge is *upadeśaḥi* it is never erroneous in matters invisible; it is authoritative in the opinion of Bādarāyaṇa by reason of its not depending on others.

कर्मैके तत्र दर्शनात् ॥६॥

6. One set says that it is an action; by reason of seeing it there.

अस्थानात् ॥७॥

7. By reason of no stability.

करोतिशब्दात् ॥८॥

8. By reason of the word 'make'.

सत्त्वान्तरे च यौगपद्यात् ॥९॥

9. By reason of its being heard simultaneously by other beings.

प्रकृतिविकृत्योश्च ॥१०॥

10. And on account of the original and modified forms.

वृद्धिश्च कर्तृभूम्नाऽस्य ॥११॥

11. Its increase by reason of many persons pronouncing it.

समं तु तत्र दर्शनम् ॥१२॥

12. On the other hand there is a reasoning of equal force.

सतः परमदर्शनं विषयानागमात् ॥१३॥

13. Disappearance after once coming into existence is by reason of the object not coming into contact.

प्रयोगस्य परम् ॥१४॥

14. After the application.

आदित्त्यवद्यौगपद्यम् ॥१५॥

15. The simultaneousness is like the sun.

वर्णान्तरमविकारः ॥१६॥

16. The change of letters is not a modification.

नादबृद्धिपरा ॥१७॥

17. The increase is with reference to the increase of the tone.

नित्यस्तु स्याद्दर्शनस्य परार्थत्वात् ॥१८॥

18. On the other hand, it is eternal by the reason of its manifestation being for the sake of others.

सर्वत्र यौगपद्यात् ॥१९॥

19. By reason of the simultaneity, it produces the same effect everywhere.

संख्याभावात् ॥२०॥

20. By reason of there being no number.

अनपेक्षत्वात् ॥२१॥

21. By reason of its being non-correlative.

प्रख्याभावाच्च योगस्य ॥२२॥

22. And by reason of no manifestation of the collection of words.

लिङ्गदर्शनाच्च ॥२३॥

23. And by seeing the force of the text.

उत्पत्तौ वाऽवचनास्स्युरर्थस्यातन्निमित्तत्वात् ॥२४॥

24. It has no meaning when manifested, because the meaning does not depend upon it.

तद्भूतानां क्रियार्थेन सामाम्नायोऽर्थस्य तन्निमित्तत्वात् ॥२५॥

25. The pronunciation of the constituent parts (words) is with the object of an action, the sense being dependent upon them.

लोके सन्नियमात्प्रयोगसन्निकर्षः स्यात् ॥२६॥

26. Just as in the world you get knowledge by having the object in contact with a sense, so you have the knowledge of a sentence by reason of the arrangement of the words which it is made up of.

वेदांश्चैके सन्निकर्षं पुरुषाख्याः ॥२७॥

27. And the one party hold that the Vedas are modern being called after human names.

अनित्यदर्शनाच्च ॥२८॥

28. And by seeing transitory things (in them).

उक्तन्तु शब्दपूर्वत्वम् ॥29॥

29. On the other hand the priority of the word is already spoken of.

आख्या प्रवचनात् ॥३०॥

30. The name is on account of their explaining them.

परन्तु श्रुतिसामान्यमात्रम् ॥३१॥

31. But the Vedic words are used in a general sense only.

कृते वा विनियोगःस्यात्कर्मणस्सम्बन्धात् ॥३२॥

32. On the other hand the inducement is for the purpose of the action, because it is connected with the sacrifice.

END OF PĀDA 1

***

PĀDA 2

आम्नायस्य क्रियार्थत्वादानर्थक्यमतदर्थानां तस्मादनित्त्यमुच्यते ॥१॥

1. The Veda being for the sacrifice, the portion which is not for the sacrifice is useless; therefore it cannot be said to be eternal.

शास्त्रदृष्टविरोधाच्च ॥२॥

2. And by reason of being contrary to the religious rules and sensuous perception.

तथाफलाभावात् ॥३॥

3. By reason of the absence of that fruit.

अन्यानर्थक्यात् ॥४॥

4. And by reason of the uselessness of others.

अभागिप्रतिषेधाच्च ॥५॥

5. By prohibiting a thing which cannot form the subject of prohibition.

अनित्त्यसंयोगात् ॥६॥

6. By reason of the connection with the transitory things.

विधिनात्त्वेकवाक्यत्वात्तुत्त्यर्थेन विधीनां स्युः ॥७॥

7. They by reason of one sentence with the injunction are with the object of the praise, parts of the injunction.

तुल्यं च साम्प्रदायिकम् ॥८॥

8. And equal is the object (of *vidhi* and *arthavāda*).

अप्राप्ता चानुपपत्तिः प्रयोगे हि विरोधस्स्याच्छब्दार्थस्त्वप्रयोगभूतस्तस्मादुपपद्येत ॥९॥

9. And no proof is wanting, there is a contradiction in the sentence; but the meaning of the word is not the sentence. Therefore the utility of *arthavāda* is established.

गुणवादस्तु ॥१०॥

10. On the other hand description of quality.

रूपात्त्प्रायात् ॥११॥

11. (*Guṇavāda*) is either by the nature or by its frequent observation.

दूरभूयस्त्वात् ॥१२॥

12. By reason of the distance.

अपराधात्त्कर्त्तुश्च पुत्रदर्शनम् ॥१३॥

13. And by reason of the fault of the wife, a son is born to her husband.

आकालिकेप्सा ॥१४॥

14. Untimely desire.

विद्याप्रशंसा ॥१५॥

15. Praise of learning.

सर्वत्वमाधिकारिकम् ॥१६॥

16. Universality is an exaggeration.

फलस्य कर्मनिष्पत्तेस्तेषां लोकवत्परिमाणतः फलविशेषस्यात् ॥१७॥

17. The fruit of the accomplishment of the act is a *guṇānuvāda* just as in the world, so in the case of the Vedas the special fruit is proportionate (to the act done).

अन्त्ययोर्यथोक्तम् ॥१८॥

18. Of the last two objections the reply is said above.

विधिर्वा स्यातपूर्वत्त्वाद्वादमात्रं ह्यनर्थकम् ॥१९॥

19. On the other hand, it may be a *vidhi* by reason of securing an unseen fruit and mere *arthavāda* is to no purpose.

लोकवदिति चेत् ॥२०॥

20. If you say that it will be like the worldly transaction.

न पूर्वत्त्वात् ॥२१॥

21. Not so; by reason of knowing it before.

उक्तन्तु वाक्यशेषत्त्वम् ॥२२॥

22. On the other hand the subordinate sentence is explained.

विधिश्चानर्थकः क्वचित्तस्मात्स्तुतिः प्रतीयेत तत्सामान्यादितरेषु तथात्त्वम् ॥२३॥

23. Somewhere the *vidhi* is without any purpose, therefore it is considered a praise (eulogy); by reason of its general nature at other place it is so considered.

प्रकरणे सम्भवन्नपकर्षो न कल्प्येत विध्यानर्थक्यं हि तं प्रति ॥२४॥

24. When the content can be construed reasonably the transference should not be made; the injunction will be useless by reason of it.

विधौ च वाक्यभेदः स्यात् ॥२५॥

25. If you consider it to be a *vidhi* then there will be splitting of a sentence.

हेतुर्वा स्यादर्थवत्त्वोपपत्तिभ्याम् ॥२६॥

26. On the other hand it is a statement containing reason by virtue of the independent signification and explanation.

स्तुतिस्तु शब्दपूर्वत्त्वादचोदनाच तस्य ॥२७॥

27. On the other hand, it is only a praise; because it presupposes an injunction and it is not commandatory in itself.

व्यर्थे स्तुतिरन्याय्येति चेत् ॥२८॥

28. If you say that the reason is useless and then the eulogy is improper.

अर्थस्तु विधिशेषत्त्वाद्यथा लोके ॥२९॥

29. The causative sentence is with an object being subordinate to another *vidhi* text, just as it happens in ordinary life.

यदि च हेतुरवतिष्ठेत निर्देशात्सामान्यादिति चेदव्यवस्था विधीनां स्यात् ॥३०॥

30. And if the reason is restricted by reason of the particular statement, it is all right; if you say that by reason of the general character of it, then the injunctive passage will be usettled.

तदर्थशास्त्रात् ॥३१॥

31. By reason of the scriptures for it.

वाक्यनियमात् ॥३२॥

32. By reason of arrangement of the sentence.

बुद्धशास्त्रात् ॥३३॥

33. By reason of laying down what is known.

अविद्यमानवचनात् ॥३४॥

34. By reason of the description of that which does not exist.

अचेतनेऽर्थबन्धनात् ॥३५॥

35. By ascribing of the object to the inanimate object.

अर्थविप्रतिषेधात् ॥३६॥

36. By reason of the contrary statement on the same subject.

स्वाध्यायवद्वचनात् ॥३७॥

37. By reason of not teaching the meaning of the *mantras* which are taught.

अविज्ञेयात् ॥३८॥

38. By reason of not knowing their meaning.

अनित्यसंयोगान्मन्त्रार्थानर्थक्यम् ॥३९॥

39. The *mantras* are meaningless by reason of the mention of the transitory things.

अविशिष्टस्तु वाक्यार्थः ॥४०॥

40. On the other hand the meaning of the sentence is essential.

गुणार्थेन पुनः श्रुतिः ॥४१॥

41. The repetition is with the object of describing the quality.

परिसंख्या ॥४२॥

42. The repetition may be by way of *parisaṃkhyā.*

अर्थवादी वा ॥४३॥

43. Or it may be an *arthavāda.*

अविरुद्धं परम् ॥४४॥

44. The other is not contrary.

संप्रैषे कर्मगर्हानुपालम्भः संस्कारत्त्वात् ॥४५॥

45. In a sacrificial command, by virtue of the purification, the reproach for a sacrifice is removed.

अभिधानेऽर्थवादः ॥४६॥

46. The figurative description is by way of *arthavāda.*

गुणादप्रतिषेधः स्यात् ॥४७॥

47. There is no contradiction if you consider it as description of a *guṇa* (subordinate quality).

विद्यावचनमसंयोगात् ॥४८॥

48. Not laying down that the meaning of the Vedic *mantras* should be understood, is by reason of their connection with the Vedic sacrifice.

सतः परमविज्ञानम् ॥४९॥

49. There is ignorance of that which is beyond the existent.

उक्तश्चाऽनित्यसंयोगः ॥५०॥

50. And the mention of the transitory things is already said.

लिङ्गोपदेशश्च तदर्थवत् ॥५१॥

51. The naming by the mark is like the object of the *mantra.*

ऊहः ॥५२॥

52. Substitution.

विधिशब्दाश्च ॥५३॥

53. And the injunctive sentences.

End of Pāda 2

***

PĀDA 3

धर्मस्य शब्दमूलत्वादशब्दमनपेक्षं स्यात् ॥१॥

1. Because *dharma* depends upon the Veda and the non-Veda is therefore not acceptable.

अपि वा कर्तृसामान्यात्प्रमाणमनुमानं स्यात् ॥२॥

2. Not so; by reason of the common author, the non-Veda may also be an authority.

विरोधे त्वनपेक्ष्यं स्यादसति ह्यनुमानम् ॥३॥

3. When there is contradiction it is not to be accepted; when there is none then there is the presumption.

हेतुदर्शनाच्च ॥४॥

4. And by seeing the selfish motive.

शिष्टाकोपे विरुद्धमिति चेत् ॥५॥

5. If you say what is not contrary to the Vedas is acceptable.

न शास्त्रपरिमाणत्वात् ॥६॥

6. No, because the system has a limit.

अपि वा कारणाग्रहणे प्रयुक्तानि प्रतीयेरन् ॥७॥

7. Not so; on not accepting the system, the meaning of the words used is known.

तेष्वदर्शनाद्विरोधस्य समा विप्रतिपत्तिः स्यात् ॥८॥

8. When there is no contradiction seen amongst them there is equal doubt on both sides.

शास्त्रस्था वा तन्निमित्तत्वात् ॥९॥

9. On the other hand they should be used in the sense in which they are used in the Veda, because they derive their origin from it.

चोदितं तु प्रतीयेताऽविरोधात्प्रमाणेन ॥१०॥

10. On the other hand that which is not opposed to authority is recognized as a duty laid down.

प्रयोगशास्त्रमिति चेत् ॥११॥

11. If you say that the treatises on the sacrifice (*kalpasūtra*) are an authority.

नाऽसन्नियमात् ॥१२॥

12. No, they are not authorities because there are no accents as we find in the Veda.

अवाक्यशेषाच्च ॥१३॥

13. And by not being supplementary to any text.

सर्वत्र च प्रयोगात्सन्निधानशास्त्राच्च ॥१४॥

14. And by their applicability everywhere and their being mere compilations.

अनुमानव्यवस्थानात्तत्संयुक्तं प्रमाणं स्यात् ॥१५॥

15. Anything established by inference and adjustment is an authority.

अपि वा सर्व धर्मः स्यात्तन्न्यायत्वाद्विधानस्य ॥१६॥

16. No, it is a universal duty because of the validity of the duty laid down.

दर्शनाद्विनियोगः स्यात् ॥१७॥

17. By reason of seeing (them in the Vedas), their applicability is (justified).

लिङ्गाभावाच्च नित्यस्य ॥१८॥

18. And by reason of the absence of the marks of the eternal.

आख्या हि देशसंयोगात् ॥१९॥

19. Because the name by reason of the connection with country.

न स्याद्देशान्तरेष्विति चेत् ॥२०॥

20. If you say that such local practice may not be in the foreign country.

स्याद्योगाख्या हि माथुरवत् ॥२१॥

21. The compound name is like the name of a Māthura man.

कर्मधर्मो वा प्रवणवत् ॥२२॥

22. No, the practice varies just as the sloping ground in (*vaiśvadeva*).

तुल्यं तु कर्तृधर्मेण ॥२३॥

23. On the other hand it is equal or analogous to the qualities of the agent.

प्रयोगोत्पत्त्यशास्त्रत्वाच्छब्देषु न व्यवस्था स्यात् ॥२४॥

24. There being no system as to the applicability and the origin of words, there is no rule as to words.

शब्दे प्रयत्ननिष्पत्तेरपराधस्य भागित्त्वम् ॥२५॥

25. On account of the effort in pronouncing a word, there is partaking of the mistake or mispronunciation.

अन्यायश्चानेकशब्दत्त्वम् ॥२६॥

26. It is improper to have several words for an idea.

तत्र तत्त्वमभियोगविशेषात्स्यात् ॥२७॥

27. On that subject correct form can be known from special dissertations.

तदशक्तिश्चानुरूपत्वात् ॥२८॥

28. And by reason of the similar forms, their incapacity (to signify the meaning).

एक देशत्वाच्च विभक्तिव्यत्यये स्यात् ॥२९॥

29. And in the forms of declensions being parts of the original, they convey sense.

प्रयोगचोदनाभावादर्थैकत्वमविभागात् ॥३०॥

30. By reason of the direction as to action there is the unity of sense, because there is no distinction.

अद्रव्यशब्दत्वात् ॥३१॥

31. Because the word does not apply to a substance.

अन्यदर्शनाच्च ॥३२॥

32. By seeing another.

आकृतिस्तु क्रियार्थत्वात् ॥३३॥

33. It is form by reason of its having an action for its object.

न क्रिया स्यादिति चेदर्थान्तरे विधानं न द्रव्यमिति चेत् ॥३४॥

34. If you say "no action is possible"; in the substitution of another object "there is not a substance" if you say.

तदर्थत्वात्प्रयोगस्याविभागः ॥३५॥

35. By reason of the word conveying a form, the performance of the act is undivided.

END OF PĀDA 3

***

PĀDA 4

उक्तं समाम्नायैदमर्थ्यं तस्मात्सर्वं तदर्थं स्यात् ॥१॥

1. It is said that the object of the Veda is sacrifice; therefore all is for that object.

अपि वा नामधेयं स्याद्यदुत्पत्तावपूर्वमविधायकत्वात् ॥२॥

2. Not so, it is a name; it is a new thing in its origin not known before, by reason of its being not injunctive.

यस्मिन्गुणोपदेशः प्रधानतोऽभिसम्बन्धः ॥३॥

3. Where there is the description of a quality it is connected with the principal.

तत्प्रख्यञ्चान्यशास्त्रम् ॥४॥

4. It is known by that name, but the description is in another book.

तद्व्यपदेशं च ॥५॥

5. And the resemblance with that.

नामधेये गुणश्रुतेः स्याद्विधानमिति चेत् ॥६॥

6. If you say that in a name there is the mention of the quality.

तुल्यत्वात्क्रिययोर्न ॥७॥

7. Not so by reason of the similarity of the acts.

ऐकशब्द्ये परार्थवत् ॥८॥

8. By reason of dependence on another, in one word (two things are meant).

तद्गुणास्तु विधीयेरन्नविभागाद्विधानार्थे न चेदन्येन शिष्टाः ॥९॥

9. On the other hand the action and its qualities are laid down because they can be separated for the purpose of laying down; otherwise the qualities will be known by another.

बर्हिराज्ययोरसंस्कारे शब्दलाभादतच्छब्दः ॥१०॥

10. The use of the terms of grass and ghee in consecrated things does not convey the meaning of consecrated things.

प्रोक्षणीष्वर्थसंयोगात् ॥११॥

11. In the terms *prokṣaṇī* &c. by reason of the meaning of the component parts.

तथानिर्मन्थ्ये ॥१२॥

12. Similarly *nirmanthya.*

वैश्वदेवे विकल्प इति चेत् ॥१३॥

13. If you say that there is option in the term *vaiśvadeva.*

न वा प्रकरणात्प्रत्यक्षविधानाच्च न हि प्रकरणं द्रव्यस्य ॥१४॥

14. Not so, by reason of the context and the direct statement because a context cannot override a statement.

मिथश्चानर्थसम्बन्धः ॥१५॥

15. If you break the component parts there will be meaninglessness.

परार्थत्वाद्गुणानाम् ॥१६॥

16. The qualities being subservient to another.

पूर्ववन्तोऽविधानार्थास्तत्सामर्थ्यं समाम्नाये ॥१७॥

17. What is known is not a *vidhi*; its force is in the Vedas.

गुणस्य तु विधानार्थे तद्गुणाः प्रयोगे स्युरनर्थका न हि तं प्रत्यर्थवत्ताऽस्ति ॥१८॥

18. No, they are qualities for the *vidhi*; its qualities are meaningless in the practical application, because it has no independent signification.

तच्छेषो नोपपद्यते ॥१९॥

19. Its subsidiary is not possible.

अविभागाद्विधानार्थे स्तुत्यर्थेनोपपद्येरन् ॥२०॥

20. In the object of the *vidhi* being indivisible, they are possible as praises.

कारणं स्यादिति चेत् ॥२१॥

21. If you say that there is a reason.

आनर्थक्यादकारणं कर्तुर्हि कारणानि गुणार्थो हि विधीयते ॥२२॥

22. They are not a reason because of the meaninglessness; because the reasons pertain to the performers, therefore they are said to be only qualities.

तत्सिद्धिः ॥२३॥

23. Its accomplishment.

जातिः ॥२४॥

24. Class.

सारूप्यात् ॥२५॥

25. By reason of similarity.

प्रशंसा ॥२६॥

26. Praise.

भूमा ॥२७॥

27. A multitude.

लिङ्गसमवायात् ॥२८॥

28. By the permanent connection with the badge or symbol.

सन्दिग्धेषु वाक्यशेषात् ॥२९॥

29. In doubtful meanings by ellipsis.

अर्थाद्वा कल्पनैकदेशत्वात् ॥३०॥

30. An ellipsis is to be determined by the power of the meaning because the adjustment of sense is the part of the Veda.

END OF PĀDA 4

***

END OF ADHYĀYA I

ADHYĀYA II

PĀDA 1

भावार्थाः कर्मशब्दास्तेभ्यः क्रिया प्रतीयेतैष ह्यर्थो विधीयते ॥१॥

1. The words signifying existence are words denoting action; from them an action is known; this object is laid down.

सर्वेषां भावोऽर्थ इति चेत् ॥२॥

2. If you say that the meaning of all words is existence.

येषामुत्पत्तौ स्वे प्रयोगे रूपोपलब्धिस्तानि नामानि तस्मात्तेभ्यः पराकाङ्क्षा भूतत्वात्स्वे प्रयोगे ॥३॥

3. The words in whose origin while used, there is the perception of the form or substance are called nouns; therefore from them dependence on others is removed by reason of the existence in their use.

येषां तूत्पत्तावर्थे स्वे प्रयोगो न विद्यते तान्याख्यातानि तस्मात्तेभ्यः प्रतीयेताऽऽश्रितत्वात्प्रयोगस्य ॥४॥

4. On the other hand the words which do not have a meaning in their use, they are verbs; therefore from them is known (action) by reason of the dependence of the use.

चोदना पुनरारम्भः ॥५॥

5. There is the exciting cause and then the commencement.

तानि द्वैधं गुणप्रधानभूतानि ॥६॥

6. They are of two kinds : principal and subordinate.

यैर्द्रव्यं न चिकीर्ष्यते तानि प्रधानभूतानि द्रव्यस्य गुणभूतत्वात् ॥७॥

7. By which no substance is desired to be acted upon, they are principal because the substance is there subordinate.

यैस्तु द्रव्यं चिकीर्ष्यते गुणस्तत्र प्रतीयेत तस्य द्रव्यप्रधानत्वात् ॥८॥

8. On the other hand, by which any substance is desired to be acted upon, there subordinate act is known because of the substance being principal.

धर्ममात्रे तु कर्म स्यादनिर्वृत्तेः प्रयाजवत् ॥९॥

9. On the other hand, in all actions there is the principal act by reason of no visible effect being produced like *prayāja.*

तुल्यश्रुतित्वाद्वेतरैः सधर्मः स्यात् ॥१०॥

10. On the other hand, by reason of the similarity of declension, they are of the same class with others.

द्रव्योपदेश इति चेत् ॥११॥

11. If it be said that there is a direct mention of the material.

न तदर्थत्वाल्लोकवत्तस्य च शेषभूतत्वात् ॥१२॥

12. No; it being for the sacrifice just as in the common life; and its being subordinate.

स्तुतशस्त्रयोस्तु संस्कारो याज्यावद्देवताभिधानत्वात् ॥१३॥

13. On the other hand the poetical and prose praises are subordinate by reason of the praises of the gods.

अर्थेन त्वपकृष्येत देवतानामचोदनार्थस्य गुणभूतत्वात् ॥१४॥

14. On the other hand there will be transference by the sense because of the mention of the deities' name being subordinate.

वशावद्वा गुणार्थं स्यात् ॥१५॥

15. Or it is subordinate like a barren goat.

न श्रुतिसमवायित्वात् ॥१६॥

16. No, by reason of the affinity of the Śruti text.

व्यपदेशभेदाच्च ॥१७॥

17. And by reason of the difference of the name.

गुणश्चानर्थकः स्यात् ॥१८॥

18. And the quality will be useless.

तथा याज्यापुरोरुचोः ॥१९॥

19. Similarly of *yājyā* and *purorūca* verses.

वशायामर्थसमवायात् ॥२०॥

20. In the case of a barren goat by the affinity of the sense.

यच्चेति वाऽर्थवत्त्वात्स्यात् ॥२१॥

21. On the other hand, which (where Indra is, there is transference), by reason of its being for some purpose.

न त्वाम्नातेषु ॥२२॥

22. On the other hand, not in the Vedic matter.

दृश्यते ॥२३॥

23. Seen.

अपि वा श्रुतिसंयोगात्प्रकरणे स्तौतिशंसती क्रियोत्पत्तिं विदध्याताम् ॥२४॥

24. Not so, by reason of the connection of the Vedic text in the same context; the terms "he praises and he extols" produce invisible result.

शब्दपृथक्त्वाच्च ॥२५॥

25. And by reason of the difference of words.

अनर्थकं च तद्वचनम् ॥२६॥

26. And the Vedic texts will be useless.

अन्यश्चार्थः प्रतीयते ॥२७॥

27. And other sense is known.

अभिधानं च कर्मवत् ॥२८॥

28. And they have names like an action.

फलनिर्वृत्तिश्च ॥२९॥

29. And the accomplishment of an object.

विधिमन्त्रयोरैकार्थ्यमैकशब्द्यात् ॥३०॥

30. The Brāhmaṇa and the Saṃhitā have the same object or sense by reason of the similarity of words.

अपि वा प्रयोगसामर्थ्यान्मन्त्रो ऽभिधानवाची स्यात् ॥३१॥

31. Not so by the force of application the mantra conveys a meaning.

तच्चोदकेषु मन्त्राख्या ॥३२॥

32. The name of a mantra applies to the instigation of that.

शेषे ब्राह्मणशब्दः ॥३३॥

33. To the remainder the word *brāhmaṇa* applies.

अनाम्नातेष्वमन्त्रत्वमाम्नातेषु हि विभागः ॥३४॥

34. The definition of mantra does not apply to that which is not in *āmnāta* and the above division is applicable to *āmnāta*.

तेषामृग्यत्रार्थवशेन पादव्यवस्था ॥३५॥

35. Of those are *ṛk* where there is a metrical arrangement by sense.

गीतिषु स माख्या ॥३६॥

36. The term *sāma* applies to songs.

शेषे यजुः शब्दाः ॥३७॥

37. In the rest the term *yajuḥ.*

निगदो वाचतुर्थं स्याद्धर्मविशेषात् ॥३८॥

38. On the other hand, *nigada* is the fourth Veda by reason of the special quality.

व्यपदेशाच्च ॥३९॥

39. And by reason of the nomenclature.

यजूंषि वा तद्रूपत्वात् ॥४०॥

40. On the other hand they are *yajuḥ* by reason of having the same form.

वचनाद्धर्मविशेषः ॥४१॥

41. By reason of the special text there is a special quality.

अर्थाच्च ॥४२॥

42. And by reason of the meaning.

गुणार्थो व्यपदेशः ॥४३॥

43. The nomenclature is with the object of quality.

सर्वेषामिति चेत् ॥४४॥

44. If you say that all mantras are Nigadas.

न, ऋग्व्यपदेशात् ॥४५॥

45. Not so; by reason of having the name of *ṛk.*

अर्थैकत्वादेकं वाक्यं साकाङ्क्षं चेद्विभागे स्यात् ॥४६॥

46. By reason of the unity of sense there is one sentence; on division it is dependent.

समेषु वाक्यभेदः स्यात् ॥४७॥

47. In equal, there is a split of sentences.

अनुषङ्गो वाक्यसमाप्तिः सर्वेषु तुल्ययोगित्वात् ॥४८॥

48. *Anuṣaṅga* is a completion of a sentence by reason of the equal fitness in all.

व्यवायान्नानुषज्येत ॥४९॥

49. There is no *anuṣaṅga* by reason of intervention.

END OF PĀDA 1

***

PĀDA 2

शब्दान्तरे कर्मभेदः कृतानुबन्धत्वात् ॥१॥

1. On having a different verb, there will be a difference of extraordinary principle by reason of having different verbs.

एकस्यैवं पुनः श्रुतिरविशेषादनर्थकं हि स्यात् ॥२॥

2. Similarly the repetition of one verb produces the invisible effect; by reason of there being no distinction, there will be meaninglessness.

प्रकरणन्तु पौर्णमास्यां रूपावचनात् ॥३॥

3. On the other hand the context is in *pūrṇamāsī yāga* by reason of there being no word indicating the form.

विशेषदर्शनाच्च सर्वेषां समेषुह्यप्रवृत्तिः स्यात् ॥४॥

4. And by reason of seeing the special description, the application of the preceding sentences cannot be co-ordinate.

गुणस्तु श्रुतिसंयोगात् ॥५॥

5. On the other hand it is a quality by reason of the connection with the text.

चोदना वा गुणानां युगपच्छास्त्राच्चोदिते हि तदर्थत्वात्तस्य तस्योपदिश्येत ॥६॥

6. On the other hand it is an injunction by reason of the simultaneous description of the qualities; and being enjoined for it, it will be an injunction for each detail.

व्यपदेशश्चतद्वत् ॥७॥

7. The naming is also like that.

लिङ्गदर्शनाच्च ॥८॥

8. And by seeing the force of the text.

पौर्णमासीवदुपांशुयाजः स्यात् ॥९॥

9. Like full moon sacrifice is the *upāṃśuyāja.*

चोदना वाऽप्रकृतत्वात् ॥१०॥

10. On the other hand it is an injunction by reason of its being described elsewhere.

गुणोपबन्धात् ॥११॥

11. By reason of describing the quality.

प्राये वचनाच्च ॥१२॥

12. And frequently by the text.

आघाराग्निहोत्रमरूपत्वात् ॥१३॥

13. The *āghāra* and *agnihotra* are not independent (*samudāyānuvāda*) by reason of there being no description (of *mantra, devatā* and *sāmagrī*).

संज्ञोपबन्धात् ॥१४॥

14. By reason of having the name.

अप्रकृतत्वाच्च ॥१५॥

15. And by reason of being not mentioned elsewhere.

चोदना वा शब्दार्थस्य प्रयोगभूतत्वात्तत्सन्निधेर्गुणार्थेन पुनः श्रुतिः ॥१६॥

16. On the other hand they are injunctions by reason of the application of the sense of the words; by reason of being in proximity with the object of the description of the quality there is repetition.

द्रव्यसंयोगाच्चोदनापशुसोमयोः प्रकरणे ह्यनर्थको द्रव्यसंयोगो न हि तस्य गुणार्थेन ॥१७॥

17. The animal and Soma Sacrifices are principal by reason of the mention of the material. In the context, mention of the material is meaningless; but it is not with the object of describing the quality.

अचोदकाश्च संस्काराः ॥१८॥

18. And purificatory acts are not injunctive.

तद्भेदात्कर्मणोऽभ्यासो द्रव्यपृथक्त्वादनर्थकं हि स्याद्भेदो द्रव्यगुणीभावात् ॥१९॥

19. By reason of their (Saṃskāras) being different, there is the repetition of the sacrifice; because by reason of the material being separate, the principal act is meaningless; the difference is by reason of the materials being subordinate.

संस्कारस्तु न भिद्येत परार्थत्वाद् द्रव्यस्य गुणभूतत्वात् ॥२०॥

20. On the other hand the purificatory rite is not divided, being subservient because the material is subordinate.

पृथक्त्वनिवेशात्संख्यया कर्मभेदः स्यात् ॥२१॥

21. Because there is separateness with the enumeration, there is a difference of action.

संज्ञा चोत्पत्तिसंयोगात् ॥२२॥

22. And name by reason of the text which lays down the action.

गुणाश्चाऽपूर्वसंयोगे वाक्ययोः समत्त्वात् ॥२३॥

23. And subordinate act in connection with the mention of the *apūrva* is independent act by reason of the two sentences being co-ordinate.

अगुणे तु कर्मशब्दे गुणस्तत्र प्रतीयेत ॥२४॥

24. On the other hand when the word denoting an act does not describe a quality, a quality is known.

फलश्रुतेस्तु कर्म स्यात्फलस्य कर्मयोगित्वात् ॥२५॥

25. On the other hand by reason of the text laying down a fruit; it is an act because a fruit fits in with an act.

अतुल्यत्वात्तु वाक्ययोर्गुणेतस्य प्रतीयेत ॥२६॥

26. On the other hand by reason of the disparity of two sentences, there its quality is recognized.

समेषु कर्मयुक्तं स्यात् ॥२७॥

27. In the co-ordinate sentences, the fruit accompanies the act.

सौभरे पुरुषश्रुतेर्निधनं कामसंयोगः ॥२८॥

28. In the song called *saubhara,* there is a text laying down the effort of the human being, and in the cadence there is the mention of the desire.

सर्वस्य वोक्तकामत्वात्तस्मिन्कामश्रुतिः स्यान्निधनार्था पुनः श्रुतिः ॥२९॥

29. Or by reason of accomplishing all desires there is a text mentioning the desires and the repetition is for the purpose of a cadence.

END OF PĀDA 2

***

PĀDA 3

गुणस्तु क्रतुसंयोगात्कर्मान्तरं प्रयोजयेत्संयोगस्याशेषभूत्वात् ॥१॥

1. On the other hand the quality by reason of the mention of the sacrifice points to another independent action because the description is not dependent on any other.

एकस्य तु लिङ्गभेदात्प्रयोजनार्थमुच्येतैकत्वं गुणावाक्यत्वात् ॥२॥

2. On the other hand, of one by different syntactical signs, the purpose is described. There is unity by reason of the sentences describing the quality.

अवेष्टौ यज्ञसंयोगात्क्रतुप्रधानमुच्यते ॥३॥

3. In aveṣṭi there is the connection with the mention of yajña; it is said to be a principal *kratu.*

आधाने सर्वशेषत्वात् ॥४॥

4. By reason of its being subsidiary to the entire act, in the establishment of fire.

अयनेषु चोदनान्तरं संज्ञोपबन्धात् ॥५॥

5. By reason of the conventional naming there is separate *codanā* in the sacrifices known as *ayana.*

अगुणाच्च कर्मचोदना ॥६॥

6. And they do not describe any quality of an act, so they are independent acts.

समाप्तं च फले वाक्यम् ॥७॥

7. And in the fruit the sentence is complete.

विकारो वा प्रकरणात् ॥८॥

8. On the other hand they are modifications by reason of the context.

लिङ्गदर्शनाच्च ॥९॥

9. And by seeing the force of the text.

गुणात्संज्ञोपबन्धः ॥१०॥

10. By reason of the quality, they have the conventional name.

समाप्तिरविशिष्टा ॥११॥

11. The end is common.

संस्कारश्चाप्रकरणेऽकर्मशब्दत्वात् ॥१२॥

12. And it is a purificatory rite without a context, by reason of no word indicating action.

यावदुक्तं वा कर्मणः श्रुतिमूलत्वात् ॥१३॥

13. Or if what is said is not acceptable, by reason of the sacrifice having its origin in the Veda.

यजतिस्तु द्रव्यफलभोक्तृसंयोगादेतेषां कर्मसम्बन्धात् ॥१४॥

14. On the other hand they mean "sacrifices" by reason of the mention of the materials; reward and agents, they are connected with the principal act.

लिङ्गदर्शनाच्च ॥१५॥

15. And by seeing the force of the text.

विषये प्रायदर्शनात् ॥१६॥

16. In a doubt, by seeing the constant use of it.

अर्थवादोपपत्तेश्च ॥१७॥

17. And by reason of the proof of *arthavāda.*

संयुक्तस्त्वर्थशब्देन तदर्थः श्रुतिसंयोगात् ॥१८॥

18. On the other hand, connected with the significant word, it is with the object by reason of its being mentioned in the Veda.

पात्नीवते तु पूर्वत्वादवच्छेदः ॥१९॥

19. On the other hand, in the *pātnīvata* by reason of the preceding description, determination should be made.

अद्रव्यत्वात्केवले कर्मशेषः स्यात् ॥२०॥

20. There being no description of any material, it is subsidiary only in name.

अग्निस्तु लिङ्गदर्शनात्क्रतुशब्दः प्रतीयेत ॥२१॥

21. On the other hand, the word *agni* by reason of the force of the text indicates the soma sacrifice.

द्रव्यं वा स्याच्चोदनायास्तदर्थत्वात् ॥२२॥

22. On the other hand, it is a material by reason of the command being for it.

तत्संयोगात्क्रतुस्तदाख्यः स्यात्तेन धर्मविधानानि ॥२३॥

23. By reason of the connection with that, the sacrifice is known by that name, therefore it is a description of qualities.

प्रकरणान्तरे प्रयोजनान्यत्वम् ॥२४॥

24. In the different contexts, there are different objects.

फलं चाकर्मसन्निधौ ॥२५॥

25. And the fruit when it is not in connection with the act.

सन्निधौत्वविभागात्फलार्थेन पुनः श्रुतिः ॥२६॥

26. On the other hand, in juxtaposition by reason of indivisibility with the object of the fruit, there is the repetition.

आग्नेयसूक्तहेतुत्वादभ्यासेन प्रतीयेत ॥२७॥

27. By reason of the *āgneya sūkta,* from repetition an independent act is inferred.

अविभागात्तुकर्मणां द्विरुक्तेर्न विधीयते ॥२८॥

28. On the other hand by reason of the indivisibility of the act, no repetition is sanctioned.

अन्यार्था वा पुनः श्रुतिः ॥२९॥

29. Or the repetition is with another object.

End of Pāda 3

***

PĀDA 4

यावज्जीविकोऽभ्यासः कर्मधर्मः प्रकरणात् ॥१॥

1. It is an essential quality of the act which is to be repeated for one's life by reason of the context.

कर्तुर्वा श्रुतिसंयोगात् ॥२॥

2. Or of the agent by reason of the mention of the text.

लिङ्गदर्शनाच्च कर्मधर्म्मे हि प्रक्रमेण नियम्येत तत्रानर्थकमन्यत्स्यात् ॥३॥

3. By reason of the force of the text, if the term be restricted with the commencement of the action to the quality of the action, then other texts will be meaningless.

व्यपवर्गं च दर्शयति कालश्चेत्कर्मभेदः स्यात् ॥४॥

4. And shows the completion; if time, there is division of the action.

अनित्यत्वात्तु नैवं स्यात् ॥५॥

5. On the other hand by reason of its being not permanent, it cannot be so.

विरोधश्चापि पूर्ववत् ॥६॥

6. And there will be a contradiction as in the preceding.

कर्तुस्तु धर्मनियमात्कालशास्त्रं निमित्तं स्यात् ॥७॥

7. On the other hand by reason of the restriction of the quality of the agent, laying down of time is a cause.

नामरूपधर्मविशेषपुनरुक्तिनिन्दाऽशक्तिसमाप्तिवचनप्रायश्चित्ता-ऽन्यार्थदर्शनाच्छाखान्तरेषु कर्मभेदः स्यात् ॥८॥

8. By seeing the name, form, peculiar qualities, repetition, censure, incapacity, final sentence, penance and different objects (it appears) that there are different acts, in different recensions of the Veda.

एकं वा संयोगरूपचोदनाख्याविशेषात् ॥९॥

9. On the other hand, it is one on account of there being no distinction of the mention in the text, laying down of the procedure and the name.

न नाम्ना स्यादचोदनाभिधानत्वात् ॥१०॥

10. Not so, by the name there is no command by reason of its laying down nothing.

सर्वेषां चैककर्म्यं स्यात् ॥११॥

11. And of all, there will be the unity of action.

कृतकं चाभिधानम् ॥१२॥

12. And the name is artificial.

एकत्वेऽपि परम् ॥१३॥

13. In unity also there is diversity.

विद्यायां धर्मशास्त्रम् ॥१४॥

14. In knowledge, there are laid down the duties.

आग्नेयवत्पुनर्वचनम् ॥१५॥

15. The repetition is like *āgneyamantras.*

अद्विर्वचनं वा श्रुतिसंयोगाविशेषात् ॥१६॥

16. On the other hand, there is no tautology because the Vedic text mentions nothing special.

अर्थसन्निधेश्च ॥१७॥

17. By reason of the non-proximity of the object.

न चैकं प्रतिशिष्यते ॥१८॥

18. Nor is it restricted to one only.

समाप्तिवच्च संप्रेक्षा ॥१९॥

19. And the assertion is like the completion.

एकत्वेऽपिपराणि निन्दाशक्तिसमाप्तिवचनानि ॥२०॥

20. In the unity also there are censure, incapacity and completion of sentences.

प्रायश्चित्तं निमित्तेन ॥२१॥

21. The penance is with an object.

प्रक्रमाद्वा नियोगेन ॥२२॥

22. On the other hand by the command from the beginning.

समाप्तिः पूर्ववत्त्वाद्यथाज्ञाते प्रतीयेत ॥२३॥

23. Completion, because of the commencement, should be inferred as known.

लिङ्गमविशिष्टं सर्वशेषत्वान्न हि तत्र कर्मचोदना तस्मात्द्वादशाहस्याहारव्यपदेशः स्यात् ॥२४॥

24. A subordinate sentence is dependent by reason of its being subsidiary; because there is no injunction as to any act, therefore there is no incongruity of procedure in *dvādaśāha*.

द्रव्ये चाचोदितत्वाद्विधीनामव्यवस्था स्यान्निर्देशाद्व्यतिष्ठेत तस्मान्नित्यानुवादः स्यात् ॥२५॥

25. And the material being not enjoined the injunctions will be in confusion, by reason of its being pointed out, it is restricted; therefore it is a permanent description.

विहितप्रतिषेधात्पक्षेऽतिरेकः स्यात् ॥२६॥

26. By reason of prohibiting the enjoined, the redundancy is optional.

सारस्वते विप्रतिषेधाद्यदेति स्यात् ॥२७॥

27. In a Sārasvata offering by reason of the prohibition the term 'when' occurs.

उपहव्येऽप्रतिप्रसवः ॥२८॥

28. In the *upahavya* Soma juice, there is no counter exception.

गुणार्था वा पुनः श्रुतिः ॥२९॥

29. On the other hand the repetition is for describing the quality.

प्रत्ययं चापि दर्शयति ॥३०॥

30. And the same conviction is also conveyed.

अपि वा क्रमसंयोगाद्विधिपृथक्त्वमेकस्यां व्यवतिष्ठेत ॥३१॥

31. Or also, by reason of the connection with the orderly description, in one there should be a difference of injunction.

विरोधिना त्वसंयोगादैककर्म्ये तत्संयोगाद्विधीनां सर्वकर्मप्रत्ययः स्यात् ॥३२॥

32. On the other hand by reason of no connection with the contradiction in one action, because the injunctions are connected with it, there is a conviction that all acts are one.

END OF PĀDA 4

***

END OF ADHYĀYA II

ADHYĀYA III

PĀDA 1

अथातः शेषलक्षणम् ॥१॥

1. Now is therefore an enquiry about accessory.

शेषः परार्थत्वात् ॥२॥

2. The accessory is by reason of its being for the sake of others.

द्रव्यगुणसंस्कारेषु बादरिः ॥३॥

3. The substance, quality and purificatory acts are *śeṣa* according to Bādari.

कर्माण्यपि जैमिनिः फलार्थत्वात् ॥४॥

4. According to Jaimini actions are also included under it by reason of their being for a fruit.

फलं च पुरुषार्थत्वात् ॥५॥

5. And fruit is by reason of its being for the object of a person.

पुरुषश्च कर्मार्थत्वात् ॥६॥

6. And a person by reason of his being for an act.

तेषामर्थेन सबन्धः ॥७॥

7. Their relationship is with the purpose.

विहितस्तु सर्वधर्मः स्यात्संयोगतोऽविशेषात्प्रकरणाविशेषाच्च ॥८॥

8. All duties are sanctioned by reason of there being nothing special about the mention and there being nothing special about the context.

अर्थलोपादकर्म स्यात् ॥९॥

9. By removal of the purpose, there is no act.

फलं तु सह चेष्टया शब्दार्थोऽभावाद्विप्रयोगेस्यात् ॥१०॥

10. On the other hand the fruit accompanies the action; in case of such non-connection, the sense of the word on the principle of *abhāva.*

द्रव्यं चोत्पत्तिसंयोगात्तदर्थमेव चोद्येत ॥११॥

11. And the material by reason of its mention in the original text, is laid down for that very object.

अर्थैकत्वे द्रव्यगुणयोरैककर्म्यान्नियमः स्यात् ॥१२॥

12. The purpose of the substance and its quality being one, there is a restriction by reason of the act being one.

एकत्वयुक्तमेकस्य श्रुतिसंयोगात् ॥१३॥

13. A singular number stands for one, by reason of the mention in the Vedic text.

सर्वेषां वा लक्षणत्वादविशिष्टं हि लक्षणम् ॥१४॥

14. On the other hand, it applies to all by reason of the general description, because the general description is not specific.

चोदितेतुपरार्थत्वाद्यथाश्रुति प्रतीयेत ॥१५॥

15. On the other hand, in a command for another object, it is known as it is in the text.

संस्काराद्वागुणानामव्यवस्था स्यात् ॥१६॥

16. On the other hand by purification, there will be an irregularity in the qualities.

व्यवस्थावाऽर्थस्य श्रुतिसंयोगात्तस्य शब्द प्रमाणत्वात् ॥१७॥

17. On the other hand there is a system in the meaning by reason of the connection with the text, because it depends for its authority on the word.

आनर्थक्यात्तदंगेषु ॥१८॥

18. It is in the parts by reason of meaninglessness.

कर्तृगुणेतुकर्मासमवायाद्वाक्यभेदः स्यात् ॥१९॥

19. On the other hand in a quality of an agent, by reason of the action being not connected, there is a split of a sentence.

साकांक्षंत्वेकवाक्यं स्यादसमाप्तं हि पूर्वेण ॥२०॥

20. On the other hand, it is dependent one sentence, because it is incomplete with the preceding.

सन्दिग्धे तु व्यवायाद्वाक्यभेदः स्यात् ॥२१॥

21. In doubtful cases by reason of intervention, there is a split of sentence.

गुणानां च परार्थत्त्वादसम्बन्धः समत्वात्स्यात् ॥२२॥

22. And the qualities being subservient to others, there is no relationship *inter se* because of the equality.

मिथश्चानर्थसम्बन्धात् ॥२३॥

23. There is mutuality to avoid meaninglessness.

आनन्तर्यमचोदना ॥२४॥

24. Close juxtaposition does not lay down.

वाक्यानां च समाप्तत्वात् ॥२५॥

25. And by reason of the completion of the sentences.

शेषस्तु गुणसंयुक्तः साधारणः प्रतीयेत मिथस्तेषामसम्बन्धात् ॥२६॥

26. On the other hand, the subsidiary connected with the quality is known to be common, because amongst themselves there is no connection.

व्यवस्था वाऽर्थसंयोगाल्लिङ्गस्यार्थेनसम्बन्धाल्लक्षणार्था गुणश्रुतिः ॥२७॥

27. On the other hand there is a rule by reason of the connection with the meaning and by reason of the force of the text being connected with the meaning, the text laying down the quality is by way of figure of speech.

END OF PĀDA 1

***

PĀḌA 2

अर्थाभिधानसामर्थ्यान्मन्त्रेषु शेषभावः स्यात्तस्मादुत्पत्तिसम्बन्धोऽर्थेन नित्यसंयोगात् ॥१॥

1. There being an inherent power of meaning in the words the mantras are subsidiary; therefore there is the relationship arising from the origin with the meaning by virtue of the everlasting connection.

संस्कारकत्वादचोदितेनस्यात् ॥२॥

2. By reason of their being purificatory they are with that which is not ordained.

वचनात्त्वयथार्थमैन्द्री स्यात् ॥३॥

3. On the other hand, by reason of the text, the verses in honour of Indra do not serve their purpose.

गुणाद्वाऽप्यभिधानं स्यात्सम्बन्धस्याशास्त्रहेतुत्वात् ॥४॥

4. On the other hand the name is by the quality, because the relationship does not depend on the textual injunction.

तथाह्वानमपीति चेत् ॥५॥

5. Similarly if it be said that the invitation mantras are also.

नकालविधिश्चोदितत्वात् ॥६॥

6. No it is an injunction about time as it is laid down.

गुणाभावात् ॥७॥

7. By reason of the absence of the quality.

लिङ्गाच्च ॥८॥

8. By reason of the force of the text.

विधिकोपश्चोपदेशे स्यात् ॥९॥

9. There will be confusion of injunction if the direction be considered (as applicable to pounding).

तथोत्थानविसर्जने ॥१०॥

10. Similarly in rising up and dismissal.

सूक्तवाके च कालविधिः परार्थत्वात् ॥११॥

11. And in the *Sūktavāka* there is an injunction as to time by reason of its being subservient to another.

उपदेशो वा याज्याशब्दो हि नाकस्मात् ॥१२॥

12. On the other hand, it is an order because the word *yājyā* is not used without a purpose.

सदेवतार्थस्तत्संयोगात् ॥१३॥

13. It (*sūktavāka*) is with the object of describing the god, because it is connected with the sacrifice.

प्रतिपत्तिरिति चेत्स्विष्टकृद्वदुभयसंस्कारः स्यात् ॥१४॥

14. If you say that it is final disposal, then like (*sviṣṭakṛt*) it serves two purposes.

कृत्स्नोपदेशादुभयत्र सर्ववचनम् ॥१५॥

15. Because it is laid down that the whole should be read, at both places, the whole should be read.

यथार्थं वा शेषभूतसंस्कारात् ॥१६॥

16. On the other hand they should be read according to the suitability of the rite, because they are purificatory of the subordinate acts.

वचनादिति चेत् ॥१७॥

17. If you say that it is so enjoined by a command.

प्रकरणाविभागादुभे प्रति कृत्स्नशब्दः ॥१८॥

18. By reason of the indivisibility of the context the word 'entire' applies to both.

लिङ्गक्रमसमाख्यानात्काम्ययुक्तं समाम्नानम् ॥१९॥

19. The description in the Veda in connection with the desire accomplishing sacrifice is known from the force of the text, the order and the classification and meaning of the division.

अधिकारे च मन्त्रविधिरतदाख्येषु शिष्टत्वात् ॥२०॥

20. And in the general description is the application of the mantras, there being nothing laid down in the classification and naming.

तदाख्योवा प्रकरणोपपत्तिभ्याम् ॥२१॥

21. On the other hand, *samākhyā* depends upon context and philosophical explanation.

अनर्थकश्चोपदेशः स्यादसम्बन्धात्फलवता न ह्युपस्थानं फलवत् ॥२२॥

22. And the direction is meaningless by reason of there being no connection with one that produces fruit; becausc the praise is not producing fruit.

सर्वेषां चोपदिष्टत्वात् ॥२३॥

23. And by reason of all being enjoined.

लिङ्गसमाख्यानाभ्यां भक्षार्थताऽनुवाकस्य ॥२४॥

24. The drinking of the soma is the object of the *anuvāka* and can be inferred by means of *liṅga* and *samākhyā*.

तस्य रूपोपदेशाभ्यामपकर्षोऽर्थस्य चोदितत्वात् ॥२५॥

25. There will be transference of sense by means of its form and direction, by reason of its being laid down.

गुणाभिधानान्मन्द्रादिरेकमन्त्रः स्यात्तयोरेकार्थसंयोगात् ॥२६॥

26. The *mantras* commencing with *mandra* by reason of ḍescribing the quality, constitute one *mantra*, because they both are connected with one object.

लिङ्गविशेषनिर्देशात्समानविधानेष्वनैन्द्राणाममन्त्रत्वम् ॥२७॥

27. By reason of the direction from the special force of the text, in things equally enjoined, the deities other than Indra are without *mantras.*

यथादेवतं वा तत्प्रकृतित्वं हि दर्शयति ॥२८॥

28. On the other hand, according to the gods; because the model sacrifice shows it.

पुनरभ्युन्नीतेषु सर्वेषामुपलक्षणं द्विशेषत्त्वात् ।२९॥

29. Again in *abhyunnīta* soma juice cups there is *upalakṣaṇa* of all by reason of the residue of two.

अपनयाद्वा पूर्वस्याऽनुपलक्षणम् ॥३०॥

30. On the other hand by setting aside there is non-mention of the foregoing deity.

ग्रहणाद्वाऽपनयः स्यात् ॥३१॥

31. On the other hand, there is setting aside by reason of taking the soma juice (remnant of Indra's drink).

पात्नीवते तु पूर्ववत् ॥३२॥

32. On the other hand, in *pātnivata* cup like the preceding.

ग्रहणाद्वाऽपनीतं स्यात् ॥३३॥

33. On the other hand, by taking there is setting aside.

त्वष्टारं तूपलक्षयेत्पानात् ॥३४॥

34. On the other hand *tvaṣṭr* should be mentioned by reason of the drink.

अतुल्यत्वात्तु नैवं स्यात् ॥३५॥

35. On the other hand, by reason of the inequality, it is not so.

त्रिंशच्च परार्थत्वात् ॥३६॥

36. And 30, by reason of being subservient to others.

वषट्कारश्च कर्त्तृवत् ॥३७॥

37. And pronouncing of *vaṣaṭakāra* is like an agent.

छन्दः प्रतिषेधस्तु सर्वगामित्वात् ॥३८॥

38. On the other hand, prohibition of *chanda* by reason of its going into all.

ऐन्द्राग्ने तु लिङ्गभावात्स्यात् ॥३९॥

39. In the cup of Indrāgnī dual gods, by the inferential power of the text, there is a *mantra.*

एकस्मिन्वा देवतान्तराद्विभागवत् ॥४०॥

40. On the other hand, one cup will be divided by reason of another deity.

छन्दश्च देवतावत् ॥४१॥

41. And *chanda* is like a deity.

सर्वेषु वाऽभावादेकच्छन्दसः ॥४२॥

42. On the other hand, in all, by reason of the absence of one metre.

सर्वेषां वैकमन्त्र्यमैतिशायनस्य भक्तिपानत्वात्सवनाधिकारोहि ॥४३॥

43. On the other hand, the view of Aitiśāyana is that there is only one *mantra* for all, by reason of the different occasions of soma drinking; because they all come under the general subject of squeezing and preparing soma.

END OF PĀDA 2

***

PĀDA 3

श्रुतेर्जाताधिकारः स्यात् ॥१॥

1. By reason of the direct text, there is a class of the Vedas.

वेदो वा प्रायदर्शनात् ॥२॥

2. On the other hand, the Veda by reason of seeing it often.

लिङ्गाच्च ॥३॥

3. And also by reason of the force of the text.

धर्मोपदेशाच्च न हि द्रव्येण सम्बन्धः ॥४॥

4. And by reason of the description of the quality; because it is not connected with the matter.

त्रयीविद्याख्या च तद्विदि ॥५॥

5. And a person who knows the three Vedas is called knower of the three Vedas.

व्यक्तिक्रमे यथाश्रुतीति चेत् ॥६॥

6. "And on confusion, it should be according to the text" if it be said.

न सर्वस्मिन्निवेशात् ॥७॥

7. Not so, by reason of inclusion in all.

वेदसंयोगान्न प्रकरणेन बाध्यते ॥८॥

8. By reason of the connection with the Vedic text, it is not violated by the context.

गुणमुख्यव्यतिक्रमे तदर्थत्वान्मुख्येन वेदसंयोगः ॥९॥

9. In the conflict between the principal and the subordinate, by reason of the latter being subservient to the former, the principal has connection with the Veda.

भूयस्त्वेनोभयश्रुति ॥१०॥

10. And act described in two Vedas is governed by one in which it is described at length.

असंयुक्तं प्रकरणादितिकर्त्तव्यतार्थित्वात् ॥११॥

11. When there is no applicability of *śruti, liṅga* and *vākya,* the context (*prakaraṇa*) will apply, because it shows how an action is to be done.

क्रमश्च देशसामान्यात् ॥१२॥

12. And *krama* (sequence) is by the place being common.

आख्या चैवं तदर्थत्वात् ॥१३॥

13. And *samākhyā* also, being subservient.

श्रुति-लिङ्ग-वाक्य-प्रकरण-स्थान-समाख्यानां समवाये पारदौर्बल्य-मर्थविप्रकर्षात् ॥१४॥

14. In the common applicability of *śruti, liṅga, vākya, prakaraṇa, sthāna* and *samākhyā,* the weakness of the latter is by reason of the distance of the sense.

अहीनो वा प्रकरणाद्गौणः ॥१५॥

15. On the other hand, *ahīna* is subordinate by reason of the context.

असंयोगात्तु मुख्यस्य तस्मादपकृष्येत ॥१६॥

16. On the other hand, being not connected with the principal, therefore there is a backward transference.

द्वित्त्वबहुत्वयुक्तं वा चोदनात्तस्य ॥१७॥

17. On the other hand, connected with two or more by reason of its being ordained.

पक्षेणार्थकृतस्येति चेत् ॥१८॥

18. If it be said that with the help of the sacrificer.

नकृतेरेकसंयोगात् ॥१९॥

19. Not so; because one sacrificer is mentioned in connection with the model sacrifice.

जाघनी चैकदेशत्वात् ॥२०॥

20. And the tail of an animal by reason of a part.

चोदना वाऽपूर्वत्वात् ॥२१॥

21. On the other hand, it is a command by reason of its being an extraordinary and invisible result.

एकदेश इति चेत् ॥२२॥

22. If you say that a part (stands for the whole).

न प्रकृतेरशास्त्रनिष्पत्तेः ॥२३॥

23. Not so; by reason of not getting the command from the model sacrifice.

सन्तर्दनं प्रकृतौ क्रयणवदनर्थलोपात्स्यात् ॥२४॥

24. In the model sacrifice, the fastening is like the purchase of soma (optional) because there is no omission of anything essential.

उत्कर्षो वा ग्रहणाद्विशेषस्य ॥२५॥

25. On the other hand, there is transference forward by virtue of a particular reference.

कर्तृतो वा विशेषस्य तन्निमित्तत्वात् ॥२६॥

26. On the other hand from the agent, there is a special reference because of his being the cause of it.

क्रतुतो वाऽर्थवादानुपपत्तेः स्यात् ॥२७॥

27. On the other hand, from the sacrifice by reason of the force of the *arthavāda.*

संस्थाश्च कर्तृवद्धारणार्थविशेषात् ॥२८॥

28. And soma sacrifices like an agent, by reason of the word *'dhāraṇā'* having no particular sense.

उक्थ्यादिषु वाऽर्थस्य विद्यमानत्वात् ॥२९॥

29. On the other hand, in *ukthya* &c. by reason of the presence of the object.

अविशेषात्स्तुतिर्व्यर्थेति चेत् ॥३०॥

30. "By reason of there being nothing particular, the praise is useless"; if it be said.

स्यादनित्यत्वात् ॥३१॥

31. It is by reason of its being not permanent.

सङ्ख्यायुक्तं क्रतोः प्रकरणात्स्यात् ॥३२॥

32. The connection of the nurmerals is with the sacrifice by reason of the context.

नैमित्तिकं वा कर्तृसंयोगाल्लिङ्गस्य तन्निमित्तत्वात् ॥३३॥

33. On the other hand, it is occasiond by reason of the connection with the agent, because the inferential sense is for it.

पौष्णं पेषणं विकृतौ प्रतीयेताऽचोदनात्प्रकृतौ ॥३४॥

34. The offering of flour to Pūṣā is known in a modified sacrifice, because there is no such direction in the model sacrifice.

तत्सर्वार्थमविशेषात् ॥३५॥

35. That is in all purposes, by reason of there being nothing particular.

चरौवाऽर्थोक्तं पुरोडाशेऽर्थविप्रतिषेधात्पशौ न स्यात् ॥३६॥

36. On the other hand, it is ordained in *caru* offering and in *puroḍāśa* offering; it is indispensable and by reason of no use, it is not to be used in animal sacrifice.

चरावपीति चेत् ॥३७॥

37. "In *caru* also", if it be said.

न पक्तिनामत्वात् ॥३८॥

38. Not so, by reason of its being a synonym for boiled rice.

एकस्मिन्नेकसंयोगात् ॥३९॥

39. In one by reason of the connection of one.

धर्मविप्रतिषेधाच्च ॥४०॥

40. And by reason of incongruity.

अपि वा सद्वितीये स्याद्देवतानिमित्तत्वात् ॥४१॥

41. Not so, it applies to dual gods because the gods are the cause.

लिङ्गदर्शनाच्च ॥४२॥

42. And there is also the figurative sense of the text.

वचनात्सर्वपेषणं तं प्रति शास्त्रवत्वादर्थाभावाद्विचरावपेषणं भवति ॥४३॥

43. To the god Pūṣā the entire offering is of flour by reason of a text, for there is a rule of the Śāstra; there being no purpose served in the dual offerings, there is no flour.

एकस्मिन्वाऽर्थधर्मत्वादैन्द्राग्नवदुभयोर्न स्याद्चोदितत्वात् ॥४४॥

44. On the other hand in one by reason of its being the quality of the sacrifice like Indrāgnī; to dual deities there is no such offering because it is not so ordained.

हेतुमात्रमदन्तत्वम् ॥४५॥

45. The toothlessness is only reason.

वचनं परम् ॥४६॥

46. Further there is a text.

END OF PĀDA 3

***

PĀDA 4

निवीतमिति मनुष्यधर्मः शब्दस्य तत्प्रधानत्वात् ॥१॥

1. 'Nivīta' is the duty of man; because of its being principal of the word (Veda).

अपदेशो वाऽर्थस्य विद्यमानत्वात् ॥२॥

2. On the other hand it is a common practice by reason of the object being present.

विधिस्त्वपूर्वत्वात्स्यात् ॥३॥

3. It is a command (*vidhi*) by reason of its being (*apūrva*) new.

स प्रायात्कर्मधर्मः स्यात् ॥४॥

4. It is a quality of the action by reason of the context.

वाक्यशेषत्वात् ॥५॥

5. By reason of the completion of a sentence.

तत्प्रकरणे यत्तत्संयुक्तमविप्रतिषेधात् ॥६॥

6. On accepting the context, there is *apūrva vidhi* because its connection with the context is not inconsistent or prohibited.

तत्प्रधाने वा तुल्यवत्प्रसंख्यानादितरस्य तदर्थत्वात् ॥७॥

7. On the other hand, if the *manuṣya dharma* is principal by reason of equal description of all three, the other is for it.

अर्थवादो वाप्रकरणात् ॥८॥

8. It is *arthavāda* by reason of the context.

विधिना चैकवाक्यत्वात् ॥९॥

9. By reason of being in harmony with the *vidhi.*

दिग्विभागश्च तद्वत्सम्बन्धस्यार्थहेतुत्वात् ॥१०॥

10. And the division of the direction is like it by reason of the relationship being for a purpose.

परुषि दितपूर्णघृतविदग्धं च तद्वत् ॥११॥

11. And similarly are *parūṣidita pūrṇa-ghṛtavidagdha* verses.

अकर्म क्रतुसंयुक्तं संयोगान्नित्यानुवादः स्यात् ॥१२॥

12. Connected with a sacrifice, it is not a duty; being connected with moral rectitude it is a permanent rule of practice.

विधिर्वा संयोगान्तरात् ॥१३॥

13. On the other hand it is *vidhi* by reason of the connection with another.

अहीनवत्पुरुषस्तदर्थत्वात् ॥१४॥

14. Like *ahīna* it is a duty of man, being subordinate to it.

प्रकरणविशेषाद्वा तद्युक्तस्य संस्कारो द्रव्यवत् ॥१५॥

15. On the other hand by reason of the particular context being connected with it, it is a purificatory rite like a material.

व्यपदेशादपकृष्येत ॥१६॥

16. There is a transference by reason of the special mention.

शंयौ च सर्वपरिदानात् ॥१७॥

17. And in the passage *śaṃyu* by reason of the application to all.

प्रागपरोधान्मलवद्वाससः ॥१८॥

18. By reason of the exclusion of a dirty woman from before.

अन्नप्रतिषेधाच्च ॥१९॥

19. And by reason of the prohibition of the food.

अप्रकरणे तु तद्धर्मस्ततो विशेषात् ॥२०॥

20. On the other hand not in any context; it is an ethical principle because of this speciality.

अद्रव्यत्वात् तु शेषः स्यात् ॥२१॥

21. On the other hand by reason of its being not a material, it is subsidiary.

वेदसंयोगात् ॥२२॥

22. By reason of the connection with the Veda.

द्रव्यसंयोगाच्च ॥२३॥

23. And by reason of the connection with the material.

स्याद्वाऽस्य संयोगवत्फलेन सम्बन्धस्तस्मात्कर्मैतिशायनः ॥२४॥

24. On the other hand, its connection with the material is as the connection with the fruit; therefore it is an ethical act. It is the view of Aitiśāyana.

शेषाः प्रकरणेऽविशेषात्सर्वकर्मणाम् ॥२५॥

25. Not in any context, it is subsidiary and by reason of no speciality it belongs to all actions.

होमास्तुव्यवतिष्ठेरन्नाहवनीयसंयोगात् ॥२६॥

26. On the other hand, the oblations are restricted by reason of the conection with *āhavanīya.*

शेषश्च समाख्यानात् ॥२७॥

27. And it is *śeṣa* by reason of *samākhyā.*

दोषात्त्विष्टिर्लौकिके स्याच्छास्त्राद्धि वैदिक न दोषः स्यात् ॥२८॥

28. On the other hand there is an expiatory rite in the secular acts by reason of the fault; therefore in the Vedic act, there is no fault, by reason of being sanctioned.

अर्थवादो वाऽनुपपातात्स्माद्यज्ञेप्रतीयेत ॥२९॥

29. On the other hand, it is commendatory to avoid any mishap, therefore it is known to be connected with the sacrifice.

अचोदित च कर्मभेदात् ॥३०॥

30. And not laid down, by reason of the difference of act.

लिङ्गादार्त्विजे स्यात् ॥३१॥

31. That, by reason of the force of the text, is in the sacrificer.

पानव्यापच्च तद्वत् ॥३२॥

32. And a mishap in drinking, like it.

दोषात्तु वैदिके स्यादर्थाद्धि लौकिके न दोषः स्यात् ॥३३॥

33. On the other hand, by reason of the fault in a Vedic rite; but by reason of the object there is no fault in the ordinary life.

तत्सर्वत्राविशेषात् ॥३४॥

34. That (offering) everywhere as there is nothing special.

स्वामिनो वा तदर्थत्वात् ॥३५॥

35. On the other hand, the lord of the sacrifice that being for his sake.

लिङ्गदर्शनाच्च ॥३६॥

36. And there is the force of the text.

सर्वप्रदानं हविषस्तदर्थत्वात् ॥३७॥

37. The whole offering should be made as it is for it.

निरवदानात्तु शेषः स्यात् ॥३८॥

38. On the other hand there will be a residue by reason of being cut up.

उपायो वा तदर्थत्वात् ॥३९॥

39. On the other hand it is a device, by reason of its being for that object.

कृतत्वात्तु कर्मणः सकृत्स्याद्द्रव्यस्यगुणभूतत्वात् ॥४०॥

40. On the other hand, by reason of the act being done, it is once because the material is subordinate.

शेषदर्शनाच्च ॥४१॥

41. And by seeing the residue.

अप्रयोजकत्वादेकस्मात्क्रियेरञ्छेषस्य गुणभूतत्वात् ॥४२॥

42. By reason of being not the means, an offering should be made from one because the residue is subordinate.

संस्कृतत्वाच्च ॥४३॥

43. And by reason of a purificatory rite being performed.

सर्वेभ्यो वा कारणाविशेषात्संस्कारस्य तदर्थत्वात् ॥४४॥

44. On the other hand from all by reason of there being no special cause because the purificatory ceremony is for that object.

लिङ्गदर्शनाच्च ॥४५॥

45. And by seeing the force of the text.

एकस्माच्चेद्यथाकाम्यमविशेषात् ॥४६॥

46. If it be taken from one, it should be according to the desire of the sacrificer by reason of there being nothing special.

मुख्याद्वा पूर्वकालत्वात् ॥४७॥

47. On the other hand from the principal, by reason of its priority.

भक्षाश्रवणाद्दानशब्दः परिक्रये ॥४८॥

48. There being no word for eating, the word 'gift' is in the sense of purchase.

तत्संस्तवाच्च ॥४९॥

49. And by reason of praising it.

भक्षार्थो वाद्रव्ये समत्वात् ॥५०॥

50. On the other hand, it is for the purpose of food; both being equal in the substance.

व्यादेशाद्दानसंस्तुतिः ॥५१॥

51. There is a praise of gift by reason of division.

End of Pāda 4

***

PĀDA 4—APPENDIX

उपवीतं लिङ्गदर्शनात्सर्वधर्मः स्यात् ॥९(अ)॥

9-A. *upavīta*, by seeing the force of the text, belongs to all ceremonies.

न वा प्रकरणात्तस्य दर्शनम् ॥९(इ)॥

9-B. Not so, by reason of the context; (the *liṅga* is) its reference only.

विधिर्वा स्यादपूर्वत्वात् ॥९(उ)॥

9-C. On the other hand, it is *vidhi* because it is a new thing.

उदक्त्वं चापूर्वत्वात् ॥९(ऋ)॥

9-D. And the quality of being north, by reason of its being a new thing.

सतो वा लिङ्गदर्शनम् ॥९(लृ)॥

9-E. On the other hand, it is already existent by seeing the force of the text.

विधिस्तु धारणेऽपूर्वत्वात् ॥९(ए)॥

9-F. On the other hand it is a *vidhi* in holding by reason of its being new.

END OF PĀDA 4—APPENDIX

***

PĀDA 5

आज्याच्च सर्वसंयोगात् ॥१॥

1. And from the clarified butter by reason of its being connected with the whole sacrifice.

कारणाच्च ॥२॥

2. And because of the reason.

एकस्मिन्त्समवत्तशब्दात् ॥३॥

3. In one, by reason of the word *samavatta* (oblation).

आज्ये च दर्शनात्स्विष्टकृदर्थवादस्य ॥४॥

4. And from seeing in clarified butter; it is *arthavāda* of *sviṣṭakṛta.*

अशेषत्वात्तु नैवं स्यात्सर्वादानादशेषता ॥५॥

5. On the other hand by reason, of there being no residue, it cannot be so; there is no residue by reason of taking the whole in use.

साधारण्यान्न ध्रुवायां स्यात् ॥६॥

6. By reason of its being common, there is not in a *dhruvā.*

अवत्तत्वाच्च जुह्वां तस्य च होमसंयोगात् ॥७॥

7. And by reason of its being taken in a *juhū* and by reason of its being connected with the homa.

चमसवदिति चेत् ॥८॥

8. If you say 'like a spoon'.

न चोदनाविरोधाद्धविःप्रकल्पनत्वाच्च ॥९॥

9. Not so; by reason of this being contrary to the command and by reason of preparing the oblation.

उत्पन्नाधिकारात्सति सर्ववचनम् ॥१०॥

10. The word 'all' applies, by reason of sanctioning the remaining rite, if there be a residue.

जातिविशेषात्परम् ॥११॥

11. And further by reason of a particular species.

अन्त्यमरेकार्थे ॥१२॥

12. The last reason (is not valid) because it is not empty.

साकम्प्रस्थाय्ये स्विष्टकृदिडश्च तद्वत् ॥१३॥

13. In a *sākamprasthāyya* sacrifice *sviṣṭakṛt* and *iḍā* are in the same way.

सौत्रामण्यां च ग्रहेषु ॥१४॥

14. And in a *sautrāmaṇī* sacrifice, in the cups.

तद्वच्च शेषवचनम् ॥१५॥

15. And the text regarding the residue is like that.

द्रव्यैकत्वे कर्मभेदात्प्रतिकर्म क्रियेरन् ॥१६॥

16. By reason of the difference of the main acts, in the unity of the materials, each act should be done.

अविभागाच्च शेषस्य सर्वान्प्रत्यविशिष्टत्वात् ॥१७॥

17. And by reason of the indivisibility of the remaining half, all are performed at once because there is no special mention about it.

ऐन्द्रवायवे तु वचनात्प्रतिकर्म भक्षः स्यात् ॥१८॥

18. On the other hand, in a cup called *aindravāyava* by reason of a text, there will be drinking with each subordinate act.

सोमेऽवचनाद्भक्षो न विद्यते ॥१९॥

19. In a Soma sacrifice by reason of no text, there is no drinking.

स्याद्वाऽन्यार्थदर्शनात् ॥२०॥

20. On the other hand, there is, by seeing the other text.

वचनानि त्वपूर्वत्वात्तस्माद्यथोपदेशं स्युः ॥२१॥

21. On the other hand, there are texts by reason of laying down something new; therefore it should be according to the direction.

चमसेषु समाख्यानात्संयोगस्य तन्निमित्तत्त्वात् ॥२२॥

22. By reason of the *samākhyā* in the case of spoons and of the mention of the connection being for it.

उद्गातृचमसमेकः श्रुतिसंयोगात् ॥२३॥

23. One should drink from the *udgātṛ* cup by reason of the Vedic text.

सर्वे वा सर्वसंयोगात् ॥२४॥

24. On the other hand, all, by reason of the mention of all.

स्तोत्रकारिणां वा तत्त्संयोगाद्बहुश्रुतेः ॥२५॥

25. On the other hand, by reason of its connection, all the singers should drink it, because the plural number is used in the Vedic text.

सर्वे तु वेदसंयोगात्त्कारणा देकदेशे स्यात् ॥२६॥

26. On the other hand, all by reason of the connection with the text and by reason that a part represents the whole.

ग्रावस्तुतो भक्षो न विद्यतेऽनाम्नानात् ॥२७॥

27. The *grāvastut* is not entitled to a drink by reason of non-mention in the Vedas.

हारियोजने वा सर्वसंयोगात् ॥२८॥

28. On the other hand, in the *hāriyojana* cup, by reason of the mention of all.

चमसिनां वा सन्निधानात् ॥२९॥

29. On the other hand, the *camasī* priests, by reason of the close proximity.

सर्वेषां तु विधित्वात्तदर्था चमसिश्रुतिः ॥३०॥

30. On the other hand, of all, by reason of the command; the mention of *camasī* in the text is with that object.

वषट्काराच्च भक्षयेत् ॥३१॥

31. And one should drink by pronouncing *vaṣaṭkāra.*

होमाऽभिषवाभ्यां च ॥३२॥

32. And by Homa and extraction of Soma juice.

प्रत्यक्षोपदेशाच्चमसानामव्यक्तः शेषे ॥३३॥

33. And by the direct command of the *camasa* cups and the general in the residue.

स्याद्वा कारणाभावादनिर्देशश्चमसानां कर्तुस्तद्वचनत्वात् ॥३४॥

34. On the other hand, there is no direct statement about the *camasa* cups because there is no reason, but there is a direct statement about one who pronounces *vaṣaṭkāra*.

चमसे चान्यदर्शनात् ॥३५॥

35. And in a *camasa* cup by reason of another Vedic text.

एकपात्रे क्रमादध्वर्युः पूर्वो भक्षयेत् ॥३६॥

36. In one cup in an order, the *adhvaryu* priest drinks first.

होता वा मन्त्रवर्णात् ॥३७॥

37. On the other hand, *hotā* by reason of his mention in the text.

वचनाच्च ॥३८॥

38. And by reason of the direct text.

कारणानुपूर्व्याच्च ॥३९॥

39. And by reason of the sequences of causes.

वचनादनुज्ञातभक्षणम् ॥४०॥

40. By the direct text, there is drinking after obtaining permission.

तदुपहूत उपह्वयस्वेत्त्यनेनानुज्ञापयेलिङ्गात् ॥४१॥

41. Then "you who are invited, invite;" from this, permission is given by reason of the force of the text.

तत्रार्थात्त्प्रतिवचनम् ॥४२॥

42. There, by the object is the reply.

तदेकत्राणां समवायात् ॥४३॥

43. That applies to those who drink from the same cup by reason of their collecting (for the object).

याज्यापनयेनापनीतो भक्षः प्रवरवत् ॥४४॥

44. When *yājyā* is not recited, there is no deprivation of food like the appointment.

यष्टुर्वा कारणागमात् ॥४५॥

45. On the other hand, of the *yajamāna* by virtue of the reason.

प्रवृत्तत्वात्प्रवरस्यानपायः ॥४६॥

46. There cannot be annulment of the appointment by reason of the commencement of the act.

फलचमसो नैमित्तिको भक्षविकारः श्रुतिसंयोगात् ॥४७॥

47. The fruit cup is a conditional substitute for food, by reason of its mention in the Vedic text.

इज्याविकारो वा संस्कारस्य तदर्थत्वात् ॥४८॥

48. On the other hand it is a substitute for oblation because the sacrificial purification is for that object.

होमात् ॥४९॥

49. By reason of the homa.

चमसैश्च तुल्यकालत्वात् ॥५०॥

50. And by reason of contemporaneousness with the cups.

लिङ्गदर्शनाच्च ॥५१॥

51. And by seeing the force of the text.

अनुप्रसर्पिषु सामान्यात् ॥५२॥

52 In the procession by reason of its being common.

ब्राह्मणा वा तुल्यशब्दत्वात् ॥५३॥

53. On the other hand the Brāhmaṇas by reason of the word 'equal'.

END OF PĀDA 5

***

PĀDA 6

तत् सर्वार्थमप्रकरणात् ॥१॥

1. That belongs to all cases by reason of the text not belonging to any context.

प्रकृतौ वाऽद्विरुक्तत्वात् ॥२॥

2. On the other hand, it applies to the model sacrifice by reason of no repetition.

तद्वर्जं तु वचनप्राप्ते ॥३॥

3. On the other hand excluding it, the direct text is applicable.

दर्शनादिति चेत् ॥४॥

4. If it be said that by reason of seeing (Vedic text).

न चोदनैकार्थ्यात् ॥५॥

5. Not, by reason of a *codanā* being for the same end.

उत्पत्तिरिति चेत् ॥६॥

6. If it be said that there is *a priori* ground.

न तुल्यत्वात् ॥७॥

7. Not by reason of parity of reasoning.

चोदनार्थकात्स्न्यीत्तु मुख्यविप्रतिषेधात्प्रकृत्यर्थः ॥८॥

8. On the other hand, a particular statement serving all purposes and the general text being applicable to both, it is applicable to the model sacrifice.

प्रकरणविशेषात्तु विकृतौ विरोधि स्यात् ॥९॥

9. On the other hand, by reason of the particular context, there will be contradictions in the modified sacrifice.

नैमित्तिकं तु प्रकृतौ तद्विकारः संयोगविशेषात् ॥१०॥

10. On the other hand, the occasional should be used in *prakṛti* and the exclusion of the other by reason of particular mention.

इष्ट्यर्थमग्न्याधेयं प्रकरणात् ॥११॥

11. By virtue of the context, the establishment of fire is for *pavamāneṣṭi.*

न वा तासां तदर्थत्वात् ॥१२॥

12. Not so, because they are for it.

लिङ्गदर्शनाच्च ॥१३॥

13. And by seeing the force of the text.

तत्प्रकृत्यर्थं यथान्येऽनारभ्यवादाः ॥१४॥

14. That is for the model sacrifice just as other general statements.

सर्वार्थं वाग्न्याधानस्य स्वकालत्वात् ॥१५॥

15. On the other hand, it is connected with all sacrifices by reason of *agnyādhāna* having its own time.

तासामग्निः प्रकृतितः प्रयाजवत्स्यात् ॥१६॥

16. Their fire from the model sacrifice like the *prayāja.*

न वा तासां तदर्थत्वात् ॥१७॥

17. Not so, their being for that.

तुल्यः सर्वेषां पशुविधिः प्रकरणाविशेषात् ॥१८॥

18. Equal is the animal ceremony in all sacrifices by reason of there being nothing special about the context.

स्थानाच्च पूर्वस्य ॥१९॥

19. By reason of location, it would apply to the first.

श्वस्त्वेकेषां तत्र प्राक्श्रुतिर्गुणार्था ॥२०॥

20. According to one, the *paśuvidhi* of the succeeding day is described first with a view to describe the quality.

तेनोत्कृष्टस्य कालविधिरिति चेत् ॥२१॥

21. "By this means, it is laying down of time of the transferred" if you say.

नैकदेशत्वात् ॥२२॥

22. Not so, by reason of the partial (context).

अर्थेनेति चेत् ॥२३॥

23. If you say by the sense.

न श्रुतिविप्रतिषेधात् ॥२४॥

24. Not so, by reason of the two Vedic texts of equal force.

स्थानात्तु पूर्वस्य संस्कारस्य तदर्थत्वात् ॥२५॥

25. On the other hand by reason of the sequence; because the former purificatory ceremonies are for it.

लिङ्गदर्शनाच्च ॥२६॥

26. And by seeing the force of the text.

अचोदना गुणार्थेन ॥२७॥

27. There is no injunction with a view to describe the quality.

दोहयोः कालभेदादसंयुक्तं शृतं स्यात् ॥२८॥

28. By reason of the difference of time in the milking, the heated milk is unconnected.

प्रकरणाविभागाद्वातत्संयुक्तस्य कालशास्त्रम् ॥२९॥

29. On the other hand by reason of the indivisibility of the context, the time of the two milkings connected with each other is pointed out.

तद्वत्सवनान्तरे ग्रहाम्नानम् ॥३०॥

30. Similarly is the description of the cups at different times of soma offering.

रशना च लिङ्गदर्शनात् ॥३१॥

31. And the bridle by seeing the force of the text.

आराच्छिष्टमसंयुक्तमितरैः सन्निधानात् ॥३२॥

32. What is laid down at a distance is not connected by reason of its proximity with others.

संयुक्तं वा तदर्थत्त्वाच्छेषस्य तन्निमित्तत्वात् ॥३३॥

33. On the other hand, they are connected by reason of their being for it; because their use is for the residual sacrificial act.

निर्देशाद्व्यवतिष्ठेत ॥३४॥

34. The interpretation of the text is to be adjusted by reason of special enunciation.

अग्न्यङ्गमप्रकरणे तद्वत् ॥३५॥

35. Though not in a context, similarly they are parts of the *agnicayana.*

नैमित्तिकमतुल्यत्वादसमानविधानं स्यात् ॥३६॥

36. The casual by reason of being not equal, there is unequal description.

प्रतिनिधिश्च ॥३७॥

37. And similarly the substitute.

तद्वत्प्रयोजनैकत्वात् ॥३८॥

38. Like it, by reason of there being one object.

अशास्त्रलक्षणत्वाच्च ॥३९॥

39. By reason of there being no distinctive quality mentioned.

नियमार्था गुणश्रुतिः ॥४०॥

40. Description of qualities is with a view to restriction.

संस्थास्तु समानविधानाः प्रकरणाविशेषात् ॥४१॥

41. On the other hand, *saṁsthās* are *samānavidhāna* by reason of their occurring in no context.

व्यपदेशश्च तुल्यवत् ॥४२॥

42. And the designation is alike.

विकारास्तु कामसंयोगे नित्यस्य समत्वात् ॥४३॥

43. On the other hand, the modifications in connection with the desire, are of the permanent (sacrifice) by reason of the equality.

अपि वा द्विरुक्तत्वात्प्रकृतेर्भविष्यन्तीति ॥४४॥

44. Or also by virtue of want of repetition they will belong to the model sacrifice.

बचनात्तु समुच्चयः ॥४५॥

45. On the other hand by reason of the Vedic text, all sacrifices collectively.

प्रतिषेधाच्च पूर्वलिङ्गानाम् ॥४६॥

46. And by reason of prohibiting the preceding texts.

गुणविशेषादेकस्य व्यपदेशः ॥४७॥

47. There is the designation of one by reason of special quality.

END OF PĀDA 6

***

PĀDA 7

प्रकरणविशेषादसंयुक्तं प्रधानस्य ॥१॥

1. By reason of the special context, the un-connected belongs to the principal.

सर्वेषां वा शेषत्वस्याऽतत्प्रयुक्तत्वात् ॥२॥

2. On the other hand, of all because of their subsidiary nature, they are not described.

आरादपीतिचेत् ॥३॥

3. If it be said by means of the proximate relationship.

न तद्वाक्यं हि तदर्थत्वात् ॥४॥

4. Not so; because that statement is for that purpose.

लिङ्गदर्शनाच्च ॥५॥

5. And by seeing the force of the text.

फलसंयोगात्तु स्वामियुक्तं प्रधानस्य ॥६॥

6. On the other hand by reason of the mention of the fruit, (all ceremonies) connected with the master are for the principal.

चिकीर्षया च संयोगात् ॥७॥

7. By reason of the connection with the volition.

तथाऽभिधानेन ॥८॥

8. Similarly by the name.

तद्युक्ते तु फलश्रुतिस्तस्मात्सर्वचिकीर्षा स्यात् ॥९॥

9. On the other hand, in connection with that there is a text about the fruit; therefore there is volition of all.

गुणाऽभिधानात्सर्वार्थमभिधानम् ॥१०॥

10. By naming the parts, the whole is named.

दीक्षादक्षिणं तु वचनात्प्रधानस्य ॥११॥

11. On the other hand initiation and donation under a text belong to the principal.

निवृत्तिदर्शनाच्च ॥१२॥

12. And by seeing the cessation.

तथा यूपस्य वेदि ॥१३॥

13. Similarly the altar is not a part of the sacrificial post.

देशमात्रं वा शिष्टेनैकवाक्यत्वात् ॥१४॥

14. On the other hand, it is only a part of the locality by reason of its being in harmony with what is incapable of being enjoined.

सामधेनीस्तदन्वाहुरिति हविर्द्धानयोर्वचनात्सामधेनीनाम् ॥१५॥

15. "Then they recite the *sāmadhenī* verses"; two carts under the word are the parts of the *sāmadhenī*.

देशमात्रं वा प्रत्यक्षं ह्यर्थकर्म सोमस्य ॥१६॥

16. On the other hand a part of the space; the object of the soma sacrifice is visible or evident.

समाख्यानं च तद्वत् ॥१७॥

17. And the naming is accordingly.

शास्त्रफलं प्रयोक्तरितल्लक्षणत्वात्तस्मात्स्वयं प्रयोगे स्यात् ॥१८॥

18. The fruit enjoined accrues to the sacrificer, by reason of his quality; therefore he must perform it personally.

उत्सर्गे तु प्रधानत्वाच्छेषकारी प्रधानस्य तस्मादन्यः स्वयं वा स्यात् ॥१९॥

19. On the other hand in donation by reason of the principal and the subsidiary acts subserve the principal, they may therefore be performed by himself or by another.

अन्यो वा स्यात्परिक्रयाम्नानाद्विप्रतिषेधात्प्रत्यगात्मनि ॥२०॥

20. Or another may perform by reason of the Veda laying down the hiring (of the priests) and by reason of the prohibition of the performance by one's self.

तत्रार्थात्कर्तृ परिमाणं स्यादनियमोऽविशेषात् ॥२१॥

21. There by reason of the object, there is a limit of the workers; there is no rule or limit by reason of there being nothing special.

अपि वा श्रुति भेदात्प्रतिनामधेयं स्युः ॥२२॥

22. Or also by reason of the different Vedic texts, there are different officiating priests named for each.

एकस्य कर्मभेदादिति चेत् ॥२३॥

23. If it be said "of one by reason of the difference of duties".

नोत्पत्तौ हि ॥२४॥

24. Not so, because at the time of appointment.

चमसाध्वर्यवश्च तैर्व्यपदेशात् ॥२५॥

25. And *camasādhvaryus* by reason of their being mentioned separately.

उत्पत्तौ तु बहुश्रुतेः ॥२६॥

26. On the other hand at the time of appointment by reason of the Vedic text mentioning many.

दशत्वं लिङ्गदर्शनात् ॥२७॥

27. Ten, by seeing the force of the text.

शमिता च शब्दभेदात् ॥२८॥

28. And *śamitā* is (different) by reason of having a separate word.

प्रकरणाद्वोत्पत्त्यसंयोगात् ॥२९॥

29. On the other hand by reason of the context and there being no original text.

उपगाश्च लिङ्गदर्शनात् ॥३०॥

30. And the assistant singers, by reason of the force of the text.

विक्रयी त्वन्यः कर्मणोऽचोदित्वात् ॥३१॥

31. On the other hand, a seller is a different person because his function is not prescribed.

कर्म्मकार्यात्सर्वेषामृत्विक्त्वमविशेषात् ॥३२॥

32. By doing the sacrificial works all are *ṛtviks*, because there is nothing special.

न वा परिसंख्यानात् ॥३३॥

33. Not so, by reason of exclusive specification.

पक्षेणेति चेत् ॥३४॥

34. If it be said "by either way".

न सर्वेषामधिकारः ॥३५॥

35. No, all are not entitled.

नियमस्तु दक्षिणाभिः श्रुतिसंयोगात् ॥३६॥

36. On the other hand, there is a (*niyama*) restrictive rule by reason of the connection of the Vedic text with the donation.

उक्त्वा च यजमानत्वं तेषां दीक्षाविधानात् ॥३७॥

37. And having described the position of the sacrificer by reason of the description of their initiation.

स्वामिसप्तदशाः कर्मसामान्यात् ॥३८॥

38. The master completes the 17th number by reason of the function being common.

ते सर्वार्थाः प्रयुक्तत्वादग्नयश्च स्वकालत्वात् ॥३९॥

39. By reason of their appointment, they perform all duties just as sacred fires by reason of their fixed time.

तत्संयोगात्त्कर्मणो व्यवस्था स्यात्संयोगास्यार्थवत्त्वात् ॥४०॥

40. By reason of its relationship, the arrangement of the duties has been made by reason of the significant power of the relationship.

तस्योपदेशसमाख्यानेन निर्देशः ॥४१॥

41. Its nature is known from the direct statement and authoritative adjustment.

तद्वच्च लिङ्गदर्शनम् ॥४२॥

42. And similarly by seeing the force of the text.

प्रैषाऽनुवचनं मैत्रावरुणस्योपदेशात् ॥४३॥

43. The command and after-repetition are the functions of the *maitrāvaruṇa*, by reason of the direct Vedic text.

पुरोऽनुवाक्याधिकारो वा प्रैषसन्निधानात् ॥४४॥

44. On the other hand he has a right to *puronuvākya*, by reason of the proximity with the sacrificial command.

प्रातरनुवाके च होतृदर्शनात् ॥४५॥

45. And in (the repetition of *prātaranuvāka*, by seeing (the text authorising) the *hotṛ*.

चमसांश्चमसाध्वर्यवः सामाख्यानात् ॥४६॥

46. The *camasādhvaryus* ought to make an oblation from the cups by reason of the authoritative adjustment.

अध्वर्युर्वा तन्न्यायत्त्वात् ॥४७॥

47. On the other hand *adhvaryu* by reason of the principle.

चमसे चान्यदर्शनात् ॥४८॥

48. And in a *camasa* cup, by seeing other (priest).

अशक्तौ ते प्रतीयेरन् ॥४९॥

49. In weakness, they are to be recognised.

वेदोपदेशात्पूर्ववद्वेदान्यत्वे यथोपदेशं स्युः ॥५०॥

50. By reason of the direct statement in the Veda like the preceding; if it be otherwise in the Veda, it should be according to the direction.

तद्गुणाद्वा स्वधर्मः स्यादधिकारसामर्थ्यात्सहांगैरव्यक्तः शेषे ॥५१॥

51. Or by accepting it, there is one's duty; by virtue of the *codaka* text, it should be along with the constituent parts; in the rest indeterminate.

END OF PĀDA 7

***

PĀDA 8

स्वामिकर्मपरिक्रयः कर्मणस्तदर्थत्वात् ॥१॥

1. The duty of the master is hiring, because the sacrifice is for his sake.

वचनादितरेषां स्यात् ॥२॥

2. By a direct text of others also.

संस्कारास्तु पुरुषसामर्थ्ये यथावेदं कर्मवद्व्यवतिष्ठेरन् ॥३॥

3. On the other hand the purificatory ceremonies are in human power; they are to be performed according to the Veda like the sacrificial act.

याजमानास्तु तत्प्रधानत्त्वात्त्कर्मवत् ॥४॥

4. On the other hand, of the sacrificer; because he is principal like the sacrifice.

व्यपदेशाच्च ॥५॥

5. And by reason of the designation.

गुणत्त्वे तस्य निर्देशः ॥६॥

6. It is prescribed in the case of being subordinate.

चोदना प्रति भावाच्च ॥७॥

7. And by reason of the connection with *codanā* or the extraordinary principle.

अतुल्यत्वादसमानविधानाः स्युः ॥८॥

8. By reason of the inequality, the directions are not of similar nature.

तपश्च फलसिद्धित्वाल्लोकवत् ॥९॥

9. And the austerities, by reason of obtaining the fruit as in ordinary life.

वाक्यशेषश्च तद्वत् ॥१०॥

10. And filling up of the ellipsis is like that.

वचनादितरेषां स्यात् ॥११॥

11. By a direct text, of others also.

गुणत्वाच्च वेदेन न व्यवस्था स्यात् ॥१२॥

12. And by reason of its being subordinate, there is no adjustment by means of the Veda.

तथा कामोऽर्थसंयोगात् ॥१३॥

13. And similarly desire, by reason of the connection with the object.

व्यपदेशादितरेषां स्यात् ॥१४॥

14. By designation of others also.

मन्त्राश्चाऽकर्मकरणास्तद्वत् ॥१५॥

15. And the mantras which do not describe the sacrificial acts are likewise.

विप्रयोगे च दर्शनात् ॥१६॥

16. And by seeing on separation.

द्व्याम्नातेषूभौ द्व्याम्नानस्याऽर्थवत्त्वात् ॥१७॥

17. When a mantra is repeated twice, it is to be used by both because there is a purpose in the repetition.

ज्ञाते च वाचनं न ह्यविद्वान्विहितोऽस्ति ॥१८॥

18. And in a literate, there is the repetition of the mantras; because an illiterate is nowhere permitted.

याजमाने समाख्यानात्कर्माणि याजमानं स्युः ॥१९॥

19. By reason of being described in the *yājamānakāṇḍa,* the sacrificial acts pertain to the sacrificer.

अध्वर्युर्वा तदर्थो हि न्यायपूर्वं समाख्यानम् ॥२०॥

20. On the other hand, *adhvaryu*; it is for him and the *samākhyā* is based on reason.

विप्रतिषेधे करणः समावायविशेषादितरमन्यस्तेषां यतो विशेषः स्यात् ॥२१॥

21. On conflict, the performance is by reason of special connection; the other by another out of them; because there is a distinction.

प्रैषेणु च पराधिकारात् ॥२२॥

22. And in commands by reason of another's right.

अध्वर्युस्तु दर्शनात् ॥२३॥

23. On the other hand, *adhvaryu* by seeing the Vedic text.

गौणो वा कर्मसामान्यात् ॥२४॥

24. On the other hand, it is subordinate by reason of the function being the same.

ऋत्विक्फलं करणेष्वर्थत्त्वात् ॥२५॥

25. In *karaṇamantras* there is the reward of the *ṛtvik*; because it is for his purpose.

स्वामिनो वा तदर्थत्वात् ॥२६॥

26. On the other hand, of the master by reason of its being for him.

लिङ्गदर्शनाच्च ॥२७॥

27. And by seeing the force of the text.

कर्मार्थं फलं तेषां स्वामिनं प्रत्यर्थवत्त्वात् ॥२८॥

28. On the other hand, their reward is the success of the sacrificial act by reason of its being for the purpose of the master.

व्यपदेशाच्च ॥२९॥

29. And by the designation also.

द्रव्यसंस्कारः प्रकरणाऽविशेषात्सर्वकर्मणाम् ॥३०॥

30. The purificatory ceremony on the materials by reason of there being no speciality in the context, belongs to all sacrificial acts.

निर्देशात्तु विकृतावपूर्वस्याऽनधिकारः ॥३१॥

31. On the other hand, by the direct Vedic statement the extraordinary principle does not apply to the modified sacrifice.

विरोधे च श्रुतिविशेषादव्यक्तः शेषे ॥३२॥

32. On the conflict, by reason of the special text and the indirect in the remainder.

अपनयस्त्वेकदेशस्य विद्यमानसंयोगात् ॥३३॥

33. On the other hand, the transference is of a portion by reason of the connection with the one existing.

विकृतौ सर्वार्थः शेषः प्रकृतिवत् ॥३४॥

34. In a modified sacrifice, the subordinate acts fulfill all objects as in a model sacrifice.

मुख्यार्थो वाऽङ्गस्याचोदितत्वात् ॥३५॥

35. On the other hand, it is for the principal because the constituent parts are not directly mentioned.

सन्निधानाविशेषादसम्भवेदतदंगानाम् ॥३६॥

36. On impossibility, by the reason of the special juxtaposition; its constituent parts.

आधानेऽपि तथेति चेत् ॥३७॥

37. If it be said "similarly in *agnyādhāna*."

नाऽप्रकरणत्वादङ्गस्यातन्निमित्तत्वात् ॥३८॥

38. Not so, by reason of the context being not similar; because the constituent parts are for the principal.

तत्काले वा लिङ्गदर्शनात् ॥३९॥

39. On the other hand, at the time by seeing the force of the text.

सर्वेषां वाऽविशेषात् ॥४०॥

40. On the other hand, of all, by reason of there being nothing special.

न्यायोक्ते लिङ्गदर्शनम् ॥४१॥

41. The inference from the text is based on reason.

मांसं तु सवनीयानां चोदनाविशेषात् ॥४२॥

42. On the other hand, the *savanīya* cakes are of flesh by reason of a special text.

भक्तिरसन्निधावन्याय्येति चेत् ॥४३॥

43. "Metonymy is improper when there is no juxtaposition" if you say.

स्यात्प्रकृतिलङ्गाद्वैराजवत् ॥४४॥

44. It may be by reason of the signs of the model sacrifice like *vairāja.*

End of Pāda 8

***

END OF ADHYĀYA III

ADHYĀYA IV

PĀDA 1

अथातः क्रत्वर्थपुरुषार्थयोर्जिज्ञासा ॥१॥

1. Now therefore is the enquiry about *kratvartha* and *puruṣārtha.*

यस्मिन्प्रीतिः पुरुषस्य तस्य लिप्साऽर्थलक्षणाऽविभक्तत्वात् ॥२॥

2. (*purṣārtha* is that) in which there is a love of a man and that love is indicated by (a certain) object (which is) inseparably connected (with it).

तदुत्सर्गे कर्माणि पुरुषार्थाय शास्त्रस्यानतिशङ्क्यत्वान्न च द्रव्यं चिकीर्ष्यते तेनार्थेनाभिसम्बन्धात्क्रियायां पुरुषश्रुतिः ॥३॥

3. (There are) actions in which there is no natural prompting (but are done on account of the infallibility of the scripture; nor is there any material substance purified (but) in an action it is connected with the object (and also) there is a direct signification that it is *puruṣārtha.*

अविशेषात्तु शास्त्रस्य यथाश्रुति फलानि स्युः ॥४॥

4. Again there being no distinction of the passages of the scripture, the fruits shall accrue as described in the text (of the Veda).

अपि वा कारणाऽग्रहणे तदर्थमर्थस्याऽनभिसम्बन्धात् ॥५॥

5. Not so; on not accepting the cause, there is the object of a person; the object being not connected (with the cause).

तथा च लोकभूतेषु ॥६॥

6. And similarly in the conduct of the worldly affairs.

द्रव्याणि त्त्वविशेषेणाऽऽनर्थक्यात्प्रदीयेरन् ॥७॥

7. Again materials should, without any distinction, be offered (in the fire to avoid) meaninglessness.

स्वेन त्वर्थेन सम्बन्धो द्रव्याणां पृथगर्थत्वात्तस्माद्यथा श्रुति स्युः ॥८॥

8. On the contrary the materials are connected with their own object. On account of their different uses, they are (to be used) according to the text (of the Veda).

चोद्यन्ते चार्थकर्मसु ॥९॥

9. The offering of the sacrificial cakes is also enjoined in the principal act.

लिङ्गदर्शनाच्च ॥१०॥

10. (There are) indications also (to that effect).

तत्रैकत्वमयज्ञाङ्गमर्थस्य गुणभूतत्वात् ॥११॥

11. There unity is not a part of a sacrifice because of its being subordinate to the main object.

एकश्रुतित्वाच्च ॥१२॥

12. And on account of one being used in the Veda.

प्रतीयते इति चेत् ॥१३॥

13. If you say that it also appears from the usage.

नाऽशब्दं तत्प्रमाणत्वात्पूर्ववत् ॥१४॥

14. Not so, that (number) is meaningless, being authoritative like the 'east.'

शब्दवत्तूपलभ्यते तदागमे हि तद्दृश्यते तस्य ज्ञानं हि यथाऽन्येषाम् ॥१५॥

15. It (number) is known along with the word; on the pronunciation of it, the number is known. Its knowledge (is obtained) just like other (things).

तद्वच्च लिङ्गदर्शनम् ॥१६॥

16. And the same (is from the) indicative power of the text.

तथा च लिङ्गम् ॥१७॥

17. In the same way, gender (is known).

आश्रयिष्वविशेषेण भावोऽर्थः प्रतीयेत ॥१८॥

18. In the constituent parts generally the purpose of the main act (sacrifice) is served.

चोदनायां त्वनारम्भोऽविभक्तत्वान्न ह्यन्येन विधीयते ॥१९॥

19. The Vedic command does not pertain to the parts on account of their being separate; nor can they be regulated by another (command).

स्याद्वा द्रव्यचिकीर्षायां भावोऽर्थे च गुणभूतताऽऽश्रयाद्धिगुणीभावः ॥२०॥

20. Not so; in the purification of the sacrificial materials, there in an invisible effect (*apūrva*); in the object (of purification) there is dependence by reason of its being subsidiary to the principal act.

अर्थे समवैषम्यतो द्रव्यकर्मणाम् ॥२१॥

21. There is a parity or disparity of sacrificial material or act in the fulfilment of the object.

एकनिष्पत्तेः सर्वं समं स्यात् ॥२२॥

22. It is a case of parity when different effects are produced by means of one act.

संसर्गरसनिष्पत्तेरामिक्षा वा प्रधानं स्यात् ॥२३॥

23. By reason of the production of whey by contact, the *āmikṣā* (curd) is principal.

मुख्यशब्दाभिसंस्तवाच्च ॥२४॥

24. By reason of the praise of the chief object.

पदकर्माप्रयोजकं नयनस्य परार्थत्वात् ॥२५॥

25. Causing a cow to walk is a subsidiary act because the bringing of it is subservient (to some other act).

अर्थाभिधानकर्म च भविष्यता संयोगस्य तन्निमित्तत्वात्तदर्थो हि विधीयते ॥२६॥

26. The action of naming *puroḍāśa kapāla* is based on the main object; on account of the connection with the future *puroḍāśa kapāla* that object is described.

पशावनालम्भाल्लोहितशकृतोरकर्मत्वम् ॥२७॥

27. When an animal is not killed, the blood and dung do not constitute the (essential) act.

एकदेशद्रव्यश्चोत्पत्तौ विद्यमानसंयोगात् ॥२८॥

28. (*sviṣṭakṛt* offering) is a portion (of the sacrificial cake) being in existence with the whole in the beginning.

निर्देशात्तस्यान्यदर्थादिति चेत् ॥२९॥

29. If it be said that on account of the special description of it; another (puroḍāśa cake should he prepared) from the object.

न शेषसन्निधानात् ॥३०॥

30. No; on account of the remnant being near.

कर्मकार्यात् ॥३१॥

31. By reason of the performance of the act.

लिङ्गदर्शनाच्च ॥३२॥

32. By reason of the suggestive sense of the Vedic text.

अभिधारणे विप्रकर्षादनुयाजवत्पात्रभेदः स्यात् ॥३३॥

33. In sprinkling of ghee by reason of distant connection, there must be a separate vessel as in an Anuyāja offering.

न वा पात्रत्वादपात्रत्वं त्वेकदेशत्वात् ॥३४॥

34. Not so; by reason of the absence of a vessel and the absence of the vessel is by reason of its being a portion (of the whole ghee).

हेतुत्वाच्च सहप्रयोगस्य ॥३५॥

35. And there is a reason for using both at the same time.

अभावदर्शनाच्च ॥३६॥

36. And by seeing its absence.

सति सव्यवचनम् ॥३७॥

37. When there is abhidhāraṇa, the term *savya* is used.

न तस्येति चेत् ॥३८॥

38. If you say that it does not pertain to it (the omentum).

स्यात्तस्य मुख्यत्वात् ॥३९॥

39. May be so, on account of its being principal.

समानयनं तु मुख्यं स्याल्लिङ्गदर्शनात् ॥४०॥

40. On the other hand, *Samānayana* is principal by virtue of the significant power of the Vedic text.

वचने हि हेत्वसामर्थ्यम् ॥४१॥

41. In the Vedic text or authority the power of the reason is absent.

तत्रोत्पत्तिरविभक्ता स्यात् ॥४२॥

42. There what is taken is undivided.

तत्र जौहवमनुयाजप्रतिषेधार्थम् ॥४३॥

43. There the ghee taken in *juhū* is for the prohibition (that it is not to be used) for *anuyāja* offerings.

औपभृतं तथेति चेत् ॥४४॥

44. If you say that the ghee taken in *upabhṛta* is similarly (prohibited).

स्याज्जुहूप्रतिषेधान्नित्यानुवादः ॥४५॥

45. By reason of the prohibition relating to *juhū*, there is permanent restatement.

तदष्टसङ्ख्यं श्रवणात् ॥४६॥

46. On account of the direct text of number eight for (clarified butter).

अनुग्रहाच्च जौहवस्य ॥४७॥

47. Because of its serving the purpose of the ghee in a *juhū.*

द्वयोस्तु हेतुसामर्थ्यं श्रवणं च समानयने ॥४८॥

48. Of the two there is the force of reason and direct authority in *samānayana.*

END OF PĀDA 1

***

PĀDA 2

स्वरुस्त्वनेकनिष्पत्तिः स्वकर्मशब्दत्वात् ॥१॥

1. Svaru is to be made from a different tree because there is a direction of its preparation.

जात्यन्तराच्च शङ्कते ॥२॥

2. Because a *svaru* is prepared from another tree, he doubts.

तदेकदेशो वा स्वरुत्वस्य तन्निमित्तत्वात् ॥३॥

3. On the other hand, the very nature of the *svaru* is a portion (of the *yūpa*) and its very purpose is for it (*yūpa*).

शकलश्रुतेश्च ॥४॥

4. And also by reason of the Vedic text to the effect that it is a portion.

प्रतियूपं च दर्शनात् ॥५॥

5. Because it is seen with each *yūpa.*

आदाने करोतिशब्दः ॥६॥

6. The word 'makes' (is used) in (the sense of) taking.

शाखायां तत्प्रधानत्वात् ॥७॥

7. In (the sense of a) branch on account of its being principal.

शाखायां तत्प्रधानत्वादुपवेषेण विभागः स्याद्वैषम्यंतत् ॥८॥

8. On account of its being principal in the branch, there is a separation with the lower portion; it is a case of disparity.

श्रुत्यपायाच्च ॥९॥

9. And by reason of the absence of the Vedic text.

हरणे तु जुहोतिर्योगसामान्याद्द्रव्याणां चार्थशेषत्वात् ॥१०॥

10. On the other hand the term 'throwing' means sacrifice by reason of its being used in common and by reason of the materials being subsidiary to the object.

प्रतिपत्तिर्वा शब्दस्य तत्प्रधानत्वात् ॥११॥

11. It is the final disposal (*pratipattikarma*) by reason of the word being principal in this connection.

अर्थेऽपि चेत् ॥१२॥

12. If you say that the sense (also indicates that it is *arthakarma*).

न तस्यानधिकारादर्थस्य च कृतत्वात् ॥१३॥

13. There being no analogy with it (*eka kapāla*) and its (*śākhā*) having fulfilled the object.

उत्पत्त्यसंयोगात्प्रणीतानामाज्यवद्विभागः स्यात् ॥१४॥

14. There being no connection with the mandatory command as to the water, there must be division as in the case of the ghee.

संयवनार्थानां वा प्रतिपत्तिरितरासां तत्प्रधानत्वात् ॥१५॥

15. On the other hand the other water (namely *ninayana*) is the *pratipatti* of the *saṃyavana* which is the principal act on account of its being principal.

प्रासनवन्मैत्रावरुणस्य दण्डप्रदानं कृतार्थत्वात् ॥१६॥

16. Handing over of the staff to the *maitrāvaruṇa* priest (is a *pratipattikarma*) by reason of its having accomplished its object just like throwing off (of the horn of the black antelope).

अर्थकर्म वा कर्तृसंयोगात्स्रग्वत् ॥१७॥

17. It is an arthakarma by reason of its connection with the sacrificer like the garland.

कर्मयुक्ते च दर्शनात् ॥१८॥

18. Because it is seen in subsequent acts.

उत्पत्तौ येन संयुक्तं तदर्थं तच्छ्रुतिहेतुत्वात्तस्यार्थान्तरगमने शेषत्वात्प्रतिपत्तिः स्यात् ॥१९॥

19. It is for that object with which it is connected in the origin for reason of direct authority; its use subsequently by reason of its being subsidiary is pratipatti.

सौमिके च कृतार्थत्वात् ॥२०॥

20. Because they have all been used up in the soma sacrifice.

अर्थकर्म वाऽभिधानसंयोगात् ॥२१॥

21. On the other hand, it is an *arthakarma* on account of its connection with the original name.

प्रतिपत्तिर्वा तन्न्यायत्वाद्देशार्थाऽवभृथश्रुतिः ॥२२॥

22. On the other hand it is *pratipatti*; by reason of the propriety of its sense; the word *avabhṛtha* signifies a place.

कर्तृदेशकालानामचोदनं प्रयोगे नित्यसमवायात् ॥२३॥

23. The agent, place and time being essentially connected with the performance of a (sacrifice) are not mandatory.

नियमार्था वा श्रुतिः ॥२४॥

24. On the other hand the Vedic text is restrictive.

तथा द्रव्येषु गुणश्रुतिरुत्पत्तिसंयोगात् ॥२५॥

25. Similarly the description of the qualities of the materials (is restrictive) by reason of its connection with the original text.

संस्कारे च तत्प्रधानत्वात् ॥२६॥

26. And in the purification of the materials by reason of its being principal.

यजति चोदनाद्रव्यदेवताक्रियं समुदाये कृतार्थत्वात् ॥२७॥

27. Command as to the sacrifice, the materials, gods and act, all collectively (constitute a sacrifice) by reason of their having accomplished their object.

तदुक्ते श्रवणाज्जुहोतिरासेचनाधिकः स्यात् ॥२८॥

28. (*yāga*) having been defined, a homa (includes) gift in addition by reason of the direct text.

विधेः कर्मापवर्गित्वादर्थान्तरे विधिप्रदेशः स्यात् ॥२९॥

29. The force of Vedic command lasts till the completion of an act; and for another act another command is required.

अपि वोत्पत्तिसंयोगादर्थसम्बन्धोऽविशिष्टानां प्रयोगैकत्वहेतुः स्यात् ॥३०॥

30. Not so; by reason of the original command (an act is enjoined); and the connection of the acts not specially described with the object is the reason of their constituting one whole act.

END OF PĀDA 2

***

PĀDA 3

द्रव्यसंस्कारकर्मसु परार्थत्वात्फलश्रुतिरर्थवादः स्यात् ॥१॥

1. The text regarding the reward as to the materials, their purification and acts by reason of their being subservient to others is recommendatory.

उत्पत्तेश्चातत्प्रधानत्वात् ॥२॥

2. In the original (Vedic text) on account of its being not principal.

फलन्तु तत्प्रधानायाम् ॥३॥

3. On the other hand, the (mention of) reward (is original) when it is principal in it.

नैमित्तिके विकारत्वात्क्रतुप्रधानमन्यत्स्यात् ॥४॥

4. On account of the procedure adopted in the performance of the occasional acts, being that of the modified sacrifice, the principal sacrifice is different.

एकस्य तूभयत्वे संयोगपृथक्त्वम् ॥५॥

5. On the other hand (when) one (substance used) in two capacities (both for *nitya* and *naimittika* acts), (there is a) split of a sentence.

शेष इति चेत् ॥६॥

6. If you say (that the separate sentence be treated as) subsidiary.

नार्थपृथक्त्वात् ॥७॥

7. No, by reason of the sense being different.

द्रव्याणान्तु क्रियार्थानां संस्कारः क्रतुधर्मः स्यात् ॥८॥

8. On the other hand, the purification of the materials for the purpose of an action is a *kratvartha.*

पृथक्त्वाद्व्यवतिष्ठेत ॥९॥

9. By reason (of the acts) being different, this rule has been laid down.

चोदनायां फलाश्रुतेः कर्ममात्रं विधीयेत न ह्यशब्दं प्रतीयते ॥१०॥

10. When there is no mention of a reward in the commandatory text, it lays down only an act, because what is not ordained is not recognised.

अपि वाऽम्नानसामर्थ्याच्चोदनार्थेनगम्येतार्थानांह्यर्थवत्त्वेन वचनानि प्रतीयन्तेऽर्थतोप्यसमर्थानामानन्तर्य्येप्यसम्बन्धस्तस्माच्छ्रुत्येकदेशस्सः ॥११॥

11. Not so; the binding force (command) is inferred from the authority of the Vedic text; the texts are recognised to be for some object by reason of their having rewards. Those that do not contain any reward and have no connection with any (sentence) in the proximity (their connection should be sought in a remote passage) because it is a portion of the Vedic text.

वाक्यार्थश्च गुणार्थवत् ॥१२॥

12. The sense of the Vedic sentence is like the sense of the subordinate act.

तत्सर्वार्थमनादेशात् ॥१३॥

13. That (*viśvajit* produces) all fruits, because no specific reward is mentioned.

एकं वा चोदनैकत्वात् ॥१४॥

14. (It produces) one fruit, because there is one command.

स स्वर्गः स्यात्सर्वान्प्रत्यविशिष्टत्वात् ॥१५॥

15. That (reward) is heaven because it is desired by all.

प्रत्ययाच्च ॥१६॥

16. And by reason of (our) experience.

क्रतौ फलार्थवादमङ्गवत्कार्ष्णाजिनिः ॥१७॥

17. It is the opinion of Kārṣṇājini that the *arthavāda* description of a fruit in a sacrifice is like that of the description of a subordinate act.

फलमात्रेयो निर्देशादश्रुतौ ह्यनुमानं स्यात् ॥१८॥

18. It is the opinion of Ātreya that there is a reward under the (Vedic) command and where there is no command, it can be inferred.

अङ्गेषु स्तुतिः परार्थत्वात् ॥१९॥

19. The praise in subordinate acts (is) by reason of being subordinate to others (for the principal).

काम्ये कर्मणि नित्यः स्वर्गो यथा यज्ञाङ्गे क्रत्वर्थः ॥२०॥

20. In a desire accomplishing sacrifice, (there) is its reward in the shape of heaven; just as a subordinate act (besides fulfilling its result) is for the sake of a sacrifice.

वीते च कारणे नियमात् ॥२१॥

21. On the cause (which actuated the act) being over by reason of the restrictive rule (the act is continued till completion).

कामो वा तत्संयोगेन चोद्यते ॥२२॥

22. On the other hand, the motive has been ordained in that connection.

अङ्गे गुणत्वात् ॥२३॥

23. In a subordinate act by reason of its being subordinate.

वीते च नियमस्तदर्थम् ॥२४॥

24. On the desire being accomplished, the rule (that it should be continued till completion) is for that object.

सर्वकाम्यमङ्गकामैः प्रकरणात् ॥२५॥

25. All desires are fulfilled by fulfilment of the desires connected with subordinate acts (as is shown) by the context.

फलोपदेशो वा प्रधानशब्दसंयोगात् ॥२६॥

26. On the other hand, (it is) a description of the reward by reason of the connection with the principal statement.

तत्र सर्वेऽविशेषात् ॥२७॥

27. There all (desires are accomplished) as no distinction is made.

योगसिद्धिर्वाऽर्थस्योत्पत्यसंयोगित्वात् ॥२८॥

28. On the other hand, the desires are fulfilled in succession by reason of their not rising simultaneously.

समवाये चोदनासंयोगस्यार्थवत्वात् ॥२९॥

29. Because the sense of the text is properly conveyed when it is connected with the permanent relationship.

कालश्रुतौ काल इति चेत् ॥३०॥

30. If you say that it indicates time under a text enjoining time.

नासमवायात्प्रयोजनेन ॥३१॥

31. Not so, because there will be no connection with the reward.

उभयार्थमिति चेत् ॥३२॥

32. If it be said that it is for both.

न शब्दैकत्वात् ॥३३॥

33. It is not so, by reason of its being one sentence.

प्रकरणादिति चेत् ॥३४॥

34. If you say that by reason of the context.

नोत्पत्तिसंयोगात् ॥३५॥

35. No; by reason of the original sentence.

अनुत्पत्तौ तु कालः स्यात्प्रयोजनेन सम्बन्धात् ॥३६॥

36. On the other hand when there is no original sentence, it is then sequence of time by virtue of its connection with the object.

उत्पत्तिकालविशये कालः स्याद्वाक्यस्य तत्प्रधानत्वात् ॥३७॥

37. When there is a doubt whether it is a relationship of a part to the whole or a sequence of time, it is a sequence of time by virtue of its being principal in the sentence.

फलसंयोगस्त्वचोदिते न स्यादशेषभूतत्वात् ॥३८॥

38. On the other hand, when there is no commandatory text, there is no reward (to the sacrificer) by virtue of there being no relationship of a part to its whole.

अङ्गानां तूपघातसंयोगो निमित्तार्थः ॥३९॥

39. On the other hand, the mention of the son's birth is for the purpose of subsidiary actions.

प्रधानेनाभिसंयोगादङ्गानां मुख्यकालत्वम् ॥४०॥

40. By reason of the connection with the principal, the time of the principal is the time of the subsidiary actions.

अपवृत्ते तु चोदना तत्सामान्यात्स्वकाले स्यात् ॥४१॥

41. On the other hand, on the completion (of a sacrifice, another sacrifice should be commenced, is) the commandatory text; by virtue of its general nature (the subsidiary sacrifices) shall be (performed) at their proper time.

END OF PĀDA 3

***

PĀDA 4

प्रकरणशब्दसामान्याच्चोदनानामनङ्गत्वम् ॥१॥

1. By virtue of the word 'context' in general, the commendatory text does not constitute subordinate acts.

अपि वाऽङ्गमनिज्याः स्युस्ततो विशिष्टत्वात् ॥२॥

2. Not so; the subordinate acts are without oblation; therefore there is a distinction.

मध्यस्थं यस्य तन्मध्ये ॥३॥

3. It belongs to that subject under which it is described.

सर्वासां वा समत्वाच्चोदनातः स्यान्न हि तस्य प्रकरणं देशार्थमुच्यते मध्ये ॥४॥

4. By virtue of the original text they are all equally important, it is not its context; it is mentioned in the middle for the purpose of direction.

प्रकरणाविभागे च विप्रतिषिद्धं ह्युभयम् ॥५॥

5. On account of the indivisibility of the context, the direct command relating to two is forbidden (by reason of the syntactical division).

अपि वा कालमात्रं स्याददर्शनाद्विशेषस्य ॥६॥

6. Not so; it (lays down) time only, by reason of the absence of any special mention.

फलवद्वोक्तहेतुत्वादितरस्य प्रधानं स्यात् ॥७॥

7. (The acts) which produce fruit are principal, by reason as given of another.

दधिग्रहो नैमित्तिकः श्रुतिसंयोगात् ॥८॥

8. The (offering of a) cup of curd is occasional by reason of its relation with the Vedic text.

नित्यश्च ज्येष्ठशब्दात् ॥९॥

9. (The *dadhigraha* is) permanent because of the word 'excellent' (used).

सार्वरूप्याच्च ॥१०॥

10. And also by reason of its being the form of all (gods).

नित्यो वा स्यादर्थवादस्तयोः कर्मण्यसम्बन्धाद्भङ्गित्वाच्चान्तरायस्य ॥११॥

11. On the other hand, it is permanent; it is *arthavāda* because of their (of the sacrificer and the priest) having no connection with the act and by reason of the impermanent nature of the impediment.

वैश्वानरश्च नित्यः स्यान्नित्यैः समानसङ्ख्यत्वात् ॥१२॥

12. Vaiśvānara is permanent by reason of its being numbered along with permanent things.

पक्षे वोत्पन्नसंयोगात् ॥१३॥

13. On the other hand, it is occasional by reason of the original authority.

षट्चितिः पूर्ववत्त्वात् ॥१४॥

14. The Ṣaṭciti sacrifice is like the former.

ताभिश्च तुल्यसंख्यानात् ॥१५॥

15. And by reason of its being reckoned among them.

अर्थवादोपपत्तेश्च ॥१६॥

16. And by reason of the satisfactory explanation of the recommendatory statement in this connection.

एकचितिर्वा स्यादपवृक्ते हि चोद्यते निमित्तेन ॥१७॥

17. On the other hand, there is only one citi on the completion (of the *agnicayana* sacrifice) because it is ordained with a purpose.

विप्रतिषेधात्ताभिः समानसङ्ख्यत्वम् ॥१८॥

18. Though opposed, they are reckoned along with them.

पितृयज्ञः स्वकालत्वादनङ्गं स्यात् ॥१९॥

19. The offering to the manes by reason of its (appointed) time is principal.

तुल्यवच्च प्रसङ्ख्यानात् ॥२०॥

20. And by reason of its being counted along with equal (things).

प्रतिषिद्धे च दर्शनात् ॥२१॥

21. And by reason of its being seen on a prohibited day.

पश्वङ्गं रशना स्यात्तदागमे विधानात् ॥२२॥

22. The rope is a part of an animal being described in that context.

यूपाङ्गं वा तत्संस्कारात् ॥२३॥

23. On the other hand, it is a part of the sacrificial post by reason of its purifying it.

अर्थवादश्च तदर्थवत् ॥२४॥

24. It has a meaning (if we take it for an) arthavāda (descriptive).

स्वरुश्चाप्येकदेशत्वात् ॥२५॥

25. And *svaru* (is a part of *yūpa*) by reason of its being a part.

निष्क्रयश्च तदङ्गवत् ॥२६॥

26. And (it is) a ransom and therefore it is a part of (the sacrificial post).

पश्वङ्गं वार्थकर्मत्वात् ॥२७॥

27. On the other hand, *svaru* is a part of animal because it is an *arthakarma.*

भक्त्या निष्क्रयवादः स्यात् ॥२८॥

28. The description about ransom is by the transferred sense.

दर्शपूर्णमासयोरिज्याः प्रधानान्यविशेषात् ॥२९॥

29. All the oblations (made) during new and full moons are principal by reason of no special mention (made about them).

अपि वाङ्गानि कानि चिद्येश्वङ्गत्वेन संस्तुतिः सामान्योह्यभिसंस्तवः ॥३०॥

30. Not so; some are parts which are praised as parts; because the praise is general.

तथा चान्यार्थदर्शनम् ॥३१॥

31. And again seeing another case.

अवशिष्टन्तु कारणं प्रधानेषु गुणस्य विद्यमानत्वात् ॥३२॥

32. The reason (given) is not distinctive by virtue of the subordinate being included in the principal.

नानुक्तेऽन्यार्थदर्शनं परार्थत्वात् ॥३३॥

33. When it is not mentioned (in the Vedas) it cannot be another case by reason of being subservient to another.

पृथक्त्वे त्वभिधानयोर्निवेशः श्रुतितो व्यपदेशाच्च तत्पुनर्मुख्यलक्षणं यत्फलवत्त्वं तत्सन्निधावसंयुक्तं तदङ्गं स्याद्भागित्वात्कारणस्याश्रुतश्चान्यसम्बन्धः ॥३४॥

34. On the other hand, by reason of the connection and sacrificial custom, when there is difference of names, (there is) connection with the reward; that which is the quality of bearing the fruit is the distinctive mark of the principal and that in its proximity is

unconnected, is a constituent part; the connection with any other is not heard.

गुणाश्च नामसंयुक्ता विधीयन्ते नाङ्गेषूपपद्यन्ते ॥३५॥

35. The qualities are ordained to be connected with the names (of the substances) and are not met with in the constituent parts.

तुल्या च कारणश्रुतिरन्यैरङ्गाङ्गिसम्बन्धः ॥३६॥

36. The text describing the main act is similar; the connection of the parts with the main act is with other (acts).

उत्पत्तावभिसम्बन्धस्तस्मादङ्गोपदेशः स्यात् ॥३७॥

37. There is a connection in the origin; therefore there is a description of the constituent part.

तथा चान्यार्थदर्शनम् ॥३८॥

38. Again, there is seen another ease.

ज्योतिष्टोमे तुल्यान्यविशिष्टं हि कारणम् ॥३९॥

39. In a jyotiṣṭoma sacrifice all are equal because the cause is not distinctive.

गुणानां तूत्पत्तिवाक्येन सम्बन्धात्कारणश्रुतिस्तस्मात्सोमः प्रधानं स्यात् ॥४०॥

40. On the other hand by reason of the connection of the qualities with the original statement there is a text describing the reward; the soma is therefore principal.

तथा चान्यार्थदर्शनम् ॥४१॥

41. And similarly there is another case seen.

END OF PĀDA 4

***

END OF ADHYĀYA IV

ADHYĀYA V

PĀDA 1

श्रुतिलक्षणमानुपूर्व्यं तत्प्रमाणत्वात् ॥१॥

1. The definition of *śruti* is the order of following in succession by virtue of its authority.

अर्थाच्च ॥२॥

2. And by purpose.

अनियमोऽन्यत्र ॥३॥

3. Sometimes it is not governed by any rule.

क्रमेण वा नियम्येत क्रत्वेकत्वे तद्गुणत्वात् ॥४॥

4. On the other hand by reason of being subordinate in one sacrifice, (the order of performance) is governed by the order (of reading).

अशाब्द इति चेत्स्याद्वाक्यशब्दत्वात् ॥५॥

5. If it be said that it is not a direct expression (of the order) by reason of the sentences.

अर्थकृते वाऽनुमानं स्यात्क्रत्वेकत्वे परार्थत्वात्स्वेन त्वर्थेन सम्बन्धस्तस्मा-त्स्वशब्दमुच्येत ॥६॥

6. On the other hand there is an inference for the sake of the sense in the unity of a sacrifice; by reason of its dependence on another, there is a relationship with its own object; it can therefore be said to be a direct expression.

तथा चान्यार्थदर्शनम् ॥७॥

7. And similarly another case is seen.

प्रवृत्त्या तुल्यकालानां गुणानां तदुपक्रमात् ॥८॥

8. By the first start (is determined the order) of the subordinate acts which are to be performed simultaneously by virtue of the first commencement.

सर्वमिति चेत् ॥९॥

9. If you say that all (should be done simultaneously).

नाकृतत्वात् ॥१०॥

10. Not so, by reason of its being not done.

क्रत्वन्तरवदिति चेत् ॥११॥

11. If you say that like another sacrifice, (*sauryayāga*)

नासमवायात् ॥१२॥

12. Not so; there being no relationship of a part with the whole.

स्थानाच्चोत्पत्तिसंयोगात् ॥१३॥

13. By position and the original text.

मुख्यक्रमेण वाऽङ्गानां तदर्थत्वात् ॥१४॥

14. The order of the subordinate acts (is governed) by the order of their principal, by reason of their being subservient to it.

प्रकृतौ तु स्वशब्दत्वाद्यथाक्रमं प्रतीयेत ॥१५॥

15. In a model sacrifice by reason of the direct authority, the order as laid down should be followed.

मन्त्रतस्तु विरोधे स्यात्प्रयोगरूपसामर्थ्यात्तस्मादुत्पत्तिदेशः सः ॥१६॥

16. Again, on conflict, (the order is governed) by the *mantra* by virtue of the power of accomplishment (of an act); because the *Brāhmaṇa* is the seat of the origin.

तद्वचनाद्विकृतौ यथा प्रधानं स्यात् ॥१७॥

17. By reason of the Vedic authority in a modified sacrifice, (the procedure is governed by that of) the principal.

विप्रतिपत्तौ वा प्रकृत्यन्वयाद्यथाप्रकृति ॥१८॥

18. On the other hand when there is a conflict, (the order) is that of the model sacrifice, it being a part of the model sacrifice.

विकृतिः प्रकृतिधर्मत्वात्तत्काला स्याद्यथा शिष्टम् ॥१९॥

19. The modified sacrifice follows the order of the model sacrifice; the time thereof is the same as laid down.

अपि वा क्रमकालसंयुक्ता सद्याः क्रियेत तत्र विधेरनुमानात्प्रकृतिधर्मलोपः स्यात् ॥२०॥

20. Not so; (the sacrifice) along with the order and time is performed immediately; there command prevails over the inference and the order of the model sacrifice is omitted.

कालोत्कर्ष इति चेत् ॥२१॥

21. If you say that the time should be transferred forward.

न तत्सम्बन्धात् ॥२२॥

22. Not so, because of its connection.

अङ्गानां मुख्यकालत्वाद्यथोक्तमुत्कर्षे स्यात् ॥२३॥

23. On the forward transference, the time of the subsidiary acts is that of the principal as laid down.

तदादि वाऽभिसम्बन्धात्तदन्तमपकर्षे स्यात् ॥२४॥

24. On the other hand, the first part is taken by reason of its connection (in the case of forward transference) and the last part is taken in the case of the transference backward.

प्रवृत्या कृतकालानाम् ॥२५॥

25. (The order of those acts) whose time is known by convention.

शब्दविप्रतिषेधाच्च ॥२६॥

26. And by inversion or prohibition of the word.

असंयोगात्तु वैकृतं तदेव प्रतिकृष्येत ॥२७॥

27. On the other hand, by reason of no connection with the modified sacrifice, that alone is transferred backward.

प्रासङ्गिकं च नोत्कर्षेदसंयोगात् ॥२८॥

28. And anything accidental should not be transferred forward, because there is no connection.

तथाऽपूर्वम् ॥२९॥

29. Similarly model sacrifice.

सान्तपनीया तूत्कर्षेदग्निहोत्रं सवनवद्वैगुणयात् ॥३०॥

30. On the transference forward of the *sāntapanīyā* the *agnihotra* is also transferred like the soma libation to avoid difference.

अव्यवायाच्च ॥३१॥

31. And in order to avoid the break of order.

असम्बन्धात्तु नोत्कर्षेत् ॥३२॥

32. On the other hand, there being no connection there should not be a forward transference.

प्रापणाच्च निमित्तस्य ॥३३॥

33. And by accrual of a reason.

सम्बन्धात्सवनोत्कर्षः ॥३४॥

34. By reason of the connection there is a forward transference of the some libation.

षोडशी चोक्थ्यसंयोगात् ॥३५॥

35. And *ṣoḍaśī* (is to be transferred forward) by reason of its connection with *ukthya.*

END OF PĀDA 1

***

PĀDA 2

सन्निपाते प्रधानानामेकैकस्य गुणानां सर्वकर्म स्यात् ॥१॥

1. On a collection of the principals, the subordinate acts should, one by one, be performed till all are over.

सर्वेषां वैकजातीयं कृतानुपूर्व्यत्वात् ॥२॥

2. On the other hand, one kind of sacrificial act be performed on all, in order to maintain the order.

कारणादभ्यावृत्तिः ॥३॥

3. There is a reason for the repetition.

मुष्टिकपालावदानाञ्जनाभ्यञ्जनवपनपावनेषु चैकेन ॥४॥

4. And in the case of taking handful of sacrificial material, sacrificial pans, oblations, collyrium, anointment, getting shaved, sprinkling of water for purification, (the procedure is) one by one.

सर्वाणि त्वेककार्यत्वादेषां तद्गुणत्वात् ॥५॥

5. On the other hand they are all (one) by reason of being one act, they being subsidiary to it.

संयुक्ते तु प्रक्रमात्तदङ्गं स्यादितरस्य तदर्थत्वात् ॥६॥

6. Again in a relationship by reason of its commencement, it is its part because it is subservient to another.

वचनात्तु परिव्याणान्तमञ्जनादिः स्यात् ॥७॥

7. Again, under a direct authority, the anointment &c., to the end of tying round of a string continue.

कारणाद्वा(न)वसर्गः स्याद्यथा पात्रवृद्धिः ॥८॥

8. Or there is relinquishment (of the past) by a special reason just as the addition of a vessel.

न वा शब्दकृतत्वान्न्यायमात्रमितरदर्थात्पात्रविवृद्धिः ॥९॥

9. Not so; by virtue of a direct authority; the other is a matter of inference only; there is a reason of an addition of a vessel.

पशुगणे तस्यतस्यापवर्जयेत्पश्वैकत्वात् ॥१०॥

10. On an assemblage of victims, each victim should have the complete performance, they being of the same class.

दैवतैर्वैककर्म्यात् ॥११॥

11. On the other hand by the *daivata*, because it is one act.

मन्त्रस्य चार्थवत्त्वात् ॥१२॥

12. And by reason of the mantra having its purpose fulfilled.

नानाबीजेष्वेकमुलूखलं विभवात् ॥१३॥

13. In the case of many seeds one mortar (is sufficient) by reason of its capacity.

विवृद्धिर्वा नियमादानुपूर्व्यस्य तदर्थत्वात् ॥१४॥

14. On the other hand there must be many, because the order based on *pāṭha* is for that purpose.

एकं वा तण्डुलभावाद्धन्तेस्तदर्थत्वात् ॥१५॥

15. On the other hand, it is one, by reason of all being rice till their preparation, because pulverisation is for it.

विकारे त्वनुयाजानां पात्रभेदोऽर्थभेदात्स्यात् ॥१६॥

16. Again in a modified sacrifice, there must be a difference of vessels for *anuyāja* offerings by reason of the difference of purpose.

प्रकृतेः पूर्वोक्तत्वादपूर्वमन्ते स्यान्नह्यचोदितस्य शेषान्मानम् ॥१७॥

17. The (*prakṛti*) model sacrifice (first), by reason of its being mentioned first; and (*vikṛti*) modified sacrifice in the end, because of that which is not mentioned is ordained as subsidiary.

मुख्यानन्तर्यमात्रेयस्तेन तुल्यश्रुतित्वादशब्दत्वात्प्राकृतानां व्यवायः स्यात् ॥१८॥

18. (In a modified sacrifice) there is an immediate sequence of the

principal; (such is the opinion of) Ātreya by reason of its equal authority with the principal. As the acts of the model sacrifice are not mentioned, there will be an intervention (break).

अन्ते तु बादरायणस्तेषां प्रधानशब्दत्वात् ॥१९॥

19. On the other hand, according to Bādarāyaṇa in the end, by reason of their being mentioned as principal.

तथा चान्यार्थदर्शनम् ॥२०॥

20. And similarly there is another case seen.

कृतदेशात्तु पूर्वेषां स देशः स्यात्तेन प्रत्यक्षसंयोगान्नयायमात्रमितरत् ॥२१॥

21. On the other hand what order has been laid down of the first, that order shall be followed; because that is directly connected and the other is only inferential.

प्रकृताच्च पुरस्ताद्यत् ॥२२॥

22. Those acts that are mentioned prior to the acts of the model sacrifice shall be performed in that order.

सन्निपातश्चेद्यथोक्तमन्ते स्यात् ॥२३॥

23. When there are several acts to be performed, they shall be performed in the end as described.

END OF PĀDA 2

***

PĀDA 3

विवृद्धिः कर्मभेदात्पृषदाज्यवत्तस्यतस्योपदिश्येत ॥१॥

1. The increase is by virtue of the difference of acts just like *pṛṣadājya*; let it be then laid down (separately) for each.

अपि वा सर्वसङ्ख्यत्वाद्विकारः प्रतीयेत ॥२॥

2. Not so; by reason of all numbers, the modification is known.

स्वस्थानात्तु विवृध्येरन्कृतानुपूर्व्यत्वात् ॥३॥

3. Again (they) should increase from their own place by reason of the order that is already established.

समिध्यमानवतीं समिद्धवतीं चान्तरेण धाय्याः स्युर्द्यावापृथिव्योरन्तरालं समर्हणात् ॥४॥

4. The dhāyyā verses should be between *samidhyamānavatī* and *samiddhavatī* verses because they are described between heaven and earth.

तच्छब्दो वा ॥५॥

5. Or that designation.

उष्णिक्ककुभोरन्ते दर्शनात् ॥६॥

6. By seeing at the end of *uṣṇik* and *kakupa.*

स्तोमविवृद्धौ वहिष्पवमाने पुरस्तात्पर्यासादागन्तवः स्युस्तथा हि दृष्टं द्वादशाहे ॥७॥

7. In a *bahiṣpavamāna* when *stoma* is enlarged, additional verses should be recited before *paryāsa*, because it is so seen in *dvādaśāha.*

पर्यास इति चाऽन्ताख्या ॥८॥

8. The word *paryāsa* is the name of the last one.

अन्ते वा तदुक्तम् ॥९॥

9. Or it is in the end as it is described.

वचनात्तु द्वादशाहे ॥१०॥

10. The case of the 12th day ceremony is based on authority.

अतद्विकारश्च ॥११॥

11. And it is not a modification of that.

तद्विकारेऽप्यपूर्वत्वात् ॥१२॥

12. In its madification also by reason of the direct statement.

अन्ते तूत्तरयोर्दध्यात् ॥१३॥

13. On the other hand, (additional verses) should be introduced at the end of the next two.

अपि वा गायत्रीबृहत्यनुष्टुप्सु वचनात् ॥१४॥

14. Under the authority (of a text, they should be introduced) in the middle of *gāyatrī, bṛhatī* and *anuṣṭup* metres.

ग्रहेष्टकमौपानुवाक्यं सवनचितिशेषः स्यात् ॥१५॥

15. The cups and bricks which are described in proximity to *anuvākya* are subordinate to *savana* and *citi.*

क्रत्वग्निशेषा वा चोदितत्वाद् अचोदनानुपूर्वस्य ॥१६॥

16. Or they are subordinate to the sacrifice and fire by reason of a direct authority. No command as to order.

अन्ते स्युरव्यवायात् ॥१७॥

17. (The *citriṇī* and *vajriṇī* bricks should be used) in the end in order to avoid the break of sequence.

लिङ्गदर्शनाच्च ॥१८॥

18. And because there is a force of the text.

मध्यमायां तु वचनाद्ब्राह्मणवत्यः ॥१९॥

19. On the other hand in the middle *brāhmaṇvatī* bricks should be laid under the authority.

प्राग्लोकम्पृणायास्तस्याः सम्पूरणार्थत्वात् ॥२०॥

20. Before *lakaṁpṛṇā* by reason of its completing (the layer).

संस्कृते कर्म संस्काराणां तदर्थत्वात् ॥२१॥

21. In a purified (fire) an act (should be performed); because the purificatory ceremonies are with that object.

अनन्तरं व्रतं तद्भूतत्वात् ॥२२॥

22. Afterwards penance, that being ready.

पूर्वं च लिङ्गदर्शनात् ॥२३॥

23. First, by virtue of the indicative texts.

अर्थवादो वाऽर्थस्य विद्यमानत्वात् ॥२४॥

24. It is a recommendatory text because the purpose is present.

न्यायविप्रतिषेधाच्च ॥२५॥

25. And by reason of the violation of the rule.

सञ्चिते त्वग्निचिद्युक्तं प्रापणान्निमित्तस्य ॥२६॥

26. On the other hand, when altar is ready a person is *agnicit*; it is proper for him (to perform penances) because occasion has arisen.

क्रत्वन्ते वा प्रयोगवचनाभावात् ॥२७॥

27. Or at the end of the sacrifice, there being no text of procedure.

अग्नेः कर्मत्वनिर्देशात् ॥२८॥

28. Of fire it has been directed to be in the accusative case.

परेणाऽऽवेदनाद्दीक्षितः स्यात्सर्वैर्दीक्षाभिसम्बन्धात् ॥२९॥

29. One is initiated when he is so declared by others; because all are connected with the initiation.

इष्ट्यन्ते वा तदर्थो ह्यविशेषार्थसम्बन्धात् ॥३०॥

30. On the other hand, when sacrifices are performed (then one becomes initiated); they are (performed) with that object because there is no connection with anything particular.

समाख्यानं च तद्वत् ॥३१॥

31. The name is also like it.

अङ्गवत्क्रतूनामानुपूर्व्यम् ॥३२॥

32. The order (of *kābhyeṣṭi*) is like that of the constituent parts of the sacrifices.

न वाऽसम्बन्धात् ॥३३॥

33. Not so; by reason of want of connection.

काम्यत्वाच्च ॥३४॥

34. And by reason of their accomplishing the desires.

आनर्थक्यान्नेति चेत् ॥३५॥

35. If you say not, because (the purpose of the order) will be fruitless.

स्याद्विद्यार्थत्वाद्यथा परेषु सर्वस्वारात् ॥३६॥

36. It may be with the object of education, just as in the opinion of others general accentuation has an object.

य एतेनेत्यग्निष्टोमः प्रकरणात् ॥३७॥

37. The words "who by this" (indicate) *agniṣṭoma*, by reason of the context.

लिङ्गाच्च ॥३८॥

38. And by force of the textual authority.

अथान्येनेति संस्थानां सन्निधानात् ॥३९॥

39. When words "now by others" are used, they mean seven big sacrifice by reason of proximity.

तत्प्रकृतेर्वाऽऽपत्तिविहारौ न तुल्येषूपपद्यते ॥४०॥

40. Or the *āpatti* and *vihāra* are seen in the modified sacrifices but not in the model sacrifice.

प्रशंसा वा विहरणाभावात् ॥४१॥

41. Or it is praise because there is absence of transference.

विधिप्रत्ययाद्वा न ह्यकस्मात्प्रशंसा स्यात् ॥४२॥

42. Or by the force of the injunction, because there can be no praise at random.

एकस्तोमे वा क्रतुसंयोगात् ॥४३॥

43. Or in those sacrifices in which *stoma* is chanted by reason of their connection with the sacrifice.

सर्वेषां वा चोदनाविशेषात्प्रशंसा स्तोमानाम् ॥४४॥

44. Or of all; because there being no special command, it is a praise of the stomas.

END OF PĀDA 3

***

PĀDA 4

क्रमकोयोऽर्थशब्दाभ्यां श्रुतिविशेषादर्थपरत्वाच्च ॥१॥

1. The *pāṭhakrama* is (set aside) by the *arthakrama* and *śrutikrama* by reason of the special text and the desired object.

अवदानाऽभिधारणाऽऽसादनेष्वानुपूर्व्यं प्रवृत्या स्यात् ॥२॥

2. In the acts of cutting a slice from the puroḍāśa cake and anointing it with the clarified ghee and placing it, the order shall be according to the inclination.

यथाप्रदानं वा तदर्थत्वात् ॥३॥

3. On the other hand, (the order will depend) on the order of the thing offered because it is with that object.

लिङ्गदर्शनाच्च ॥४॥

4. And by the force of the text.

वचनादिष्टिपूर्वत्वम् ॥५॥

5. According to the text the *iṣṭi* (new and full moon sacrifice) has priority.

सोमश्चैकेषामग्न्याधेयस्यर्तुनक्षत्राऽतिक्रमवचनात्तदन्तेनानर्थकं हि स्यात् ॥६॥

6. According to one party, soma sacrifice comes after the preparation of fire, because there is a text for non-observance of season and

constellation; with that object the Vedic text does not become meaningless.

तदर्थवचनांच्च नाविशेषात्तदर्थत्वं ॥७॥

7. And that (*agnyādhāna*) being for that (*somayāga*) under a text and if not for particular (*somayāga*) the object of that will not be served.

अयक्ष्यमाणस्य च पवमानहविषां कालनिर्देशादानन्तर्याद्विशङ्का स्यात् ॥८॥

8. By reason of the direction as to time for performance of *pavamāna* offering for a person not performing *somayāga*; the doubt as to the validity of the practice of *ānantarya* (immediateness) is removed.

इष्टिरयक्ष्यमाणस्य तादर्थ्ये न सोमपूर्वत्वम् ॥९॥

9. For a man who does not perform *somayāga*, the *iṣṭi* (should be performed after *agnyādhāna*); but if it (*agnyādhāna*) is for that object (performance of *somayāga*) then *somayāga* must be performed first.

उत्कर्षाद्ब्राह्मणस्य सोमः स्यात् ॥१०॥

10. By transference forward (of *iṣṭi*) of a Brāhmaṇa, soma (sacrifice should be performed first).

पौर्णमासी वा श्रुतिसंयोगात् ॥११॥

11. Not so; the full moon sacrifice, as there is a direct Vedic authority.

सर्वस्य वैककर्म्यात् ॥१२॥

12. On the other hand, all constitute one act.

स्याद्वा विधिस्तदर्थेन् ॥१३॥

13. On the other hand, it is a command for the object.

प्रकरणात्तु कालः स्यात् ॥१४॥

14. On the other hand, time is (known) by context.

स्वकाले स्यादविप्रतिषेधात् ॥१५॥

15. At its own time, because there is no prohibition.

अपनयो वाऽऽधानस्य सर्वकालत्वात् ॥१६॥

16. On the other hand, the prohibition (relates to *somayāga*) because the establishment of fire can be done at all time.

पौर्णमास्यूर्ध्वं सोमाद्ब्राह्मणस्य वचनात् ॥१७॥

17. (Performance of) the full moon sacrifice for a Brāhmaṇa is after the *somayāga* by reason of the Vedic text.

एकं वा शब्दसामर्थ्यात्प्राक् कृत्स्नविधानम् ॥१८॥

18. By force of the text, one offering (should be made) before (*somayāga*) by virtue of all being prescribed.

पुरोडाशस्त्वनिर्देशे तद्युक्ते देवताभावात् ॥१९॥

19. On the other hand, when there is no direction the (offering shall be of) *puroḍāśa*; on the connection with that, by reason of being a deity.

आज्यमपीतिचेत् ॥२०॥

20. If you say that it may be an offering of clarified butter.

न मिश्रदेवतत्वादैन्द्राग्नवत् ॥२१॥

21. No; by reason of the mixed deity just as in the case of the offerings to gods Indra and Agni.

विकृतेः प्रकृतिकालत्वात्सद्यस्कालोत्तरा विकृतिस्तयोः प्रत्यक्ष-शिष्टत्वात् ॥२२॥

22. The time of the modified sacrifice is that of the model sacrifice; the modified sactifice should be performed immediately. Both of them being enjoined by the direct Vedic authority.

द्वैयहकाल्ये तु यथान्यायम् ॥२३॥

23. On the other hand, two days' time is proper.

वचनाद्वैककाल्यं स्यात् ॥२४॥

24. There is only one time by reason of the direct authority.

सन्नाय्याग्नीषोमीयविकाराऊर्ध्वं सोमात्प्रकृतिवत् ॥२५॥

25. The modified sacrifices *sannāya* and *agnīṣomīya* should be performed after *somayāga* like the model sacrifice.

तथा सोमविकारादर्शपूर्णमासाभ्याम ॥२६॥

26. Similarly the modifications of soma are performed after the new and full moon sacrifices.

END OF PĀDA 4

***

END OF ADHYĀYA V

ADHYĀYA VI

PĀDA 1

द्रव्याणां कर्मसंयोगे गुणत्वेनाऽभिसम्बन्धः ॥१॥

1. The relation of the materials in connection with an act is subordinate.

असाधकं तु तादर्थ्यात् ॥२॥

2. On the other hand, it is not a means by reason of its being for that object.

प्रत्यर्थं चाऽभिसंयोगात्कर्मतो ह्यभिसम्बन्धस्तस्मात्कर्मोपदेशः स्यात् ॥३॥

3. By reason of the connection with the object, there is relationship with the act; so there is a direction for the act.

फलार्थत्वात्कर्मणः शास्त्रं सर्वाधिकारं स्यात् ॥४॥

4. Because the reward of an action is desired, all are entitled to perform it.

कर्तुर्वाश्रुतिसंयोगाद्विधिः कात्स्न्र्येन गम्यते ॥५॥

5. On the other hand, the command by reason of its connection with the Veda, applies to a doer who can complete the whole.

लिङ्गविशेषनिर्देशात्पुंयुक्तमैतिशायनः ॥६॥

6. The view of Aitiśāyana is that a man alone is entitled, there being a mention of a special gender.

तदुक्तित्वाच्च दोषश्रुतिरविज्ञाते ॥७॥

7. By reason of the mention of it (masculine gender) there is a text which lays down sin on (the sex) being not known.

जातिं तु बादरायणोऽविशेषात्तस्मात्स्त्र्यपि प्रतीयेत जात्यर्थस्या-ऽविशिष्टत्वात् ॥८॥

8. On the other hand, the view of Bādarāyaṇa is that it refers to a class without any distinction; therefore a woman is also included; the object of the class is without distinction.

चोदितत्वाद्यथाश्रुति ॥९॥

9. Being enjoined it should be performed, according to the direction of the Veda.

द्रव्यवत्त्वात्तु पुंसां स्याद्द्रव्यसंयुक्तं क्रयविक्रयाभ्यामद्रव्यत्वं स्त्रीणां द्रव्यैः समानयोगित्वात् ॥१०॥

10. On the other hand, on account of the male possessing wealth (is competent to perform the sacrifice) dependent on wealth; by reason of sale and purchase of females, they are devoid of wealth, they being on the same level as property.

तथा चान्यार्थदर्शनम् ॥११॥

11. Similarly there is another text.

तादर्थ्यात्कर्मतादर्थ्यम् ॥१२॥

12. Being for his object, the act is all for him.

फलोत्साहविशेषात्तु ॥१३॥

13. On the other hand there being no distinction of the desire for the reward.

अर्थेन च समवेतत्वात् ॥१४॥

14. And being always connected with wealth.

क्रयस्य धर्ममात्रत्वम् ॥१५॥

15. The sale is only a religious form.

स्ववत्तामपिदर्शयति ॥१६॥

16. (The Veda) shows that they have capacity to possess wealth.

स्ववतोस्तु वचनादैककर्म्यं स्यात् ॥१७॥

17. On the other hand, the husband and wife possessed of wealth are entitled to perform the one and the same sacrificial act.

लिङ्गदर्शनाच्च ॥१८॥

18. And there is also an inference from the text.

क्रीतत्वात्तु भक्त्या स्वामित्वमुच्यते ॥१९॥

19. By reason of purchase, (she is not independent); by way of figurative speech (her) ownership is described.

फलार्थित्वात्तु स्वामित्वेनाभिसम्बन्धः ॥२०॥

20. On the other hand, by reason of having a desire for a reward, there is a connection with the ownership.

फलवत्तां च दर्शयति ॥२१॥

21. The text shows that (she) obtains a fruit.

द्व्याधानं च द्वियज्ञवत् ॥२२॥

22. An *agnyādhāna* is to be performed by two persons, just like sacrifices which are performed by two persons.

गुणस्यतु विधानत्वात्पत्न्या द्वितीयशब्दः स्यात् ॥२३॥

23. On the other hand by reason of enjoining a quality, the dual shall be made up by the wife.

तस्या यावदुक्तमाशीर्ब्रह्मचर्यमतुल्यत्वात् ॥२४॥

24. For her, are all (acts) laid down (such as) paring of nails and celibacy, being not equal.

चातुर्वर्ण्यमविशेषात् ॥२५॥

25. All the four castes, there being no distinction.

निर्देशाद्वा त्रयाणां स्यादग्न्याधेये ऽसम्बन्धः क्रतुषुब्राह्मणश्रुतेरित्यात्रेयः ॥२६॥

26. On the other hand, under a command, the three castes are entitled to the establishment of fire; he has no connection with the sacrifice. This is the Brāhmaṇa text. It is the opinion of Ātreya.

निमित्तार्थेन बादरिस्तस्मात्सर्वाधिकारं स्यात् ॥२७॥

27. "For special reason", says Bādari "all are, therefore, equally entitled."

अपि वाऽन्यार्थदर्शनाद्यथाश्रुति प्रतीयेत ॥२८॥

28. Or by seeing other text also; according to the Vedic text it is laid down.

निर्देशात्तु पक्षे स्यात् ॥२९॥

29. On the other hand, by reason of the direction, there is the other side.

वैगुण्यान्नेति चेत् ॥३०॥

30. If it be said that by reason of the disability, he is not (entitled).

न काम्यत्वात् ॥३१॥

31. Not so, by reason of possessing a desire.

संस्कारे च तत्प्रधानत्वात् ॥३२॥

32. And in purificatory operation, by reason of that being principal.

अपि वा वेदनिर्देशादपशूद्राणां प्रतीयेत ॥३३॥

33. Not so, by the direction of the Vedas, only non-śūdras are meant.

गुणार्थित्वान्नेति चेत् ॥३४॥

34. If it be said, not by reason of his desire to acquire knowledge.

संस्कारस्य तदर्थत्वाद्विद्यायां पुरुषश्रुतिः ॥३५॥

35. The purificatory ceremony is with that object; there is a Vedic text about a man in connection with learning.

विद्यानिर्देशान्नेति चेत् ॥३६॥

36. If it be said not, because there is a direction for learning.

अवैद्यत्वादभावः कर्मणि स्यात् ॥३७॥

37. By reason of his being not entitled to be taught, he is incapable to perform a sacrifice.

तथा चान्यार्थदर्शनम् ॥३८॥

38. Similarly there is another text seen.

त्रयाणां द्रव्यसम्पन्नः कर्मणो द्रव्यसिद्धित्वात् ॥३९॥

39. Of the three first castes, only a person possessed of wealth (is entitled to perform a sacrifice); because accomplishment of an act depends on wealth.

अनित्यत्वात्तु नैवं स्यादर्थाद्धि द्रव्यसंयोगः ॥४०॥

40. On the other hand, it is not so, by reason of its being not permanent. Wealth can be obtained from a motive.

अङ्गहीनश्च तद्धर्मा ॥४१॥

41. And person deprived of limbs or senses is also of the same quality (or nature).

उत्पत्तौ नित्यसंयोगात् ॥४२॥

42. A person born (deprived of senses or limbs is not entitled to perform a sacrifice) by reason of the permanent connection.

अत्र्यार्षेयस्य हानं स्यात् ॥४३॥

43. A person who has not three *pravaras* has a disability (to perform a sacrifice).

वचनाद्रथकारस्याधाने ऽस्यसर्वशेषत्वात् ॥४४॥

44. By a text, a *rathakāra's* right to *agnyādhāna* (is recognised), he being excluded from the four castes.

न्याय्यो वा कर्मसंयोगाच्छूद्रस्य प्रतिषिद्धत्वात् ॥४५॥

45. On the other hand, it is proper (to regard him belonging to the three higher castes) by reason of his profession, because a *śūdra* is prohibited.

अकर्मत्वात्तु नैवं स्यात् ॥४६॥

46. On the other hand, he cannot be of higher caste, having accepted a profession prohibited (by the Vedas).

आनर्थक्यं च संयोगात् ॥४७॥

47. And there will be meaninglessness by reason of the connection (with time).

गुणार्थेनेति चेत् ॥४८॥

48. If you say that it is with the object (of mentioning) a quality.

उक्तमनिमित्तत्वम् ॥४९॥

49. It is said already that an accident does not apply.

सौधन्वनास्तु हीनत्वान्मन्त्रवर्णात्प्रतीयेरन् ॥५०॥

50. On the other hand the chariot-builders, by virtue of their inferiority and the Vedic text, ought to be considered (to be outside the pale of the three higher castes).

रथपतिर्निषादः स्याच्छब्दसामर्थ्यात् ॥५१॥

51. *Rathapati* is *niṣāda* by force of the word.

लिङ्गदर्शनाच्च ॥५२॥

52. And by seeing force of the Vedic text.

END OF PĀDA 1

***

PĀDA 2

पुरुषार्थैकसिद्धित्वात्तस्यतस्याधिकारः स्यात् ॥१॥

1. By reason of one end of the purpose of life (*puruṣārtha*), each one is entitled (to the fruit of an act).

अपि चोत्पत्तिसंयोगोयथा स्यात्सत्वदर्शनं तथाभावो विभागे स्यात् ॥२॥

2. And also the connection with the original text; just as on seeing a being a concept is formed, in the same way, is the invisible result in a separate (individual).

प्रयोगे पुरुषश्रुतेर्यथाकामी प्रयोगे स्यात् ॥३॥

3. By reason of a text laying down a rule as to person in a sacrifice any number desirous of a fruit is (entitled to join) the sacrifice.

प्रत्यर्थं श्रुतिभाव इतिचेत् ॥४॥

4. If you say that the object of the text is for each separately.

तादर्थ्ये न गुणार्थताऽनुक्तेऽर्थान्तरत्वात्कर्तुः प्रधानभूतत्वात् ॥५॥

5. On the reward being for him, he is not subordinate; as there is no direct text by reason of other proofs, the agent is principal.

अपि वा कामसंयोगे सम्बन्धात्प्रयोगायोपदिश्येत प्रत्यर्थं हि विधिश्रुतिर्विषाणावत् ॥६॥

6. Not so; by reason of the relationship in connection with the desire, the performance is directed; because the injunctive text for each and distinct individual is just like the text (which lays down) a horn.

अन्यस्यस्यादिति चेत् ॥७॥

7. If it be said that fruit may accrue to another.

अन्यार्थेनाभिसम्बन्धः ॥८॥

8. There is no connection in the case where the fruit is to accrue to another.

फलकामो निमित्तमिति चेत् ॥९॥

9. If you say that desire to obtain fruit is an essential condition.

न नित्यत्वात् ॥१०॥

10. Not, by reason of the permanency.

कर्म तथेति चेत् ॥११॥

11. If you say that there are acts similarly.

न समवायात् ॥१२॥

12. No, by reason of the connection.

प्रक्रमात्तु नियम्येतारम्भस्य क्रियानिमित्तत्वात् ॥१३॥

13. On the other hand, by reason of the commencement, it is ruled

(that an act commenced should be completed) because the commencement is for the sake of an act.

फलार्थित्वाद्वाऽनियमो यथानुपक्रान्ते ॥१४॥

14. On the other hand, by reason of a desire for a fruit, there is no rule just as in the case of an act not commenced.

नियमो वा तन्निमित्तत्वात्कर्तुस्तत्कारणं स्यात् ॥१५॥

15. On the other hand there is a rule for its sake and it is the cause of the agent.

लोके कर्माणि वेदवत्ततोऽधिपुरुषज्ञानम् ॥१६॥

16. In the world, the acts are like those enjoined in the Veda; from them there is a knowledge of the excellent man.

अपराधेऽपि च तैः शास्त्रम् ॥१७॥

17. And on fault also, by them regulated.

अशास्त्रात्तूपसम्प्राप्तिः शास्त्र स्यान्न प्रकल्पकं तस्मादर्थेन गम्येताप्राप्ते शास्त्रमर्थवत् ॥१८॥

18. On the other hand the fruit is obtained even without a code; a code is not the cause; therefore it follows from an inference that a code is helpful in cases where the subject is not known.

प्रतिषेधेष्वकर्मत्वात्क्रिया स्यात्प्रतिषिद्धानां विभक्तत्वादकर्मणाम् ॥१९॥

19. In the forbidden acts, by reason of non-action, an act is performed, there being a difference between an act forbidden and non-act.

शास्त्राणां त्वर्थवत्त्वेन पुरुषार्थो विधीयते तयोरसमवायित्वात्तादर्थ्ये विध्यतिक्रमः ॥२०॥

20. On the other hand, the injunction being for a purpose the duty of man is laid down; by reason of their being not in harmony, for that object, there is a violation of the rule.

तस्मिंस्तु शिष्यमाणानि जननेन प्रवर्त्तेरन् ॥२१॥

21. On the other hand, the duties that are laid down (for a disciple) arise in him from birth.

अपि वा वेदतुल्यत्वादुपायेन प्रवर्त्तेरन् ॥२२॥

22. Not so; by reason of the equality with the Vedas, the observance of duties arise from the time of *upanayana* (initiation ceremony).

अभ्यासोऽकर्मशेषत्वात्पुरुषार्थो विधीयते ॥२३॥

23. Because of being not subsidiary to any act and as it is the purpose of a person, the repetition is laid down.

तस्मिन्नसंभवन्नर्थात् ॥२४॥

24. In him it is impossible by necessity.

न कालेभ्य उपदिश्यन्ते ॥२५॥

25. Not so; time has been laid down.

दर्शनात्काललिङ्गानां कालविधानम् ॥२६॥

26. By seeing he Vedic texts laying down time, time has been fixed.

तेषामौत्पत्तिकत्वादागमेन प्रवर्त्तेत ॥२७॥

27. On account of the original text about them, repetition should commence (they should be repeated).

तथा हि लिङ्गदर्शनम् ॥२८॥

28. Similarly there is the force of the text.

तथान्तःक्रतुप्रयुक्तानि ॥२९॥

29. Similarly, when those (vessels) that are used in a sacrifice (are broken or their contents spilled, the repetition should be made).

आचाराद्गृह्यमाणेषु तथा स्यात्पुरुषार्थत्वात् ॥३०॥

30. In the cases of social etiquette recognised, the same is the rule because they are the duties of a man.

ब्राह्मणस्य तु सोमविद्याप्रजमृणवाक्येन संयोगात् ॥३१॥

31. On the other hand, of a Brāhmaṇa soma sacrifice, acquisition of knowledge and production of progeny (are essential duties) on account of their relationship with the text which enjoins the debt.

END OF PĀDA 2

***

PĀDA 3

सर्वशक्तौ प्रवृत्तिः स्यात्तथाभूतोपदेशात् ॥१॥

1. If one has a capacity, he should perform the whole as there is a direction in the Veda to that effect.

अपि वाऽप्येकदेशेस्यात्प्रधाने ह्यर्थनिर्वृत्तिर्गुणमात्रमितरत् तदर्थत्वात् ॥२॥

2. Not so; performance of some parts is sufficient; because in the performance of the principal, the object is accomplished; others are only subordinate being subservient to it.

तदकर्मणि च दोषस्तस्मात्ततो विशेषः स्यात्प्रधानेनाऽभिसम्बन्धात् ॥३॥

3. And on non-performance of it, there is a sin; therefore it is distinguishable from the subsidiary acts, because of the connection with the principal.

कर्माऽभेदं तु जैमिनिः प्रयोगवचनैकत्वात्सर्वेषामुपदेशः स्यादिति ॥४॥

4. "On the other hand, the view of Jaimini is that there is no difference of the act by reason of the oneness of the text laying down the rule of performance under which all are directed." If you say.

अर्थस्य व्यपवर्गित्वादेकस्यापि प्रयोगेस्याद्यथा क्रत्वन्तरेषु ॥५॥

5. On account of the main part being distinct, on the performance of one act only, the fruit may result as in another sacrifice.

विध्यपराधे च दर्शनात्समाप्तेः ॥६॥

6. And on the violation of the rule by seeing the completion.

प्रायश्चित्तविधानाच्च ॥७॥

7. And by reason of the expiatory ceremony being prescribed.

काम्येषु चैवमर्थित्वात् ॥८॥

8. And in the desire-accomplishing sacrifice the same (principle applies) by reason of the desire.

असंयोगात्तु नैवं स्याद्विधेः शब्दप्रमाणत्वात् ॥९॥

9. On the other hand there being no connection, the same principle does not apply; the command being based on the text of the Veda.

अकर्मणि चाप्रत्यवायात् ॥१०॥

10. And there is no calamity in not performing it.

क्रियाणामाश्रितत्वाद्द्रव्यान्तरे विभागः स्यात् ॥११॥

11. By reason of the actions being dependent, there is a change on the change of materials.

अपि वाऽव्यतिरेकाद्रूपशब्दाविभागाच्च गोत्ववदैककर्म्यं स्यान्नामधेयं च सत्त्ववत् ॥१२॥

12. Not so; by reason of the absence of dimiuntion or augmentation

and the indivisibility of the word expressing the form, there is a unity of action like the quality of being a cow and the name is like an animal.

श्रुतिप्रमाणत्वाच्छिष्टाभावेऽनागमोऽन्यस्याऽशिष्टत्वात् ॥१३॥

13. On account of the Veda being an authority, in the absence of the material sanctioned, no other material (shall be used as) substitute by reason of its being not sanctioned.

क्वचिद्विधानाच्च ॥१४॥

14. And somewhere by laying down a command.

आगमो वा चोदनार्थाविशेषात् ॥१५॥

15. On the other hand, there is a substitute on account of the object of the command being general.

नियमार्थः क्वचिद्विधिः ॥१६॥

16. Somewhere a command is with an object for restriction.

तन्नित्यं तच्चिकीर्षा हि ॥१७॥

17. That (statement) is permanent and because that is a desire.

न देवताग्निशब्दक्रियमन्यार्थसंयोगात् ॥१८॥

18. There is no substitute for deity, fire, mantra and act by reason of the connection with other object.

देवतायां च तदर्थत्वात् ॥१९॥

19. And in case of a deity, by reason of its being for that object.

प्रतिषिद्धं चाविशेषेण हि तच्छ्रुतिः ॥२०॥

20. And a forbidden material generally, because there is a Vedic text about it.

तथा स्वामिनः फलसमवायात्फलस्य कर्मयोगित्वात् ॥२१॥

21. Similarly of a master by reason of the connection with the act.

बहूनां तु प्रवृत्तेऽन्यमागमयेदवैगुण्यात् ॥२२॥

22. On the other hand when many are engaged, another may be brought in to avoid failure.

स स्वामी स्यात्संयोगात् ॥२३॥

23. He is a master by reason of the connection with it.

कर्मकरो वा भृतत्वात् ॥२४॥

24. On the other hand, he is a servant by reason of his being maintained.

तस्मिंश्च फलदर्शनात् ॥२५॥

25. And in him, seeing the fruit.

स तद्धर्मा स्यात्कर्मसंयोगात् ॥२६॥

26. He becomes like him, by reason of his connection with the act.

सामान्यं तच्चिकीर्षा हि ॥२७॥

27. Anything of the same class, because there is a want of it.

निर्देशात्तु विकल्पे यत्प्रवृत्तम् ॥२८॥

28. By reason of the direction of the Veda, when commenced with the optional material, (the material resembling it should be used).

अशब्दमिति चेत् ॥२९॥

29. If you say that it is not sanctioned.

नाऽनङ्गत्वात् ॥३०॥

30. No, by reason of its being not a part.

वचनाच्चाऽन्याय्यमभावे तत्सामान्येन प्रतिनिधिरभावादितरस्य ॥३१॥

31. By reason of the command of the code, it is unreasonable (not to use the substitute) in the absence (of the original). By reason of the absence of the other, it is a substitute by coming under the same class.

न प्रतिनिधौ समत्वात् ॥३२॥

32. No (substitute) in (place of) a substitute by reason of the equality.

स्याच्छ्रुतिलक्षणे नियतत्वात् ॥३३॥

33. A substitute like the substitute should be used according to the signs mentioned in that Veda; because that is the restrictive rule.

न तदीप्सा हि ॥३४॥

34. Because there is no desire for it.

मुख्याधिगमे मुख्यमागमो हि तदभावात् ॥३५॥

35. On securing the principal, the principal should be used because a substitute is used in its absence.

प्रबृत्तेऽपीति चेत् ॥३६॥

36. Even if a sacrifice is commenced.

नानर्थकत्वात् ॥३७॥

37. No, by reason of its being useless.

द्रव्यसंस्कारविरोधे द्रव्यं तदर्थत्वात् ॥३८॥

38. On conflict between a substance and the purificatory rite, the substance is preferable because the purificatory rite is for the sake of the material.

अर्थद्रव्यविरोधेऽर्थो द्रव्याभावे तदुत्पत्तेर्द्रव्याणामर्थशेषत्वात् ॥३९॥

39. When there is a conflict between the object and the material, the object is to prevail; because in the absence of the material, the substitute is used; the material being subordinate to the object.

विधिरप्येकदेशे स्यात् ॥४०॥

40. The command of the text also (applies in the case) when the original material is sufficient to accomplish a part.

अपि वाऽर्थस्यशक्यत्वादेकदेशेन निर्वर्तेतार्थानामविभक्तत्वाद्गुणमात्र-मितरत्तदर्थत्वात् ॥४१॥

41. Not so; if by performance of a part, the object is fulfilled by its being sufficient for it; the objects being indivisible, the other are only subordinate, being subservient to it.

End of Pāda 3

***

PĀDA 4

शेषाद् द्व्यवदाननाशे स्यात्तदर्थत्वात् ॥१॥

1. On the destruction of the double oblation, (the offering should be made) from the remainder because it is with that object.

निर्देशाद्वाऽन्यदागमयेत् ॥२॥

2. On the other hand, by reason of the direct authority, another should be introduced.

अपि वा शेषभाजां स्याद्विशिष्टकारणत्वात् ॥३॥

3. Not so, the offering should be of the remainder for a special cause.

निर्देशाच्छेषभक्षोऽन्यैः प्रधानवत् ॥४॥

4. By reason of the direction, the remnant should be eaten by others as in the case of the principal.

सर्वैर्वा समवायात्स्यात् ॥५॥

5. On the other hand, they should be eaten by all being connected with it.

निर्देशस्य गुणार्थत्वम् ॥६॥

6. The direction is with a view to be of benefit.

प्रधाने श्रुतिलक्षणम् ॥७॥

7. In the case of the principal oblation, there is the direct text.

अर्थवदितिचेत् ॥८॥

8. If it be said that it is for a purpose.

न चोदनाविरोधात् ॥९॥

9. Not so; being contrary to the original command.

अर्थसमवायात्प्रायश्चित्तमेकदेशेऽपि ॥१०॥

10. By reason of the connection with the object, there is a penance on a partial breaking also.

न त्वशेषे वैगुण्यात्तदर्थंहि ॥११॥

11. On the other hand none on the total destruction, by reason of the total failure, because that is with the object.

स्याद्वा प्राप्तनिमित्तत्वादतद्धर्मो नित्यसंयोगान्न हितस्य गुणार्थेनानित्यत्वात् ॥१२॥

12. Not so; because when an occasion arises, (the penance is performed); it does not partake of its nature by reason of the permanent connection, because it is not a quality by being not permanent.

गुणानां च परार्थत्वाद्वचनाद्व्यपाश्रय स्यात् ॥१३॥

13. By reason of the subordinate action, being subservient to other, there can be a connection by reason of the Vedic text.

भेदार्थमिति चेत् ॥१४॥

14. If it be said that the penance is to avoid any calamity arising from the breakage.

न शेषभूतत्वात् ॥१५॥

15. Not, by reason of its being subordinate.

अनर्थकश्च सर्वनाशे स्यात् ॥१६॥

16. It is useless on the total destruction.

क्षामे तु सर्वदाहे स्यादेकदेशस्याऽवर्जनीयत्वात् ॥१७॥

17. On the other hand on the total burning (of the *puroḍāśa* cake, a penance is to be performed), because partial burning (of the same) cannot be avoided.

दर्शनादेकदेशे स्यात् ॥१८॥

18. On the other hand, there is a text that there is a penance on the partial burning of the *puroḍāśa* cake.

अन्येन वैतच्छास्त्राद्धि कारणप्राप्तिः ॥१९॥

19. On the other hand, by another (a sacrifice) should be performed; this (is a rule) from the text; because of an occasion arising.

तद्धविःशब्दान्नेतिचेत् ॥२०॥

20. If it be said, not so, because of the term 'the offering'.

स्यादन्यायत्वादिज्यागामी हविः शब्दस्तल्लिङ्गसंयोगात् ॥२१॥

21. In order to avoid unreasonableness, the term *homa* means the whole sacrifice by force of metonymy.

यथाश्रुतीति चेत् ॥२२॥

22. If it be said that (one should act) according to the Veda.

न तल्लक्षणत्वादुपपातो हि कारणम् ॥२३॥

23. Not so, by reason of the general description of it; the spoiling is the occasion.

होमाभिषवभक्षणं च तद्वत् ॥२४॥

24. And similarly in the case of a person who can perform *homa* or extract some juice.

उभाभ्यां वा न हि तयोर्धर्मशास्त्रम् ॥२५॥

25. On the other hand, both of them constitute the occasion; because their relation is not laid down.

पुनराधेयमोदनवत् ॥२६॥

26. (The same principle applies in the case of) the re-establishment of fire as in the case of the offering of the boiled rice.

द्रव्योत्पत्तेर्वोभयोः स्यात् ॥२७॥

27. On account of the production of the materials of the two, the two together cause the occasion.

पञ्चशरावस्तु द्रव्यश्रुतेः प्रतिनिधिः स्यात् ॥२८॥

28. On the other hand, (the offering of the) five dishes (full of rice) is a substitute, because of the direct text about the material.

चोदना वा द्रव्यदेवताविधिरवाच्ये हि ॥२९॥

29. On the other hand, it is a command; because a text about materials and deïty can be laid down (in the same act).

स प्रत्यामनेत्स्थानात् ॥३०॥

30. It comes in the place, by reason of its collocation.

अङ्गविधिर्वा निमित्तसंयोगात् ॥३१॥

On the other hand (it should be regarded as a) statement about a constituent part by reason of its connection with the occasion.

विश्वजित्वप्रवृत्ते भावः कर्मणि स्यात् ॥३२॥

32. On the other hand when (the *satra*) is not commenced, a *viśvajit* sacrifice should be performed, for the fruit is in the act.

निष्क्रयवादाच्च ॥३३॥

33. And by reason of the text about ransom.

वत्ससंयोगे व्रतचोदना स्यात् ॥३४॥

34. When the term 'calf' is used, it directs the breaking of the fast.

कालो वोत्पन्नसंयोगाद्यथोक्तस्य ॥३५॥

35. On the other hand, it is time by reason of the connection with the restatement of what is previously stated.

अर्थापरिमाणाच्च ॥३६॥

36. And by reason of the sense being not determined.

वत्सस्तु श्रुतिसंयोगात्तदङ्गं स्यात् ॥३७॥

37. The term 'calf' by reason of its occurring in the Vedic text, is its part.

कालस्तु स्यादचोदनात् ॥३८॥

38. On the other hand, it means time, being not previously enjoined.

अनर्थकश्च कर्मसंयोगे ॥३९॥

39. And it will be meaningless in connecting it with the act.

अवचनाच्च स्वशब्दस्य ॥४०॥

40. By reason of not having the meaning of the term.

कालश्चेत्सन्नयत्पक्षे तल्लिङ्गसंयोगात् ॥४१॥

41. If it indicates time, it applies to one who has performed *sannāya* by reason of its connection with its description.

कालार्थत्वाद्वोभयोः प्रतीयेत ॥४२॥

42. On the other hand the time of both should be known, by reason of its being used to mean time.

प्रस्तरे शाखाश्रयणवत् ॥४३॥

43. In the bunch of grass, there is the branch like the case of mixture.

कालविधिर्वोभयोर्विद्यमानत्वात् ॥४४॥

44. On the other hand, it is a rule for time, both being present.

अतत्संस्कारार्थत्वाच्च ॥४५॥

45. And by reason of no purificatory ceremony performed on them.

तस्माच्च विप्रयोगे स्यात् ॥४६॥

46. And because there is separation also.

उपवेषश्च पक्षे स्यात् ॥४७॥

47. And the wooden poker is used in the alternative case.

END OF PĀDA 4

***

PĀDA 5

अभ्युदये कालापराधादिज्याचोदना स्याद्यथा पञ्चशरावे ॥१॥

1. On rising of the moon, by reason of missing the time, there is a direction about a sacrifice as in the case of five dishes.

अपनयो वा विद्यमानत्वात् ॥२॥

2. On the other hand, it is only a transference of the deities by reason of the existence.

तद्रूपत्वाच्च शब्दानाम् ॥३॥

3. And by reason of the same conclusion from the Vedic words.

आतञ्चनाभ्यासस्य दर्शनात् ॥४॥

4. By seeing of the repetition (division) of the milk.

अपूर्वत्वाद्विधानं स्यात् ॥५॥

5. By reason of its producing an invisible effect, it may be an (independent) injunction.

पयोदोषात्पञ्चशरावेऽदुष्टं हीतरत् ॥६॥

6. In the case of the five dishes, by reason of the defect in the milk; because the other has no defect.

सन्नायेऽपि तथेति चेत् ॥७॥

7. If it be said that in *sannāya* oblation, the same is (true).

न तस्यादुष्टत्वादविशिष्टं हि कारणम् ॥८॥

8. No. By reason of its being not impure, because there is no special reason.

लक्षणार्था शृतश्रुतिः ॥९॥

9. The word *śṛta* (heated) is by way of metonymy.

उपांशुयाजेऽवचनाद्यथाप्रकृति ॥१०॥

10. There being no text, in *upāṃśuyāja* (the deity shall be) that of the model sacrifice.

अपनयो वा प्रवृत्त्या यथेतरेषाम् ॥११॥

11. On the other hand, there will be a change (of deities) as in the case of others, by performance.

निरुप्ते स्यात्तत्संयोगात् ॥१२॥

12. On consecration, there will be (a moon-rise-sacrifice), by reason of the Vedic authority.

प्रवृत्ते वा प्रापणान्निमित्तस्य ॥१३॥

13. On the other hand, on commencement, by reason of the cause arising.

लक्षणमात्रमितरत् ॥१४॥

14. The rest is only by way of indication.

तथा चान्यार्थदर्शनम् ॥१५॥

15. And similarly seeing the other texts.

अनिरुप्तेऽभ्युदिते प्राकृतीभ्यो निर्वपेदित्याश्मरथ्यस्तण्डुलभूतेष्वपनयात् ॥१६॥

16. "When the materials are not consecrated and the moon rises, the offering should be made to the deities of the model sacrifice". This is the view of Āśmarathya, by reason of the change of deities on the preparation of the rice.

व्यूर्ध्वभाग्भ्यस्त्वालेखनस्तत्कारित्वाद्देवतापनयस्य ॥१७॥

17. On the other hand, the view of Ālekhana is that to the deities who come afterwards (the offering should be made) by reason of his own action being the cause of the change of deities.

विनिरुप्ते न मुष्टीनामपनयस्तद्गुणत्वात् ॥१८॥

18. When the handfuls (of offerings) are half consecrated there is no change of deities, because of that being subordinate to it.

अप्राकृतेन हि संयोगस्तत्स्थानीयत्वात् ॥१९॥

19. Because there is a connection with the deities of the modified sacrifice by reason of their coming in their place.

अभावाच्चेतरस्य स्यात् ॥२०॥

20. And by reason of the absence of the others.

सान्नाय्यसंयोगान्नासन्नयतः स्यात् ॥२१॥

21. A person who has not performed a *sannāya* shall not perform (the *abhyudayeṣṭi*) by reason of the connection of the text with the *sannāya.*

औषधसंयोगाद्वोभयोः ॥२२॥

22. On the other hand, both (should perform the *abhyudayeṣṭi*) by reason of the text mentioning annuals (*auṣadha*).

वैगुण्यान्नेति चेत् ॥२३॥

23. 'By reason of the failure, no', if it be said.

नातत्संस्कारत्वात् ॥२४॥

24. Not so, by reason of the purificatory ceremony not performed upon it.

साम्युत्थाने विश्वजित्क्रीते विभागसंयोगात् ॥२५॥

25. One should perform *viśvajit* on his not completing the *satra* after the purchase of *soma* by reason of the text which mentions the division of *soma.*

प्रवृत्ते वा प्रापणान्निमित्तस्य ॥२६॥

26. On the other hand, on undertaking (to perform a *satra*) by reason of the cause arising.

आदेशार्थेतरा श्रुतिः ॥२७॥

27. The rest of the text is for the general purpose.

दीक्षापरिमाणे यथाकाम्यविशेषात् ॥२८॥

28. In numbering the days for the initiation ceremony, one should be guided according to his desire, as there is no special text.

द्वादशाहस्तु लिङ्गात्स्यात् ॥२९॥

29. On the other hand, the initiation ceremony should last for 12 days by force of the Vedic text.

पौर्णमास्यामनियमोऽविशेषात् ॥३०॥

30. No rule as to the full moon day because there is no special text.

आनन्तर्यात्तु चैत्री स्यात् ॥३१॥

31. On the other hand, it may be the full moon day of the Caitra by reason of the immediate sequence (of the text).

माघी वैकाष्टकाश्रुतेः ॥३२॥

32. On the other hand, the full moon day of *Māgha* because the Vedic text refers to the 8th day of *Māgha.*

अन्या अपीति चेत् ॥३३॥

33. If it be said that *ekāṣṭakā* may mean the *aṣṭamī* of another month.

न भक्तित्वादेषा हि लोके ॥३४॥

34. No, by reason of the secondary sense, because it is so known in common parlance.

दीक्षापराधे चानुग्रहात् ॥३५॥

35. And on the failure of the initiation ceremony, by reason of the release (provided).

उत्थाने चानुप्ररोहात् ॥३६॥

36. And on the completion, the springing up (of the plants and herbs).

अस्यां च सर्वलिङ्गानि ॥३७॥

37. And the force of all the texts points to it.

दीक्षाकालस्य शिष्टत्वादतिक्रमे नियतानामनुत्कर्षः प्राप्तकालत्वात् ॥३८॥

38. Because the time of the initiation ceremony is laid down; on the time being allowed to pass away, the necessary acts connected with it are not transferred forward because their time has arrived.

उत्कर्षो वा दीक्षितत्वादविशिष्टं हि कारणम् ॥३९॥

39. On the other hand by reason of being initiated, they will be transferred forward because there is no special reason.

तत्र प्रतिहोमो न विद्यते यथा पूर्वेषाम् ॥४०॥

40. There does not exist *pratihoma* as in the case of the former.

कालप्राधान्याच्च ॥४१॥

41. And by reason of the time being principal.

प्रतिषेधाच्चोर्ध्वमवभृथादिष्टेः ॥४२॥

42. And by reason of the prohibition after the bath till (*udavasānīya*) sacrifice.

प्रतिहोमश्चेत्सायमग्निहोत्रप्रभृतीनि हूयेरन् ॥४३॥

43. If *pratihoma* is performed, the *agnihotra* &c., should be performed in the evening.

प्रातस्तु षोडशिनि ॥४४॥

44. On the other hand morning, in the case of *ṣoḍaśī* sacrifice.

प्रायश्चित्तमधिकारे सर्वत्रदोषसामान्यात् ॥४५॥

45. In the context it is a penance, in all cases the default being common.

प्रकरणे वा शब्दहेतुत्वात् ॥४६॥

46. On the other hand in the context, by reason of the word.

अतद्विकारश्च ॥४७॥

47. And they are not the modifications of it.

व्यापन्नस्याप्सु गतौ यदभोज्यमार्याणां तत्प्रतीयेत् ॥४८॥

48. On throwing the defiled things in the water that which is not eatable by the Aryas should be known.

विभागश्रुतेः प्रायश्चित्तं यौगपद्ये न विद्यते ॥४९॥

49. On account of the text laying down separation, there is a penance; but there is none if they are left off simultaneously.

स्याद्वा प्राप्तनिमित्तत्वात्कालमात्रमेकम् ॥५०॥

50. On the other hand, it must be done by reason of the accrual of the cause; the time is only one.

तत्र विप्रतिषेधाद्विकल्पः स्यात् ॥५१॥

51. By reason of the conflict of texts, there is option.

प्रयोगान्तरे वोभयानुग्रहः स्यात् ॥५२॥

52. On the other hand, in another sacrifice, both (penances) are accomplished.

न चैकसंयोगात् ॥५३॥

53. Not so, because the sacrifice has been laid down to be one.

पौर्वापर्ये पूर्वदौर्बल्यं प्रकृतिवत् ॥५४॥

54. When the clothes are let go one after the other the rule becomes weak in the first, like the model sacrifice.

यद्युद्गाता जघन्यः स्यात्पुनर्यज्ञे सर्ववेदसं दद्याद्यथेतरस्मिन् ॥५५॥

55. When the *udgātā* lets go his tucked up clothes being last, the whole wealth shall be given in another sacrifice as in the case of the other.

अहर्गणे यस्मिन्नपच्छेदस्तदावर्त्तेत कर्मपृथक्त्वात् ॥५६॥

56. In a soma sacrifice extending for more than a day, that act in which the hold of the tucked up clothes is let go, should be changed by reason of the act being separate.

END OF PĀDA 5

***

PĀDA 6

सन्निपाते वैगुण्यात् प्रकृतिवत्तुल्यकल्पा यजेरन् ॥१॥

1. In an assembly all who belong to the same *kalpa* should perform a sacrifice to avoid failure, just as in a model sacrifice.

वचनाद्वाशिरोवत्स्यात् ॥२॥

2. On the other hand by reason of an authority, it may be like the soma mixture.

न वाऽनारभ्यवादत्वात् ॥३॥

3. Not so, by reason of the general statement.

स्याद्वा यज्ञार्थत्वादौदुम्बरीवत् ॥४॥

4. On the other hand, it may be by virtue of the object of the sacrifice like the twig of an *odambara* tree.

न तत्प्रधानत्वात् ॥५॥

5. Not so; by reason of that being principal.

औदुम्बर्याः परार्थत्वात्कपालवत् ॥६॥

6. By reason of the twig of the *odambara* tree being subordinate like an earthen pan.

अन्येनापीति चेत् ॥७॥

7. If it be said that by any other also.

नैकत्वात्तस्य चानधिकाराच्छब्दस्य चाविभक्तत्वात् ॥८॥

8. Not so, by reason of his *yajamāna* being one and their (the sacrificers) having no right and the word being indivisible.

सन्निपातात्तु निमित्तविघातः स्याद्बृहद्रथन्तरवद्विभक्तशिष्टत्वाद्वसिष्ठ-निर्वर्त्ये ॥९॥

9. On the other hand by reason of the fusion, the cause of distinction should be removed just as in a *bṛhadrathantara* songs, by reason of the text laying down the fusion of different persons, in a sacrifice to be performed by *Vasiṣtha* priests.

अपि वा कृत्स्नसंयोगादविघातः प्रतीयेत स्वामित्वेनाभि-संबन्धात् ॥१०॥

10. Not so, by reason of the connection of the entirety, the non-removal of the distinction is inferred because it is connected with ownership.

साम्नोः कर्मवृद्ध्यैकदेशेन संयोगे गुणत्वेनाभिसंबन्धस्तस्मात्तत्र विघातः स्यात् ॥११॥

11. On the connection with a portion of the two songs with the increase of the sacrifice, it is connected as subordinate, therefore there may be be an annulment.

वचनात्तु द्विसंयोगस्तस्मादेकस्य पाणिवत् ॥१२॥

12. On the other hand by reason of the connection with two (they are) of one like the hand.

अर्थाभावात्तु नैवं स्यात् ॥१३॥

13. On the other hand, by reason of the absence of the purpose, this cannot be.

अर्थानाञ्च विभक्तत्वान्न तच्छ्रुतेन संबंधः ॥१४॥

14. And by reason of the difference of the purpose, it is not connected with its fruit (which is laid down).

पाणेः प्रत्यङ्गभावादसंबन्धः प्रतीयेत ॥१५॥

15. By reason of the component parts of the hand, there appears to be no connection.

सत्राणि सर्ववर्णानामविशेषात् ॥१६॥

16. All castes are entitled to perform sacrificial sessions, there being no special (restriction).

लिङ्गदर्शनाच्च ॥१७॥

17. And by seeing the force of the text.

ब्राह्मणानां वेतरयोरार्त्विज्याभावात् ॥१८॥

18. On the other hand only Brāhmaṇa are entitled; the other two being not entitled to be *ṛtvik.*

वचनादिति चेत् ॥१९॥

19. If you say that under the Vedic authority.

न स्वामित्वं हि विधीयते ॥२०॥

20. No, because it lays down ownership.

गार्हपते वा स्यातामविप्रतिषेधात् ॥२१॥

21. On the other hand, they (kṣatriya and vaiśya) may be entitled in the ceremonies connected with the *gṛhapati*, because there is prohibition.

न वा कल्पविरोधात् ॥२२॥

22. Not so, by reason of the difference of the sacrificial system.

स्वामित्वादितरेषामहीने लिङ्गदर्शनम् ॥२३॥

23. There is inference from the text in the sacrificial sessions extending over a period of 12 days by reason of the two other castes being the masters.

वासिष्ठानां वा ब्रह्मत्वनियमात् ॥२४॥

24. On the other hand, the Vāsiṣṭhas by reason of their appointment as *Brahmā*.

सर्वेषां वा प्रतिप्रसवात् ॥२५॥

25. On the other hand all, by reason of the probability of the recurrence of the prohibited.

विश्वामित्रस्य हौत्रनियमाद्भृगुशुनकवसिष्ठानामनधिकारः ॥२६॥

26. By reason of a Viśvāmitra being appointed a *hotā*, Bhṛgu, Śaunaka and *Vasiṣṭha* are not entitled.

विहारस्य प्रभुत्वादनग्नीनामपि स्यात् ॥२७॥

27. By reason of the common property of the temple, even a person who has not performed *agnyādhāna* is entitled.

सारस्वते च दर्शनात् ॥२८॥

28. And by seeing in a *sārasvata* sacrifice.

प्रायश्चित्तविधानाच्च ॥२९॥

29. And by reason of prescribing a penance.

साग्नीनां वेष्टिपूर्वत्वात् ॥३०॥

30. On the other hand, only those persons who have established their sacred fire, are entitled to perform a *satra*, because the *iṣṭi* is performed previously.

स्वार्थेन च प्रयुक्तत्वात् ॥३१॥

31. And by reason of being engaged for one's own object.

सन्निवापं च दर्शयति ॥३२॥

32. And mixture of all fires shows.

जुह्वादीनामप्रयुक्तत्वात्संदेहे यथाकामी प्रतीयेत ॥३३॥

33. It appears that one should act according to his desires on a doubt arising by reason of the sacrificial spoons &c., being not used.

अपि वाऽन्यानि पात्राणि साधारणानि कुर्वीरन्विप्रतिषेधाच्छास्त्रकृतत्वात् ॥३४॥

34. Not so, other new vessels should be made by reason of the prohibition and the object of the holy scripture.

प्रायश्चित्तमापदि स्यात् ॥३५॥

35. There is a penance in a calamity.

पुरुषकल्पेन विकृतौ कर्तृनियमः स्याद्यज्ञस्य तद्गुणत्वादभावादितरान्प्रत्येकस्मिन्नधिकारः स्यात् ॥३६॥

36. On the other hand by reason of the act to be performed by a person in a modified sacrifice, the restriction is as to the agent because that is subordinate to the sacrifice; being not applicable to the other, the right is vested in one only.

लिङ्गाच्चेज्याविशेषवत् ॥३७॥

37. And also from the force of the texts like a particular fire offering.

न वा संयोगपृथक्त्वाद् गुणस्येज्याप्रधानत्वादसंयुक्ता हि चोदना ॥३८॥

38. Not so, by reason of the subordinate being separately connected and the fire offering being the principal, the command is therefore disconnected.

इज्यायां तद्गुणत्वाद्विशेषेण नियम्येत ॥३९॥

39. In a fire oblation by reason of its being subordinate, it is specially restricted.

END OF PĀDA 6

***

PĀDA 7

स्वदाने सर्वमविशेषात् ॥१॥

1. In giving the property (as fee) the whole should be paid by reason of there being nothing special.

यस्य वा प्रभुः स्यादितरस्याऽशक्यत्वात् ॥२॥

2. On the other hand, (he can give all) of which he is owner, because he has no power over others.

न भूमिः स्यात्सर्वान्प्रत्यविशिष्टत्वात् ॥३॥

3. Not land (to be given) by reason of its being not special of any.

अकार्यत्वाच्च ततः पुनर्विशेषः स्यात् ॥४॥

4. (Horses &c. should not be given) by reason of their being of no use (to the priest); therefore they are distinguishable (from other wealth).

नित्यत्वाच्चानित्यैर्नास्ति संबंधः ॥५॥

5. (Only things in existence should be given) by reason of their being permanent; there is no connection with things uncertain.

शूद्रश्च धर्मशास्त्रत्वात् ॥६॥

6. And a servant should not be given by reason of his service out of piety.

दक्षिणाकाले यत्स्वं तत्प्रतीयेत तद्दानसंयोगात् ॥७॥

7. The wealth (which is in existence) at the time of gift is meant, because that can form a subject of gift.

अशेषत्वात्तदन्तः स्यात्कर्मणो द्रव्यसिद्धित्वात् ॥८॥

8. By reason of there being no remainder, it should be considered to be an end of it, because the success of an act depends on wealth (money).

अपि वा शेषकर्म स्यात्क्रतोः प्रत्यक्षशिष्टत्वात् ॥९॥

9. Not so; the remaining act of the sacrifice should be (finished) being laid down directly.

तथा चान्यार्थदर्शनम् ॥१०॥

10. And similarly seeing other texts.

अशेषं तु समञ्जसादानेन शेषकर्म स्यात् ॥११॥

11. On the other hand, (the gift of the) whole is proper; the remaining act should be completed with the new acquisition of wealth.

नादानस्यानित्यत्वात् ॥१२॥

12. By reason of no certainty of the fresh acquisition.

दीक्षासु विनिर्देशादक्रत्वर्थेन संयोगस्तस्मादविरोधः स्यात् ॥१३॥

13. On the other hand by reason of the direction, there is no connection with the wealth reserved for the sacrifice; therefore there is no contradiction.

अहर्गणे च तद्धर्मः स्यात्सर्वेषामविशेषात् ॥१४॥

14. And in an *ahargaṇa* sacrifice, the same rule applies, being applicable to all.

द्वादशशतं वा प्रकृतिवत् ॥१५॥

15. On the other hand, the fee may be 1200, just like the model sacrifice.

अतद्गुणत्वात् नैवं स्यात् ॥१६॥

16. On the other hand, being not subordinate to it, it can never be so.

लिङ्गदर्शनाच्च ॥१७॥

17. And by seeing the force of the text.

विकारः सन्नुभयतोऽविशेषात् ॥१८॥

18. The viśvajit is a modified sacrifice; so both can, by reason of there being nothing special.

अधिकं वा प्रतिप्रसवात् ॥१९॥

19. On the other hand, above 1200 by reason of the possibility of recurrence of the prohibited.

अनुग्रहाच्च पादवत् ॥२०॥

20. And by inclusion just like one quarter.

अपरिमिते शिष्टस्य सङ्ख्याप्रतिषेधस्तच्छ्रुतित्वात् ॥२१॥

21. When it is laid down that unlimited should be given, it means the prohibition of number by reason of the direct text.

कल्पान्तरं वा तुल्यवत्प्रसङ्ख्यानात् ॥२२॥

22. On the other hand, it means another gift, by reason of mentioning the equal.

अनियमोऽविशेषात् ॥२३॥

23. There is no rule, by reason of there being nothing special.

अधिकं वा स्याद्बह्वर्थत्वादितरेषां सन्निधानात् ॥२४॥

24. On the other hand, *aparimita* means above 1000 by reason of the meaning of 'many'; on account of its being in proximity with other numerals.

अर्थवादश्च तदर्थवत् ॥२५॥

25. And the commendatory text is like it.

परकृतिपुराकल्पं च मनुष्यधर्मः स्यादर्थाय ह्यनुकीर्त्तनम्ः ॥२६॥

26. The acts of one individual or of many individuals is a duty imposed upon man, the narration of the acts is for fruit or reward.

तद्यक्ते च प्रतिषेधात् ॥२७॥

27. And on being connected with the (*nindā*), by reason of the prohibition.

निर्देशाद्वा तद्धर्मः स्यात्पञ्चावत्तवत् ॥२८॥

28. On the other hand, by mentioning (a particular clan) it may belong to that (clan) like the division of rice into 5 portions.

विधौ तु वेदसंयोगादुपदेशः स्यात् ॥२९॥

29. On the other hand, a command by reason of its connection with the scripture, is a general statement.

अर्थवादो वा विधिशेषत्वात्तस्मान्नित्यानुवादः स्यात् ॥३०॥

30. On the other hand, it is only a recommendation being subordinate to a command, therefore it is a permanent re-statement.

सहस्त्रसंवत्सरं तदायुषामसंभवान्मनुष्येषु ॥३१॥

31. One thousand years; by reason of that age being impossible amongst men.

अपिवा तदधिकारान्मनुष्यधर्मः स्यात् ॥३२॥

32. Not so; being mentioned in connection with man's duties, it is his duty to perform it.

नासामर्थ्यात् ॥३३॥

33. No; by reason of the powerlessness.

सम्बन्धादर्शनात् ॥३४॥

34. By seeing no connection.

स कुलकल्पः स्यादिति कार्ष्णाजिनिरेकस्मिन्नसंभवात् ॥३५॥

35. "It may be the performance of a generation" says Kārṣṇājini by reason of the impossibility in one man.

अपि वा कृत्स्नसंयोगादेकस्यैव प्रयोगः स्यात् ॥३६॥

36. Not so, by reason of the connection with the completion of the whole, the performance is by one alone.

विप्रतिषेधात्तु गुण्यन्यतरः स्यादिति लावुकायनः ॥३७॥

37. "On the other hand", says Lāvukāyana "to avoid contradiction the other is in a secondary sense."

संवत्सरो विचालित्वात् ॥३८॥

38. (There may be secondary sense attached to) year by reason of changeability.

सा प्रकृतिः स्यादधिकारात् ॥३९॥

39. That (secondary sense) is accepted, it would be the sense in which it is used in a model sacrifice by reason of the right.

अहानि वाऽभिसंख्यत्वात् ॥४०॥

40. On the other hand, it means a day by reason of enumeration.

END OF PĀDA 7

***

PĀDA 8

इष्टिपूर्वत्वादक्रतुशेषो होमः संस्कृतेष्वाग्निषु स्यादपूर्वोऽप्याधानस्य सर्वशेषत्वात् ॥१॥

1. By reason of the fire-offerings being in the beginning, the homa which is not subordinate to any sacrifice is to be performed in a consecrated fire, though independent in itself by reason of the *agnyādhāna* being subordinate to all.

इष्टित्वेन तु संस्तवश्चतुर्होतृनसंस्कृतेषु दर्शयति ॥२॥

2. On the other hand, the praises are of *iṣṭi*; it appears that the *caturhotṛ homa* is to be performed in the non-consecrated fire.

उपदेशस्त्वपूर्वत्वात् ॥३॥

3. The injunction (as to its being subordinate to no sacrifice) is to avoid fruitlessness.

स सर्वेषामविशेषात् ॥४॥

4. The injunction refers to all, because there is nothing special about it.

अपि वा क्रत्वभावादनाहिताग्नेरशेषभूतानिर्देशः ॥५॥

5. Not so, it is to be performed by a person who has not performed *agnyādhāna* by reason of there being no sacrifice; there is a direction of its being not subordinate to any sacrifice.

जपो वाऽनग्निसंयोगात् ॥६॥

6. On the other hand, it is only a repetition of the mantras because there is a mention of the unconsecrated fire.

इष्टित्वेन संस्तुते होमः स्यादनारभ्याग्निसंयोगादितरेषामवाच्यत्वात् ॥७॥

7. On the other hand, on its being praised as *iṣṭi* it is homa by reason of the general statement; in the other case to avoid meaninglessness.

उभयोः पितृयज्ञवत् ॥८॥

8. Of both, like the offering to the manes.

निर्देशों वाऽनाहिताग्नेरनारभ्याग्निसंयोगात् ॥९॥

9. On the other hand, the direction is as to the person who has not established fire, by reason of the connection of the fire with the general statement.

पितृयज्ञे संयुक्तस्य पुनर्वचनम् ॥१०॥

10. Again in a *pitṛyajña* there is a text which applies to both.

उपनयन्नादधीत होमसंयोगात् ॥११॥

11. A person whose *upanayana* ceremony is to be performed should establish fire by reason of the connection with homa.

स्थपतीष्टवल्लौकिके वा विद्याकर्मानुपूर्वत्वात् ॥१२॥

12. On the other hand, it should be performed in the unconsecrated fire like the *sthapatīṣṭi*, by reason of the knowledge and act preceding the *agnyādhāna*.

आधानं च भार्य्यासंयुक्तम् ॥१३॥

13. And the consecration of fire is in the company of his wife.

अकर्म चोर्ध्वमाधानात्तत्समवायो हि कर्मभिः ॥१४॥

14. And marriage after the establishment of fire is not for the sacrificial act, because its affinity is with the act.

श्राद्धवदिति चेत् ॥१५॥

15. If you say that it is like the offerings to the manes.

न श्रुतिविप्रतिषेधात् ॥१६॥

16. No, by reason of the prohibition enjoined by the Veda.

सर्वार्थत्वाच्च पुत्रार्थो न प्रयोजयेत् ॥१७॥

17. And by reason of fulfilling all objects, one desirous of procreation only, should not engage.

सोमपानात्तु प्रापणं द्वितीयस्य तस्मादुपयच्छेत् ॥१८॥

18. On the other hand, by reason of drinking soma, there is the marriage with a second wife; therefore one should marry.

पितृयज्ञे तु दर्शनात्प्रागाधानात्प्रतीयेत ॥१९॥

19. On the other hand, in the *pitṛyajña* by seeing (the text) it appears that it can be performed even before the establishment of fire.

स्थपतीष्टिः प्रयाजवदग्न्याधेयं प्रयोजयेत्तादर्थ्याच्चापवृज्येत ॥२०॥

20. The *sthapatīṣṭi* should be performed like the *prayāja* offerings in the consecrated fire and for that object, the offerings be consigned to the fire.

अपि वा लौकिऽग्नौ स्यादाधानस्यासर्वशेषत्वात् ॥२१॥

21. Not sŏ, it should be made in the unconsecrated fire, because the *agnyādhāna* is not subordinate to any sacrifice.

अवकीर्णिपशुश्च तद्वदाधानस्याप्राप्तकालत्वात् ॥२२॥

22. And the animal to be offered as a penance for a breach of the vow by a religious student is to be done like it, because the time for the establishment of fire has not arrived.

उदगयनपूर्वपक्षाहः पुण्याहेषु दैवानि स्मृतिरूपान्यार्थ दर्शनात् ॥२३॥

23. All the domestic ceremonies should be performed when the sun is in the north and in the first half of the month, during the day on some auspicious occasion, because there is a smṛti text.

अहनि च कर्म्मसाकल्यम् ॥२४॥

24. And the whole ceremony should be performed during the day.

इतरेषु तु पित्र्याणि ॥२५॥

25. On the other hand, the offerings to the manes should be made in the other.

याच्ञाक्रयणमविद्यद्यमाने लोकवत् ॥२६॥

26. Begging and purchasing should be done when one has not, just as it happens in the worldly affairs.

नियतं वार्थवत्वात्स्यात् ॥२७॥

27. On the other hand, they are to be done always by reason of their being for a purpose.

तथा भक्षप्रैषाच्छादनसंज्ञप्तहोमद्वेषम् ॥२८॥

28. Similarly food, command, dress, *saṃjñaptanahoma* and enmity.

अनर्थकं त्वनित्यं स्यात् ॥२९॥

29. On the other hand, (when it is apprehended that it will be) fruitless, it is not permanent.

पशुचोदनायामनियमोऽविशेषात् ॥३०॥

30. Where it is laid down as to an offering of an animal, there is no rule for want of anything special.

छागो वा मन्त्रवर्णात् ॥३१॥

31. On the other hand, it is goat by the force of the text.

न चोदनाविरोधात् ॥३२॥

32. Not so; by reason of its being contrary to the direct command.

आर्षेयवदिति चेत् ॥३३॥

33. If you say that it is like *ārṣeya homa.*

न तत्र ह्यचोदितत्वात् ॥३४॥

34. Not so, because it is not commanded there.

नियमो वैकार्थ्यं ह्यर्थभेदाद्भेदः पृथक्त्वेनाभिधानात् ॥३५॥

35. On the other hand, there is a restrictive rule as they convey one meaning; by reason of the difference of meaning and naming, there is a difference.

अनियमो वार्थान्तरत्वादन्यत्वं व्यतिरेकशब्दभेदाभ्याम् ॥३६॥

36. On the other hand there is no rule on account of the difference of meaning; there is (other-ness) difference on account of words.

रूपाल्लिङ्गाच्च ॥३७॥

37. By reason of the form and gender.

छागे न कर्माख्या रूपलिङ्गाभ्याम् ॥३८॥

38. In the goat the naming is not from form and gender.

रूपान्यत्वान्न जातिशब्दः स्यात् ॥३९॥

39. By reason of the difference of form, it does not denote a class.

विकारो नौत्पत्तिकत्वात् ॥४०॥

40. The modified form is also not meant, because of the significant power of the word.

स नैमित्तिकः पशोर्गुणस्याचोदितत्वात् ॥४१॥

41. That is accidental, because the quality of the animal is not laid down.

जातेर्वा तत्प्रायवचनार्थवत्वाभ्याम् ॥४२॥

42. On the other hand, it is also genus by reason of the constant conventional use and consistent meaning.

END OF PĀDA 8

***

END OF ADHYĀYA 6

ADHYĀYA VII

PĀDA 1

श्रुतिप्रमाणत्वाच्छेषाणां मुख्यभेदे यथाधिकारं भावः स्यात् ॥१॥

1. By reason of the authority of the Veda the extraordinary principle of the subordinate acts in the difference of the principal shall be according to the context.

उत्पत्त्यर्थाविभागाद्वा सत्त्ववदैकधर्म्यं स्यात् ॥२॥

2. On the other hand, by reason of the indivisibility of the object of the original, like an animal, they belong to all.

चोदनाशेषाभावाद्वा तद्भेदाद्व्यवतिष्ठेरन्नुत्पत्तेर्गुणभूतत्वात् ॥३॥

3. On the other hand, by reason of the partial nature of the injunction and its variety there is a rule laid down; because of the extraordinary principle being subordinate.

सत्वे लक्षणसंयोगात्सार्वत्रिकं प्रतीयेत ॥४॥

4. In an animal, by reason of the connection with the characteristic peculiarity, it is known everywhere.

अविभागात्तु नैवं स्यात् ॥५॥

5. On the other hand, by reason of the indivisibility it is not so.

द्व्यर्थत्वं च विप्रतिषिद्धम् ॥६॥

6. And double object is forbidden.

उत्पत्तौ विध्यभावाद्वा चोदनायां प्रवृत्तिः स्यात्ततश्च कर्मभेदः स्यात् ॥७॥

7. On the other hand, there being no general command in the origin, there is a natural inclination for the special command; therefore there is a variety of actions.

यदि वाऽप्यभिधानवत्सामान्यात्सर्वधर्मः स्यात् ॥८॥

8. Or if like a name, by reason of its being common, it is the peculiarity of all.

अर्थस्य त्वविभक्तत्वात्तथा स्यादभिधानेषु पूर्ववत्त्वात्प्रयोगस्य कर्मणः शब्दभाव्यत्वाद्विभागाच्छेषाणामप्रवृत्तिः स्यात् ॥९॥

9. On the other hand, by reason of the indivisibility of the object, the

same shall be in the case of the names; and of the sacrificial act being founded on the word, and being divided, the subordinate acts are applied.

स्मृतिरितिचेत् ॥१०॥

10. "There is a tradition" if you say.

न पूर्ववत्वात् ॥११॥

11. Not so, by reason of being like the previous.

अर्थस्य शब्दभाव्यत्वात्प्रकरणनिबन्धनाच्छब्दादेवान्यत्र भावः स्यात् ॥१२॥

12. The object (of any sacrificial act) being founded on the Vedic text and being connected with the context only, can have its existence elsewhere by reason of the Vedic text only.

सामाने पूर्ववत्वादुत्पन्नाधिकारः स्यात् ॥१३॥

13. In equal sacrifices by reason of having their previous model, the original is the context.

श्येनस्येति चेत् ॥१४॥

14. If you say 'of *śyena.*'

नासन्निधान्नात् ॥१५॥

15. Not so, by reason of no proximity.

अपि वा यद्यपूर्वत्वादितरदधिकार्थे ज्यौतिष्टोमिकाद्विधेस्तद्वाचकं समानं स्यात् ॥१६॥

16. Or also if by reason of the nature of the invisible principle, the word 'other' is used in the meaning 'over and above' the commands pertaining to the *jyotiṣṭoma*; that meaning is then similar.

पञ्चसञ्चरेष्वर्थवादातिदेशः सन्निधानात् ॥१७॥

17. In the five offerings, there is a transference of *arthavāda* by reason of the proximity.

सर्वस्य वैकशब्द्यात् ॥१८॥

18. On the other hand, of all by reason of the unity of sentence.

लिङ्गदर्शनाच्च ॥१९॥

19. By seeing the force of the text.

विहिताम्नानान्नेति चेत् ॥२०॥

20. If you say 'it cannot be by reason of the repetition of what is laid down.'

नेतरार्थत्वात् ॥२१॥

21. Not so, by reason of being for the object of another.

एककपालैन्द्राग्नौ च तद्वत् ॥२२॥

22. And similarly like it, in *eka kapālaindrāgni.*

एककपालानां वैश्वदेविकः प्रकृतिराग्रयणे सर्वहोमापरिवृत्तिदर्शनादवभृथे च सकृद् द्व्यवदानस्य वचनात् ॥२३॥

23. Of the sacrifices in which a cake baked on one earthen pan is offered, the *vaiśvadeva* is the model; in the first offering, by not seeing the completion of the whole homa and by reason of the text for the double offering at a time on the occasion of the sacrificial bath.

END OF PĀDA 1

***

PĀDA 2

साम्नोऽभिधानशब्देन प्रवृत्तिः स्याद्यथाशिष्टम् ॥१॥

1. By the word indicating a name of a psalm, there is inclination according to the instruction given by a preceptor.

शब्दैस्त्वर्थविधित्वादर्थान्तरेऽप्रवृत्तिः स्यात्पृथग्भावात्क्रियाया ह्यभिसम्बन्धः ॥२॥

2. On the other hand, by means of the words, the meaning being laid down, there cannot be the use in a different sense; because of the difference, there is a connection with the action.

स्वार्थे वा स्यात् प्रयोजनं क्रियाया स्तदंगभावेनोप दिश्येरन् ॥३॥

3. On the other hand, in its own end there is a purpose of the action; it is laid down by its being a constituent part.

शब्दमात्रमितिचेत् ॥४॥

4. If it be said that only verbal.

नौत्पत्तिकत्वात् ॥५॥

5. No, by reason of the eternal connection.

शास्त्रंचैवमनर्थकं स्यात् ॥६॥

6. And in this way the code of rule will be meaningless.

स्वरस्येतिचेत् ॥७॥

7. If it be said 'of *swara*'.

नार्थाभावा छ्रुतेरसंबंधः ॥८॥

8. No, by reason of the want of sense, there is no relationship with the text.

स्वरस्तूत्पत्तिषुस्यान्मात्रावर्णाविभक्तत्वात् ॥९॥

9. On the other hand, the *svara* is in the origin; because the mark and letter are indivisible.

लिङ्गदर्शनाच्च ॥१०॥

10. And by seeing the force of the text.

अश्रुतेस्तुविकारस्योत्तरासु यथाश्रुति ॥११॥

11. On the other hand, because in uttarā (a number of songs) no modulation is laid down, it is according to instruction.

शब्दानां चासामञ्जस्यम् ॥१२॥

12. And there is no significant power of the word.

अपि तु कर्मशब्दः स्याद्भावोऽर्थः प्रसिद्धग्रहणत्वाद्विकारो ह्यवि-शिष्टोऽन्यैः ॥१३॥

13. On the other hand, it is a word indicating action; this is the real sense by accepting the popular sense; because it a modification without any difference with others.

अद्रव्यं चापि दृश्यते ॥१४॥

14. And a song without a *ṛk* is also seen.

तस्य च क्रिया ग्रहणार्था नानार्थेषु विरूपित्वादर्थो ह्यासामलौकिको विधानात् ॥१५॥

15. Its action (when there is no application) is for practice by reason of its being manifested in many forms; because the object of all these, is extraordinary by reason of being ordained.

तस्मिन्संज्ञाविशेषाः स्युर्विकारपृथक्त्वात् ॥१६॥

16. In it, there are particular names by reason of the difference of the modifications.

योनिशस्याश्च तुल्यवदितराभिर्विधीयन्ते ॥१७॥

17. And the verses that are not to be sung are equally ordained with others that are sung.

अयोनौ चापि दृश्यतेऽतथायोनि ॥१८॥

18. In the verses that are not set to tune, is seen the song of not similar origin.

ऐकार्थ्ये नास्ति वैरूप्यमिति चेत् ॥१९॥

19. If you say that there is no variety in one object.

स्यादर्थान्तरेष्वनिष्पत्तेर्यथा पाके ॥२०॥

20. There is, by reason of not practising in other verses just as in cooking.

शब्दानाञ्च सामञ्जस्यम् ॥२१॥

21. And the significance of the word.

END OF PĀDA 2

***

PĀDA 3

उक्तं क्रियाभिधानं तच्छ्रुतावन्यत्र विधिप्रदेशः स्यात् ॥१॥

1. It is stated to be a name of an action; it is elsewhere mentioned; it is a transfer of the qualities.

अपूर्वे वापि भागित्वात् ॥२॥

2. On the other hand, by reason of the fitness in the extraordinary principle.

नाम्नस्त्वौत्पत्तिकत्वात् ॥३॥

3. By reason of the eternal connection of the name.

प्रत्यक्षाद्गुणसंयोगात्क्रियाभिधानं स्यात्तदभावेऽप्रसिद्धं स्यात् ॥४॥

4. It is a name of an action by reason of the visible connection with the qualities; in the absence of them, it is not known.

अपि वा सत्रकर्मणि गुणार्थैषा श्रुतिः स्यात् ॥५॥

5. On the other hand, in a sacrificial session the text is descriptive of the qualities.

विश्वजिति सर्वपृष्ठे तत्पूर्वकत्वाज्ज्यौतिष्टोमिकानि पृष्ठान्यस्ति पृष्ठशब्दः ॥६॥

6. In a *viśvajit* sacrifice in *sarvapṛṣṭha*, by reason of its being a model, the *pṛṣṭhas* of the *jyotiṣṭoma* are intended; there is the word *pṛṣṭhas*.

षडहाद्वा तत्र हि चोदना ॥७॥

7. Or from the *ṣaḍaḥ* sacrifice because there is a command.

लिङ्गाच्च ॥८॥

8. And by the force of the text.

उत्पन्नाधिकारो ज्योतिष्टोमः ॥९॥

9. The *jyotiṣṭoma* is the class in which many songs occur.

द्वयोर्विधिरिति चेत् ॥१०॥

10. If it be said that it is a command relating to both.

न व्यर्थत्वात् सर्वशब्दस्य ॥११॥

11. No, by reason of the meaninglessness of the word 'all'.

तथावभृथः सोमात् ॥१२॥

12. In the same way, the sacrificial bath from *soma.*

प्रकृतेरिति चेत् ॥१३॥

13. If it be said "from the model sacrifice".

न भक्तित्वात् ॥१४॥

14. Not so, by reason of the secondary sense.

लिङ्गदर्शनाच्च ॥१५॥

15. And by seeing the force of the text.

द्रव्यादेशेतद्द्रव्यः श्रुतिसंयोगात्पुरोडाशस्त्वनादेशे तत्प्रकृतित्वात् । ॥१६॥

16. When a substance is mentioned, then that substance by reason of its connection with the text; and a *puroḍāśa* cake, if there be no mention, by reason of its being of model sacrifice.

गुणविधिस्तु न गृह्णीयात्समत्वात् ॥१७॥

17. On the other hand, it is *guṇavidhi* (laying down of qualities) and does not borrow them, being equal.

निर्मन्थ्यादिषु चैवम् ॥१८॥

18. And similarly in *nirmanthya* &c.

प्रणयनन्तु सौमिकमवाच्यं हीतरत् ॥१९॥

19. On the other hand, carrying of the fire pertains to *somayāga*, because the other is not ordained.

उत्तरवेदिप्रतिषेधश्च तद्वत् ॥२०॥

20. And the prohibition of *uttaravedi* is like it.

प्राकृतं वाऽनामत्वात् ॥२१॥

21. Or belonging to the model sacrifice by reason of having no name of any particular.

परिसङ्ख्यार्थं श्रवणं गुणार्थमर्थवादो वा ॥२२॥

22. The text is for *parisaṁkhyā* or descriptive of quality or recommendation.

प्रथमोत्तमयोः प्रणयनमुत्तरवेदिप्रतिषेधात् ॥२३॥

23. The carrying of the fire is of the first and the last by reason of the prohibition of *uttaravedi.*

मध्यमयोर्वा गत्यर्थवादात् ॥२४॥

24. On the other hand, of the middle two by reason of the description of the motion.

औत्तरवेदिकोऽनारभ्यवादप्रतिषेधः ॥२५॥

25. As to that pertaining to *uttaradevi*, it is a prohibition of the general text.

स्वरसामैककपालामिक्षं च लिङ्गदर्शनात् ॥२६॥

26. And the *svarasāma*, *ekakapāla* and *āmikṣā* by reason of the force of the text.

चोदनासामान्याद्वा ॥२७॥

27. Or by reason of the general command.

कर्मजे कर्म यूपवत् ॥२८॥

28. In a thing which is produced by an act, it is an act like a sacrificial post.

रूपं वाऽशेषभूतत्वात् ॥२९॥

29. On the other hand, it is form by reason of nothing left (of action).

विशये लौकिकः स्यात्सर्वार्थत्वात् ॥३०॥

30. In a doubt the common fire, by reason of its accomplishing all objects.

न वैदिकमर्थनिर्देशात् ॥३१॥

31. Not the consecrated fire, being ordained for a particular object.

तथोत्पत्तिरितरेषां समत्वात् ॥३२॥

32. By the reason of the equality of its origin with others.

संस्कृतं स्यात्तच्छब्दत्वात् ।'३३॥

33. Consecrated by reason of that word.

भक्त्या वाऽयज्ञशेषत्वाद्गुणानामभिधानत्वात् ॥३४॥

34. It is by the secondary sense being not subsidiary to the sacrifice and by describing the qualities.

कर्मणः पृष्ठशब्दः स्यात्तथाभूतोपदेशात् ॥३५॥

35. The word *pṛṣṭha* denotes an action by laying down similar direction.

अभिधानोपदेशाद्वा विप्रतिषेधादद्रव्येषु पृष्ठशब्दः स्यात् ॥३६॥

36. On the other hand, by mentioning the name and prohibition, the word *pṛṣṭha* is used in the sense of substance.

END OF PĀDA 3

***

PĀDA 4

इतिकर्तव्यताविधेर्यजतेः पूर्ववत्त्वम् ॥१॥

1. The model of the sacrifice by reason of the subordinate acts being not prescribed.

स लौकिकः स्याददृष्टप्रवृत्तित्वात् ॥२॥

2. It it wordly, by seeing its application.

वचनात्तु ततोऽन्यत्वम् ॥३॥

3. On the other hand, it is regulated by the force of the text since it is the characteristic of the force of the text.

लिङ्गेन वा नियम्येत लिङ्गस्य तद्गुणत्वात् ॥४॥

4. On the other hand, by the text, it is otherwise.

अपि वाऽन्यायपूर्वत्वाद्यत्र नित्यानुवादवचनानि स्युः ॥५॥

5. Not so, being based on unreasonableness, when there is permanent restatement.

मिथो विप्रतिषेधाच्च गुणानां यथार्थकल्पना स्यात् ॥६॥

6. And by reason of mutual incompatibility, there is the real applicability of the subordinate.

भागित्वात्तु नियम्येत गुणानामभिधानत्वात्सम्बन्धादभिधानवद्यथा धेनुः किशोरेण ।।७।।

7. On the other hand, it is limited by reason of participating in the extraordinary principle because it indicates the subordinate acts. By virtue of relationship, it is like a name just as mare by the colt.

उत्पत्तीनां समत्वाद्वा यथाधिकारं भावः स्यात् ।।८।।

8. On the other hand, by virtue of the equality of the origin, they are regulated by the context.

उत्पत्तिशेषवचनं च विप्रतिषिद्धमेकस्मिन् ।।९।।

9. In one sentence, the principal and the subordinate acts are prohibited.

विध्यन्तो वा प्रकृतिवच्चोदनायां प्रवर्त्तेत तथा हि लिङ्गदर्शनम् ।।१०।।

10. On the other hand, it is the end of the *vidhi*; like the model sacrifice, it is applicable in *codanā* text; similarly is the force of the text.

लिङ्गहेतुत्वादलिङ्गे लौकिकं स्यात् ।।११।।

11. By virtue of the *liṅga* being the cause, in a case where there is no *liṅga*, it will be profane.

लिङ्गस्य पूर्ववत्त्वाच्चोदनाशब्दसामान्यादेकेनापि निरूप्येत यथा स्थालीपुलाकेन ।१२।।

12. By reason of the priority of *liṅga* and the *codanā* being common, one only determines just as one (grain of) rice in a cauldron.

द्वादशाहिकमहर्गणे तत्प्रकृतित्वादैकाहिकमधिकागमात्तदाख्यं स्यादेकाहवत् ।।१३।।

13. In a sacrifice lasting for several days, the twelve days' sacrifice by reason of being the model of it; exceeding the songs of one day, they will be so-called like a sacrifice for a day.

लिङ्गाच्च ।।१४।।

14. And by force of the text.

न वा क्रत्वभिधानादधिकानामशब्दत्वम् ।।१५।।

15. Not so, by reason of the name of the sacrifice; and of the more songs there is no authority.

लिङ्गं संघातधर्मः स्यात्तदर्थापत्तेर्द्रव्यवत् ।।१६।।

16. The *liṅga* is the characteristic of the collection of sacrifices by reason of securing the object like the material.

न वार्थधर्मत्वात्संघातस्य गुणत्वात् ॥१७॥

17. Not so, by reason of partaking the characteristic of the reward, the aggregate being subordinate.

अर्थापत्तेर्द्रव्येषु धर्मलाभः स्यात् ॥१८॥

18. By reason of securing the object, there is transference of the characteristics in the materials.

प्रवृत्त्या नियतस्य लिङ्गदर्शनम् ॥१९॥

19. Fixed by the application, there is the symbol or mark.

विहारदर्शनं विशिष्टस्यानारभ्यवादानां प्रकृत्यर्थत्वात् ॥२०॥

20. Seeing the 12th day ceremony of animal sacrifice which is special, by virtue of the general statement being for the model sacrifice.

END OF PĀDA 4

* * *

END OF ADHYĀYA VII

ADHYĀYA VIII

PĀDA 1

अथ विशेषलक्षणम् ॥१॥

1. Now is the definition of the special.

यस्य लिङ्गमर्थसंयोगादभिधानवत् ॥२॥

2. Whose mark by reason of the connection with the object like a name.

प्रवृत्तित्वादिष्टेः सोमे प्रवृत्तिः स्यात् ॥३॥

3. In a *soma* sacrifice, the procedure of *iṣṭi* applies by reason of the application.

लिङ्गदर्शनाच्च ॥४॥

4. And there is also an inference.

कृत्स्नविधानाद्वाऽपूर्वत्वम् ॥५॥

5. On the other hand, by laying down all the details, there is the peculiarity of an extraordinary principle.

स्रुगभिधारणाभावस्य च नित्यानुवादात् ॥६॥

6. And there are no spoon and sprinkling of ghee by virtue of the permanent restatement.

विधिरिति चेत् ॥७॥

7. If it be said that it is a prohibition.

न वाक्यशेषत्वात् ॥८॥

8. No, by reason of completing the sentence.

शङ्कते चानुपोषणात् ॥९॥

9. And he doubts by reason of not fasting.

दर्शनमैष्टिकानां स्यात् ॥१०॥

10. There are minor offerings seen.

इष्टिषु दर्शपूर्णमासयोः प्रवृत्तिः स्यात् ॥११॥

11. In *iṣṭis* there is the application of full and new moon sacrifices.

पशौ च लिङ्गदर्शनात् ॥१२॥

12. And in an animal sacrifice, by seeing the inference from the text.

दैक्षस्य चेतरेषु ॥१३॥

13. And of *agniṣomīya*, in others.

ऐकादशिनेषु सौत्यस्य द्वैरशन्यस्य दर्शनात् ॥१४॥

14. By seeing the time for preparing the soma and two ropes in *aikādaśinī* animal sacrifice.

तत्प्रवृत्तिर्गणेषु स्यातप्रतिपशु यूपदर्शनात् ॥१५॥

15. In the collection of animals, that applies by reason of seeing separate sacrificial posts for each animal.

अव्यक्तासु तु सोमस्य ॥१६॥

16. On the other hand in indefinite sacrifices of the soma.

गणेषु द्वादशाहस्य ॥१७॥

17. In sacrifices which last for days, of the *dvādaśāha.*

गव्यस्य च तदादिषु ॥१८॥

18. And in sacrifices like that &c., of the *gavāmayana.*

निकायिनां च पूर्वस्योत्तरेषु प्रवृत्तिः स्यात् ॥१९॥

19. And of assemblage of days, the procedure of the first applies to the latter part.

कर्मणस्त्वप्रवृत्तित्वात्फलनियमकर्तृसमुदायस्यानन्वयस्तद्बन्धनत्वात् ॥२०॥

20. By reason of the non-application of the principal act, the fruit, the rule, the agent and the aggregate are not transferred, because they depend on it.

प्रवृत्तौ चापि तादर्थ्यात् ॥२१॥

21. And in the application also by reason of its being for the object of that.

अश्रुतित्वाच्च ॥२२॥

22. And by reason of being not laid down.

गुणकामेष्वाश्रितत्वात्प्रवृत्तिः स्यात् ॥२३॥

23. In the subordinate acts which are ends in themselves, by reason of dependence there is application.

निवृत्तिर्वा कर्मभेदात् ॥२४॥

24. On the other hand, there is non-application by reason of difference of the act.

अपि वाऽतद्विकारत्वात्क्रत्वर्थत्वात्प्रवृत्तिः स्यात् ॥२५॥

25. On the other hand, by reason of its being not modified and being for the sacrifice, there is the application.

एककर्मणि विकल्पोऽविभागो हि चोदनैकत्वात् ॥२६॥

26. In one action, there is option because it is indivisible by reason of one command.

लिङ्गसाधारण्याद्विकल्पः स्यात् ॥२७॥

27. There is option by reason of the *liṅga* being common.

ऐकार्थ्याद्वा नियम्येत पूर्ववत्त्वाद्विकारो हि ॥२८॥

28. On the other hand, it is regulated by reason of its being for one object; because it has a model, therefore it is a modified sacrifice.

अश्रुतित्वान्नेति चेत् ॥२९॥

29. If you say "by reason of not hearing it".

स्याल्लिङ्गभावात् ॥३०॥

30. There is one deity by the force of the text.

तथा चान्यार्थदर्शनम् ॥३१॥

31. Similarly there are other texts.

विप्रतिपत्तौ हविषा नियम्येत कर्मणस्तदुपाख्यत्वात् ॥३२॥

32. In case of conflict, it is regulated by the offering, by reason of the action being the integral part of it.

तेन च कर्मसंयोगात् ॥३३॥

33. And with that, by reason of its connection with the action.

गुणत्वेनदेवताश्रुतिः ॥३४॥

34. As a quality there is the mention of the deity.

हिरण्यमाज्यधर्मस्तेजस्त्वात् ॥३५॥

35. The golden sacrifice partakes of the procedure of the ghee offerings by reason of the splendour.

धर्मानुग्रहाच्च ॥३६॥

36. And by partaking of the quality.

औषधं वा विशदत्वात् ॥३७॥

37. On the other hand, it partakes of the procedure of the sacrifice in which wild rice is used by reason of its expansion.

चरुशब्दाच्च ॥३८॥

38. And by reason of the word 'boiled rice'.

तस्मिंश्च श्रपणश्रुतेः ॥३९॥

39. And in it, there is mention of boiling.

मधूदके द्रव्यसामान्यात्पयोविकारः स्यात् ॥४०॥

40. In honey mixed with water by similarity of fluidity, there is the modification of milk.

आज्यं वा वर्णसामान्यात् ॥४१॥

41. It is the procedure applicable to the ghee oblations that regulates it, by reason of the similarity of colour.

धर्मानुग्रहाच्च ॥४२॥

42. And by reason of partaking of its quality.

पूर्वस्य चाविशिष्टत्वात् ॥४३॥

43. And of the former being common.

END OF PĀDA 1

***

PĀDA 2

वाजिने सोमपूर्वत्वं सौत्रामण्याञ्च ग्रहेषु ताच्छब्द्यात् ॥१॥

1. In *vājinejyā* and in the cups of *sautrāmaṇi*, the soma yāga is the model by reason of the word 'soma'.

अनुवषट्काराच्च ॥२॥

2. And by reason of pronouncing the word '*vaṣaṭkāra*' in the end.

समुपहूय भक्षणाच्च ॥३॥

3. And by eating after invitation.

क्रयणश्रपणपुरोरुगुपयामग्रहणासादनवासोपनहनञ्च तद्वत् ॥४॥

4. Purchasing, boiling, offering, reciting (of *upayāma* &c.) partaking, placing and tying in a cloth, are like it.

हविषा वा नियम्येत तद्विकारत्वात् ॥५॥

5. On the other hand, it is regulated by the offering by reason of its modification.

प्रशंसा सोमशब्दः ॥६॥

6. The word 'soma' is by way of praise.

वचनानीतराणि ॥७॥

7. Others are mere words.

व्यपदेशश्च तद्वत् ॥८॥

8. And the naming is like it.

पशुपुरोडाशस्य च लिङ्गदर्शनम् ॥९॥

9. And by seeing the marks of animal *puroḍāśa.*

पशुः पुरोडाशविकारः स्याद्देवतासामान्यात् ॥१०॥

10. Animal sacrifice is the modification of *puroḍāśa* by reason of the similarity of the deity.

प्रोक्षणाच्च ॥११॥

11. And by sprinkling water.

पर्य्यग्निकरणाच्च ॥१२॥

12. And by surrounding it with fire on all sides.

सान्नाय्यं वा तत्प्रभवत्वात् ॥१३॥

13. On the other hand, it is the modification of *sannāya* by reason of its being produced from it.

तस्य च पात्रदर्शनात् ॥१४॥

14. And by seeing its vessel.

दध्नः स्यान्मूर्त्तिसामान्यात् ॥१५॥

15. Of the curd by reason of the similarity of the form.

पयो वा कालसामान्यात् ॥१६॥

16. On the other hand, milk by reason of time being common.

पश्वानन्तर्यात् ॥१७॥

17. By reason of the animal being proximate.

द्रवत्वं चाविशिष्टम् ॥१८॥

18. And motion being common.

आमिक्षोभयभाव्यत्वादुभयविकारः स्यात् ॥१९॥

19. *āmikṣā* is the modification of both by reason of being produced from both.

एकं वा चोदनैकत्वात् ॥२०॥

20. On the other hand, by reason of one command.

दधिसंघातसामान्यात् ॥२१॥

21. It is curd by reason of solidity being common.

पयो वा तत्प्रधानत्वाल्लोकवद्दध्नस्तदर्थत्वात् ॥२२॥

22. On the other hand, it is milk, by reason of its being principal as in ordinary life because curd is for it.

धर्म्मानुग्रहाच्च ॥२३॥

23. And by partaking of its quality.

सत्रमहीनश्च द्वादशाहस्तस्योभयथा प्रवृत्तिरैककर्म्यात् ॥२४॥

24. Sacrificial sessions and the sacrifice lasting for more than one day are *dvādaśāha*; its application is both ways by reason of the action being one.

अपि वा यजतिश्रुतेरहोनभूतप्रवृत्तिः स्यात्प्रकृत्या तुल्य शब्दत्वात् ॥२५॥

25. On the other hand, by hearing '*yajati*', the application is of *ahīna*, because of the equality of the word with the model.

द्विरात्रादीनामेकादशरात्रादहीनत्वं यजतिचोदनात् ॥२६॥

26. Of *dvirātra* &c. up to sacrifices lasting for eleven nights are *ahīna* by reason of the command expressed in *yajati.*

त्रयोदशरात्रादिषु सत्रभूतस्तेष्वासनोपायिचोदनात् ॥२७॥

27. In those sacrifices which last for 13 nights and upwards, the procedure of *satra* applies by reason of the words "*upeyuḥ*" and '*upāsīran*'.

लिङ्गाच्च ॥२८॥

28. And by reason of a mark.

अन्यतरतोऽतिरात्रत्वात् पंचदशरात्रस्याहीनत्वं कुण्डगयिनामयनस्य च तद्भूतेष्वहीनत्वस्य दर्शनात् ॥२९॥

29. By reason of being other and being *atirātra*, the *pañcadaśarātra*

and *kuṇḍapāyināmayana* are *ahīna* because the *ahīna* nature is seen their dependence on it.

अहीनवचनाच्च ॥३०॥

30. By reason of the text mentioning it to be *ahīna.*

सत्रे वोपायिचोदनात् ॥३१॥

31. On the other hand, in a *satra* by reason of the command containing the form of the verb '*upāyi*'.

सत्रलिङ्गञ्चदर्शयति ॥३२॥

32. And there is the mark of a *sātra.*

END OF PĀDA 2

***

PĀDA 3

हविर्गणे परमुत्तरस्य देशसामान्यात् ॥१॥

1. In the case of the manifold offerings, the subsequent to the subsequent by reason of the common sequence.

देवतया वा नियम्येतशब्दत्त्वादितरस्याश्रुतित्वात् ॥२॥

2. On the other hand, it is regulated by the deity by reason of the nature of the word and of the other, there is no text.

गणचोदनायां यस्य लिङ्गं तदावृत्तिः प्रतीयेताग्नेयवत् ॥३॥

3. In a command relating to multiplicity, it appears that that cone is to be repeated whose mark is like *āgneya.*

नानाहानि वा संघातत्वात्प्रवृत्तिलिङ्गेन चोदनात् ॥४॥

4. On the other hand, many days (*dvādaśāha*) by reason of the collection, because the command is regulated by the mark of commencement.

तथा चान्यार्थदर्शनम् ॥५॥

5. And similarly there is another text.

कालाभ्यासेऽपि बादरिः कर्मभेदात् ॥६॥

6. In the repetition of time also, the view of Bādri is (the same) by reason of the difference of action.

तदावृत्तिं तु जैमिनिरह्नामप्रत्यक्षसंख्यत्वात् ॥७॥

7. On the other hand, according to Jaimini, it is the repetition of it (*ṣaḍaha*) because the number of days is inferential.

संस्थागणेषु तदभ्यासः प्रतीयेत कृतलक्षणग्रहणात् ॥८॥

8. In the collection of songs, it appears to be a repetition of the model because it partakes of its peculiarities.

अधिकाराद्वा प्रकृतिस्तद्विशिष्टा स्यादभिधानस्य तन्निमित्तत्वात् ॥९॥

9. On the other hand, the model is characterised by it (*ukthya*) by virtue of the *codanā* text and the name is for its sake.

गणादुपचयस्तत्प्रकृतित्वात् ॥१०॥

10. There is a transference from the collection of days (*dvādaśāha*) by reason of its being a model.

एकाहाद्वा तेषां समत्त्वात्स्यात् ॥११॥

11. On the other hand, from the one day ceremony, because they are equal with the modified.

गायत्रीषु प्राकृतीनामवच्छेदः प्रकृत्त्याधिकात्संख्या त्वादग्निष्टोम-वदव्यतिरेकात्तदाख्यत्वम् ॥१२॥

12. In the *gāyatrī* metre the letters are dropped from those metres coming from the model by virtue of borrowing from the model and by reason of the number, like the *agniṣṭoma*; because that name invariably applies.

तन्नित्यवच्च प्रथक्सतीषु तद्वचनम् ॥१३॥

13. And it is permanent and the word applies in other than this.

न विंशतौ दशेति चेत् ॥१४॥

14. If it be said that in twenty, there is no ten.

न विंशतौ दशेति चेत् ॥

14. If it be said "no, in twenty ten is included".

ऐकसंख्यमेव स्यात् ॥१५॥

15. Then there would be only one numeral.

गुणाद्वाद्रव्यशब्दः स्यादसर्वविषयत्वात् ॥१६॥

16. On the other hand, by reason of a quality, it is a word denoting substance; it does not apply to all.

गोत्ववच्च समन्वयः ॥१७॥

17. And the application like the ('*cowness*') cow.

संख्यायाश्च शब्दत्वात् ॥१८॥

18. And because of the numeral being a word.

इतरस्याश्रुतित्वाच्च ॥१९॥

19. And because of the other having no name.

द्रव्यान्तरेऽनिवेशादुक्थ्यलोपैर्विशिष्टं स्यात् ॥२०॥

20. By reason of not applying it to any other substance, it is particularised by dropping the songs.

अशास्त्रलक्षणत्वाच्च ॥२१॥

21. And by reason of the characteristics not being laid down.

उत्पत्तिनामधेयत्वाद्भक्तया पृथक्सतीषु स्यात् ॥२२॥

22. By reason of the permanent nature of the name, the use in a separate thing is by way of figure of speech.

वचनमिति चेत् ॥२३॥

23. If it be a command.

यावदुक्तम् ॥२४॥

24. When the whole is uttered.

अपूर्वे च विकल्पः स्याद्यदि संख्याविधानम् ॥२५॥

25. And in the model sacrifice, there will be an option, if the number be considered to be commanded.

ऋग्गुणत्वान्नेति चेत् ॥२६॥

26. If you say that it cannot be so, by reason of being a quality of the *ṛk*.

तथा पूर्ववति स्यात् ॥२७॥

27. The same will happen in the modified sacrifice.

गुणावेशश्च सर्वत्र ॥२८॥

28. And the introduction of a quality every where.

निष्पन्नग्रहणान्नेति चेत् ॥२९॥

29. If you say "not so, by reason of accepting the conventional sense."

तथेहापिस्यात् ॥३०॥

30. Similarly here also.

यदि वाऽविशये नियमः प्रकृत्युपबन्धाच्छरेष्वपि प्रसिद्धः स्यात् ॥३१॥

31. If the term, the sense of which is certain by reason of the *codaka* text (is applied elsewhere), then the term *śara* may be used for grass.

दृष्टः प्रयोग इतिचेत् ॥३२॥

32. If you say that the application is seen.

तथा शरेष्वपि ॥३३॥

33. The same is the case in the term *śara*.

भक्त्येति चेत् ॥३४॥

34. If you say, it is by way of figure of speech.

तथेतरस्मिन् ॥३५॥

35. So in the other.

अर्थस्य चासमाप्तत्वान्न तासामेकदेशे स्यात् ॥३६॥

36. And by reason of non-completion of the sense, they cannot apply to a portion.

END OF PĀDA 3

***

PĀDA 4

दर्विहोमो यज्ञाभिधानं होमसंयोगात् ॥१॥

1. *darvihoma* is the name of a sacrifice by reason of he connection of the word *homa*.

स लौकिकानां स्यात्कर्त्तुस्तदाख्यत्वात् ॥२॥

2. It is secular by reason of its name after the agent.

सर्वेषां वा दर्शनाद्वास्तुहोमे ॥३॥

3. On the other hand, it is of all, by seeing it in the religious *homa*.

जुहोतिचोदनानां वा तत्संयोगात् ॥४॥

4. On the other hand, it is a command relating to *juhoti* verb by reason of its connection with it.

द्रव्योपदेशाद्वा गुणाभिधानं स्यात् ॥५॥

5. On the other hand, by reason of laying down the material, it is a name of material.

न लौकिकानामाचारग्रहणत्वाच्छब्दवतां चान्यार्थविधानात् ॥६॥

6. Not so, by reason of the acceptance of the procedure of the profane people and by laying down other things for those who follow the word of the Veda.

दर्शनाच्चान्यपात्रस्य ॥७॥

7. And by seeing other vessels.

तथाग्निहविषोः ॥८॥

8. Similarly in fire and offering.

उक्तश्चार्थसम्बन्धः ॥९॥

9. And the connection with the object is stated.

तस्मिन्सोमः प्रवर्त्तेताव्यक्तत्वात् ॥१०॥

10. In it, soma (procedure) applies by reason of the indistinctness.

न वा स्वाहाकारेण संयोगाद्वषट्कारस्य च निर्देशात्तन्त्रे तेन विप्रतिषेधात् ॥११॥

11. Not by reason of its connection with the word *svāhā* and by reason of ordaining *vaṣaṭkāra* in the original ritual and consequent prohibition of *svāhā.*

शब्दान्तरत्वात् ।१२॥

12. By use of a different word.

लिङ्गदर्शनाच्च ॥१३॥

13. And by seeing the indicative mark.

उत्तरार्थस्तु स्वाहाकारो यथा साप्तदश्यं तत्राविप्रतिषिद्धा पुनः प्रवृत्तिर्लिङ्गदर्शनात्पशुवत् ॥१४॥

14. On the other hand, the term *svāhā* is for other than the model sacrifice just as 17 *samādhenīs* though not prohibited there (in the model sacrifice), their reappearance is in the animal sacrifice.

अनुत्तरार्थो वाऽर्थवत्त्वादानर्थक्याद्धि प्राकृतस्योपरोधः स्यात् ॥१५॥

15. It is not for any other than the model, by reason of its being for a purpose; because by reason of being without a purpose, it is obstructed in the model.

न प्रकृतावपीति चेत् ॥१६॥

16. If you say "it is not in the model sacrifice also".

उक्तं समवाये पारदौर्बल्यम् ॥१७॥

17. It is said in a collection, the latter becomes weak.

तच्चोदना वेष्टेः प्रवृत्तित्वाद्विधिः स्यात् ॥१८॥

18. On the other hand, the command relating to it, applies by reason of its applicability to *iṣṭi*. It is presumed to be an injunction.

शब्दसामर्थ्याच्च ॥१९॥

19. And by the power of the command.

लिङ्गदर्शनाच्च ॥२०॥

20. And there is an indicative mark also.

तत्राभावस्य हेतुत्वाद्गुणार्थेस्याददर्शनम् ॥२१॥

21. There by reason of the absence, the procedure does not apply.

विधिरिति चेत् ॥२२॥

22. If you say "it is a *vidhi*".

न वाक्यशेषत्वाद्गुणार्थे च समाधानं नानात्वेनोपपद्यते ॥२३॥

23. Not so, by reason of its being a supplementary sentence; if you remove the doubt by holding it to be a *guṇavidhi*, there will be a multiplicity of sentences.

येषां वाऽपरयोर्होमस्तेषां स्यादविरोधात् ॥२४॥

24. Of those sacrifices in which a homa is performed in the *gārhapatya* and *dakṣiṇāgni* fires, their procedure will apply by reason of no contradiction.

तत्रौषधानि चोद्यन्ते तानि स्थानेन गम्येरन् ॥२५॥

25. There the herbs are ordained; they will be substituted by the material of the model.

लिङ्गनद्वा शेषहोमयोः ॥२६॥

26. On the other hand, by the marks of the remaining Homas.

प्रतिपत्ती तु ते भवतस्तस्मादतद्विकारत्वम् ॥२७॥

27. They finally dispose of the homas and so it is not their modified form.

सन्निपाते विरोधिनामप्रवृत्तिः प्रतीयेत विध्युत्पत्तिव्यवस्था-नादर्थस्यापरिणेयत्वाद्वचनादतिदेशः स्यात् ॥२८॥

28. There appears to be an inapplicability in a case of collection of the contraries by reason of the reading of the origin of the command in some context and by reason of the non-transferability of the object. The transfer therefore takes place under a text.

END OF PĀDA 4

* * *

END OF ADHYĀYA VIII

ADHYĀYA IX

PĀDA 1

यज्ञकर्म प्रधानं तद्धि चोदनाभूतं तस्य द्रव्येषु संस्कारस्तत्प्रयुक्तस्तदर्थत्वात् ॥१॥

1. The action of a sacrifice is principal. It depends on an injunction. The purificatory rite is performed on its materials. It is performed because it is for it.

संस्कारे युज्यमानानां तादर्थ्यात्तत्प्रयुक्तं स्यात् ॥२॥

2. Those applied in the purificatory ceremony being for it, there application is for it.

तेन त्वर्थेन यज्ञस्य संयोगाद्धर्मसम्बन्धस्तस्माद्यज्ञप्रयुक्तं स्यात्संस्कारस्य तदर्थत्वात् ॥३॥

3. On the other hand, the sacrifice being connected with the object, the procedure is connected. It is applied to the sacrifice because the purificatory rite is for it.

फलदेवतयोश्च ॥४॥

4. And of the fruit and the deity.

न चोदनाती हि तादगुण्यम् ॥५॥

5. Not so; by virtue of the command, it partakes of its quality.

देवता वा प्रयोजयेदतिथिवद्भोजनस्यतदर्थत्वात् ॥६॥

6. On the other hand, the deity should be entertained like a religious mendicant by reason of the food being for him.

अर्थापत्याच ॥७॥

7. And by reason of securing the object.

ततश्च तेन सम्बन्धः ॥८॥

8. And therefore the deity is connected with it.

अपि वा शब्दपूर्वत्वाद्यज्ञकर्म प्रधानं स्याद्गुणत्वे देवताश्रुतिः ॥९॥

9. On the other hand, by reason of being based on the word, the sacrifice is principal and the mention of a deity is subordinate.

अतिथौ तत्प्रधानत्वमभावः कर्मणि स्यात्तस्य प्रीति प्रधानत्वात् ॥१०॥

10. In the case of a religious mendicant he is principal, the action is absent by reason of his love being principal.

द्रव्यसंख्याहेतुसमुदायं वा श्रुतिसंयोगात् ॥११॥

11. On the other hand, material, number, reason and aggregate by reason of the connection with the text.

अर्थकारिते च द्रव्येण न व्यवस्था स्यात् ॥१२॥

12. And if the object had been to attain the extraordinary principle, there would have been no arrangement with the material.

अर्थो वा स्यात्प्रयोजनमितरेषामचोदनात्तस्य च गुणभूतत्वात् ॥१३॥

13. On the other hand the extraordinary principle is the object; the others are not ordained, by reason of being subordinate to it.

अपूर्वत्वाद्व्यवस्था स्यात् ॥१४॥

14. By reason of the *apūrva*, there is a rule of guidance.

तत्प्रयुक्तत्वे च धर्म्मस्य सर्वविषयत्वम् ॥१५॥

15. And on its being applied, the procedure will apply to all.

तद्युक्तस्येति चेत् ॥१६॥

16. If you say, it will apply to the one of the context.

नाश्रुतित्वात् ॥१७॥

17. Not so, by reason of there being nothing stated.

अधिकारादिति चेत् ॥१८॥

18. If you say, by division.

तुल्येषु नाधिकारः स्यादचोदितश्च सम्बन्धः पृथक् सतां यज्ञार्थे-नाभिसम्बन्धस्तस्माद्यज्ञप्रयोजनम् ॥१९॥

19. In equal, there is no division (difference). No relationship is pointed out; nor is there any separate existence. There is relationship with the sacrifice, therefore the sacrifice is the purpose.

देशबद्धमुपांशुत्वं तेषां स्याछ्रुतिनिर्देशात्तस्य च तत्र भावात् ॥२०॥

20. The silence relating to it, is restricted to the place by reason of the direction of the text and because that exists there.

यज्ञस्य वा तत्संयोगात् ॥२१॥

21. On the other hand, of the sacrifice by reason of its mention.

अनुवादश्च तदर्थवत् ॥२२॥

22. And the restatement is with that object.

प्रणीतादि तथेति चेत् ॥२३॥

23. If you say, that similarly in the case of sacrificial water.

न यज्ञस्याश्रुतित्वात् ॥२४॥

24. Not so, there is no mention of the sacrifice.

तद्देशानां वा संघातस्यचोदितत्वात् ॥२५॥

25. On the other hand, the procedure is of that particular locality, because the aggregate is nowhere laid own.

अग्निधर्मः प्रतीष्टकं संघातात्पौर्णमासीवत् ॥२६॥

26. The fire ceremony whould be performed on each brick, by reason of collection as in a full moon ceremony.

अग्नेर्वा स्याद्द्रव्यैकत्वादितरासां तदर्थ त्वात् ॥२७॥

27. On the other hand, it is Agni by reason of the material being one and the others being for it.

चोदनासमुदायात्तु पौर्णमास्यां तथा स्यात् ॥२८॥

28. On the other hand, by reason of the number of commands; in the full moon ceremony that is so.

पत्नीसंयाजान्तत्वं सर्वेषामविशेषात् ॥२९॥

29. The term *patnīsaṃyāja* applies to all (the days), because there is nothing special in it.

लिङ्गाद्वा प्रागुत्तमात् ॥३०॥

30. On the other hand by reason of the inference (it appears that the end of *patnīsaṃyāja* is) before the final day.

अनुवादो वा दीक्षा यथा नक्तं संस्थापनस्य ॥३१॥

31. On the other hand, it is a restatement, just as initiation is of nocturnal sitting.

स्याद्वाऽनारभ्य विधानादन्ते लिङ्ग विरोधात् ॥३२॥

32. On the other hand it may be so, by reason of the general text but in the end by reason of the opposition to the inference.

अभ्यासः सामिधेनीनां प्राथम्यात्स्थानधर्मःस्यात् ॥३३॥

33. The repetition of *sāmadhenī* verses by reason of being first, is of that which is there in order.

इष्ट्यावृतौ प्रयाजवदावर्त्तेतारम्भणीया ॥३४॥

34. On the repetition of the *darśapūrṇamāseṣṭi*, like *prayāja*, the *āraṁbhaṇīyā* should be repeated.

सकृद्वाऽऽरम्भसंयोगादेकः पुनरारम्भो यावज्जीवप्रयोगात् ॥३५॥

35. On the other hand, once by reason of the mention of (*āraṁbha*) beginning; there is only one beginning by reason of the use of 'as long as one lives'.

अर्थाभिधानसंयोगान्मन्त्रेपु शेषभावः स्यात्तत्राचोदितमप्राप्तं चोदिताभि-धानात् ॥३६॥

36. By reason of the connection with the meaning, there is a subordinate nature in the mantras; there is no adaptation without a command because the naming is under a command.

ततश्चावचनंतेषामितरार्थं प्रयुज्यते ॥३७॥

37. And therefore there is no authority for those (that are not laid down); they are applied in the other sense.

गुणशब्दस्तथेति चेत् ॥३८॥

38. "And the subordinate word is likewise" if you say.

नसमवायात् ॥३९॥

39. Not so, by reason of close affinity.

चोदिते तु परार्थत्वाद्विधिवदविकारः स्यात् ॥४०॥

40. On the other hand, on being commanded by reason of its being dependent, like the *vidhi* it will be not modified.

विकारस्तत्प्रधानेस्यात् ॥४१॥

41. It will be modified, on its being principal.

असंयोगात्तदर्थेषु तद्विशिष्टं प्रतीयेत ॥४२॥

42. By reason of there being no connection with the sense of that, it appears to be particularised with it.

कर्माभावादेवमिति चेत् ॥४३॥

43. If you say, it is so by reason of the absence of exploit.

न परार्थत्वात् ॥४४॥

44. Not so, by reason of their being subservient to others.

लिङ्गविशेषनिर्देशात्समानविधानेष्वप्राप्ता सारस्वती स्त्रीत्वात् ॥४५॥

45. By reason of mention of a particular gender where the command is equally applicable, it does not apply to the sacrifice called *sarasvati*.

पश्वभिधानाद्वा तद्धि चोदनाभूतं पुंविषयं पुनः पशुत्वम् ॥४६॥

46. On the other hand by reason of the general denomination of animal and because that is a command and applicable to a male and to the state of an animal.

विशेषो वा तदर्थनिर्देशात् ॥४७॥

47. On the other hand it is particular by reason of its pointing out that object.

पशुत्वं चैकशब्द्यात् ॥४८॥

48. And animal nature by reason of one word.

यथोक्तं वा सन्निधानात् ॥४९॥

49. On the other hand, it is as said by reason of the proximity.

आम्नातादन्यदधिकारे वचनाद्विकारः स्यात् ॥५०॥

50. In connection with one sacrifice laid down as otherwise, it is modified under an authority.

द्वैधं वा तुल्यहेतुत्वात्सामान्याद्विकल्पः स्यात् ॥५१॥

51. On the other hand, it should be two-fold by virtue of equal reasons; and by reason of common meaning there is option.

उपदेशाच्च साम्नः ॥५२॥

52. And by reason of the direct command of the song.

नियमो वा श्रुतिविशेषादितरत्साप्तदश्यवत् ॥५३॥

53. On the other hand, it is a restrictive rule by reason of the special text; and the other is like the seventeen Sāmadhenī verses.

अप्रगाणाच्छब्दान्यत्वे तथाभूतोपदेशः स्यात् ॥५४॥

54. By reason of being not capable of singing, and on the word being changed into another form, the direction is in accordance with it.

यत्स्थाने वा तद्गीतिः स्यात्पदान्यत्वप्रधानत्वात् ॥५५॥

55. On the other hand, one in whose place the word is substituted will be sung by the rule of music by reason of the modified form being principal.

गानसंयोगाच्च ॥५६॥

56. And by reason of its being connected with the music.

वचनमिति चेत् ॥५७॥

57. If you say that it is a precept.

न तत्प्रधानत्वात् ॥५८॥

58. Not so, by reason of its being principal.

END OF PĀDA 1

***

PĀDA 2

सामानि मन्त्रमेके स्मृत्युपदेशाभ्याम् ॥१॥

1. Verses set to music are *sāma* according to one by the tradition and instruction.

तदुक्तदोषम् ॥२॥

2. There is the defect as stated.

कर्म वा विधिलक्षणम् ॥३॥

3. On the other hand, it is the principal act being characterised by command.

तादृग्द्रव्यं वचनात्पाकयज्ञवत् ॥४॥

4. Therefore the material is *ṛk* under a text, just as in a cooking sacrifice.

तत्राविप्रतिषिद्धो द्रव्यान्तरे व्यतिरेकः प्रदेशश्च ॥५॥

5. There in a different material though the transference is not prohibited, it is separate.

शब्दार्थत्वात्तुनैवं स्यात् ॥६॥

6. It can not be so by reason of its being for the object of the word.

परार्थत्वाच्च शब्दानाम् ॥७॥

7. And of the words being for the object of others.

असम्बन्धश्च कर्मणा शब्दयोः पृथगर्थत्वात् ॥८॥

8. And it is not connected with the action, there being different objects of the two words.

संस्कारश्चाप्रकरणेऽग्निवत्स्यात्प्रयुक्तत्वात् ॥९॥

9. It is a purificatory act, at a non-sacrificial time like the fire by reason of being applied.

अकार्य्यत्वाच्च शब्दानामप्रयोगः प्रतीयेत ॥१०॥

10. And by reason of the words being for no purpose, it appears that they were not used.

आश्रितत्वाच्च ॥११॥

11. And by reason of being dependent.

प्रयुज्यत इति चेत् ॥१२॥

12. "It should be practised" if you say.

ग्रहणार्थं प्रयुज्येत ॥१३॥

13. It should be practised for acquisition.

तृचे स्याच्छ्रुतिनिर्देशात् ॥१४॥

14. In a group of three *ṛk* verses by reason of the command of the vedic text.

शब्दार्थत्वाद्विकारस्य ॥१५॥

15. By reason of the modification being for the purpose of the word.

दर्शयति च ॥१६॥

16. And it shows.

वाक्यानां तु विभक्तत्वात्प्रतिशब्दं समाप्तिः स्यात्सं स्कारस्य तदर्थत्वात् ॥१७॥

17. On the other hand by reason of the division of the sentence, there is a completion at every word by reason of the purificatory rite being for it.

तथा चान्यार्थदर्शनम् ॥१८॥

18. And similarly there is another text.

अनवानोपदेशश्च तद्वत् ॥१९॥

19. And similarly the instruction as to the song in one breath is like it.

अभ्यासेनेतरा श्रुतिः ॥२०॥

20. The other text is by repetition.

तदभ्यासः समासु स्यात् ॥२१॥

21. Then the repetition is to be made in equal (measures).

लिङ्गदर्शनाच्च ॥२२॥

22. And by seeing the inference from the text.

नैमित्तिकं तूत्तरात्वमानन्तर्यात्प्रतीयेत ॥२३॥

23. On the other hand, the word *uttarā* appears correlative by reason of its immediateness.

ऐकार्थ्याच्च तदभ्यासः ॥२४॥

24. And by reason of the unity of sense, its repetition.

प्रागाथिकं तु ॥२५॥

25. On the other hand, the song should be intertwined.

स्वे च ॥२६॥

26. And in itself.

प्रगाथे च ॥२७॥

27. And in singing by *pragātha.*

लिङ्गदर्शनाव्यतिरेकाच्च ॥२८॥

28. And by seeing the invariable marks of inference from the text.

अर्थैकत्वाद्विकल्पः स्यात् ॥२९॥

29. By reason of the unity of the purpose, there is option.

अर्थैकत्वाद्विकल्पः स्यादृक्सामयोस्तदर्थत्वात् ॥३०॥

30. By reason of the unity of the purposes, there is option because the *ṛk* and *sāma* are for that object.

वचनाद्विनियोगः स्यात् ॥३१॥

31. Application should be according to the text.

सामप्रदेशे विकारस्तदपेक्षः स्याच्छास्त्रकृतत्वात् ॥३२॥

32. In the transference of a song, the alteration depends on the first part, by reason of the Śāstric command.

वर्णे तु बादरिर्यथाद्रव्यं द्रव्यव्यतिरेकात् ॥३३॥

33. On the other hand, the view of Bādari is that the change is in the letter according to the matter because it differs.

स्तोभस्यैके द्रव्यान्तरे निवृत्तिमृग्वत् ॥३४॥

34. According to one, a musical pause is the cessation into another verse like a *ṛk* verse.

सर्वातिदेशस्तु सामान्याल्लोकवद्विकारः स्यात् ॥३५॥

35. On the other hand, the whole is transferable by reason of its being included in the general; the modification is just as is in the ordinary music.

अन्वयश्चापि दर्शयति ॥३६॥

36. And the invariable connection also shows.

निवृत्तिर्वाऽर्थलोपात् ॥३७॥

37. On the other hand, the completion of musical sentences is to avoid meaninglessness.

अन्वयोवार्थवादः स्यात् ॥३८॥

38. On the other hand, the invariable affinity is by way of supplementary sentence.

अधिकश्च विवर्णश्च जैमिनिः स्तोभशब्दत्वात् ॥३९॥

39. According to jainini, by the word *stobha* is meant redundant and meaningless.

धर्मस्यार्थकृतत्वाद्द्रव्यगुणविकारव्यतिक्रमप्रतिषेधे चोदनानुबन्धः समवायात् ॥४०॥

40. The function being for an object, there is a series of commands in substance, quality, modification, transgression and prohibition because there is a close affinity.

तदुत्पत्तेस्तु निवृत्तिस्तत्कृतत्वात्स्यात् ॥४१॥

41. On the other hand on its being made, there is a cessation by reason of the procedure (relating to *yūpa*) being over.

आवेश्येरन्वार्थवत्त्वात्संस्कारस्य तदर्थत्वात् ॥४२॥

42. On the other hand of the purificatory rite being for it, the function should be performed, so that it may be for a purpose.

आख्यां चैवं तदावेशाद्विकृतौ स्यादपूर्वत्वात् ॥४३॥

43. And by adoption of the ceremony, the name is in the modified sacrifice by reason of the extraordinary principle.

परार्थेन त्वर्थसामान्यं संस्कारस्य तदर्थत्वात् ॥४४॥

44. On the other hand, the common object is with the purpose for others, because the purificatory rite is for the object of it.

क्रियेरन्वार्थनिर्वृत्तेः ॥४५॥

45. On the other hand, they should be performed for the completion of the object.

एकार्थत्वादविभागः स्यात् ॥४६॥

46. There is no division by reason of having one object.

निर्देशाद्वा व्यवतिष्ठेरन् ॥४७॥

47. On the other hand by direction, a rule is fixed.

अप्राकृते तद्विकाराद्विरोधाद्व्यवतिष्ठेरन् ॥४८॥

48. In the modified sacrifice, by reason of the modification, there is a rule because of the contrary.

उभयसाम्नि चैवमेकार्थापत्तेः ॥४९॥

49. And similarly in double songs, by reason of having one object.

स्वार्थत्वाद्वा व्यवस्था स्यात्प्रकृतिवत् ॥५०॥

50. On the other hand, by reason of having their object, there is a fixed rule like the model.

पार्वणहोमयोस्त्वप्रवृत्तिः समुदायार्थसंयोगात्तदभीज्या हि ॥५१॥

51. There is the non-application of *pārvaṇahoma* by its connection with the collective sense, because the oblation is with that object.

कालस्येति चेत् ॥५२॥

52. 'Of time' if you say.

नाप्रकरणत्वात् ॥५३॥

53. Not so, by reason of no context.

मन्त्रवर्णाच्च ॥५४॥

54. And from the inference from the mantras.

तदभावेऽग्निवदिति चेत् ॥५५॥

55. "In its absence like fire" if you say.

नाधिकारिकत्वात् ॥५६॥

56. Not so, by reason of pertaining to the subject.

उभयोरविशेषात् ॥५७॥

57. Of both, by reason of there being nothing special.

यदभीज्या वा तद्विषयौ ॥५८॥

58. On the other hand, that sacrifice should be performed of whose subject it is.

प्रयाजेऽपीति चेत् ॥५९॥

59. In *prayāja* also, if you say.

नाचोदितत्वात् ॥६०॥

60. Not so by reason of there being no order.

END OF PĀDA 2

***

PĀDA 3

प्रकृतौ यथोत्पत्तिवचनमर्थानां तथोत्तरस्यां ततौ तत्प्रकृतित्वादर्थे चाकार्यत्वात् ॥१॥

1. In the model sacrifice just as is the original word of the object, so also in the subsequent sacrifice by reason of its being the model and in the purpose by reason of its being of no use.

लिङ्गदर्शनाच्च ॥२॥

2. And by seeing the *liṅga*.

जातिनैमित्तिकं यथास्थानम् ॥३॥

3. The common noun and the adjective according to their respective place.

अविकारमेकेऽनार्षत्वात् ॥४॥

4. According to one school, it is transferred unmodified by reason of its being not human.

लिङ्गदर्शनाच्च ॥५॥

5. And by seeing the *liṅga*.

विकारो वातदुक्तहेतुः ॥६॥

6. On the other hand, there is adaptation for the said reason.

लिङ्ग मन्त्रचिकीर्षार्थम् ॥७॥

7. The *liṅga* is with the object for the desire for the *mantra*.

नियमो वोभयभागित्वात् ॥८॥

8. On the other hand, it is a rule by reason of partaking of both.

लौकिके दोषसंयोगादपवृक्ते हिचोद्यते निमित्तेन प्रकृतौ स्यादभागित्वात् ॥९॥

9. In the wordly *yūpa* by reason of the connection with the sin on prohibiting touch, there is a direction for a cause; in the model sacrifice by reason of not partaking of it.

अन्यायस्त्वाविकारेणा दृष्टप्रतिघातित्वादविशेषाच्च तेनास्य ॥१०॥

10. On the other hand, it is improper; it therefore applies unmodified by reason of its not obstructing the seen and there being nothing special of it.

विकारो वा तदर्थत्वात् ॥११॥

11. On the other hand, modification by reason of its being for it.

अपित्वन्यायसम्बन्धात्प्रकृतिवत्परेषवपियथार्थं स्यात् ॥१२॥

12. On the other hand, being connected with impropriety, like model, it will become significant in the modified sacrifice also.

यथार्थं त्वन्यायस्याचोदितत्वात् ॥१३॥

13. On the other hand, correct form should be used; because the improper form in not ordained.

छन्दसि तु यथादृष्टम् ॥१४॥

14. On the other hand, in the Veda like the seen.

विप्रतिपत्तौ विकल्पः स्यात्तत्सत्वाद्गुणे त्वन्यायकल्पनैकदेशत्वात् ॥१५॥

15. On contradiction, there is option by reason of equality, because of the partial nature of the supposition of impropriety in the subordinate act.

प्रकरणविशेषाच्च ॥१६॥

16. And by reason of the special context.

अर्थाभावात्तु नैवं स्याद्गुणमात्रमितरत् ॥१७॥

17. On the other hand, by reason of the want of an object it cannot be so and the other is merely subordinate.

द्यावोस्तथेति चेत् ॥१८॥

18. "Similarly the heaven and earth" if you say.

नोत्पत्तिशब्दत्वात् ॥१९॥

19. Not so, by reason of the word being connected with the origin.

अपूर्वे त्वविकारोऽप्रदेशात्प्रतीयेत ॥२०॥

20. On the other hand, there appears to be no modification in the model sacrifice by reason of no transference.

विकृतौ चापि तद्वचनात् ॥२१॥

21. And in the modified sacrifice, by reason of that authority.

अध्रिगुः सवनीयेषु तद्वत्समानविधानाश्चेत् ॥२२॥

22. The command to the animal killer is similar in *savanīya* animal by reason of the similar rules.

प्रतिनिधौ चाविकारात् ॥२३॥

23. And in a substitute by reason of no change.

अनाम्नानादशब्दत्वमभावाच्चेतरस्य स्यात् ॥२४॥

24. There will no *ūha*, if there had been no word *brīhi* and by reason of there being no other word.

तादर्थ्याद्वा तदाख्यंस्यात्संस्कारैरविशिष्टत्वात् ॥२५॥

25. On the other hand, that name is for its object by reason of the purificatory ceremony being common.

उक्तञ्च तत्त्वमस्य ॥२६॥

26. And its real nature is also described.

संसर्गिषु चार्थस्यास्थितपरिमाणत्वात् ॥२७॥

27. And in bodily organs by reason of the multiplicity of the objects.

लिङ्गदर्शनाच्च ॥२८॥

28. And by seeing the force of the text.

एकधेत्येकसंयोगादभ्यासेनाभिधानं स्यात् ॥२९॥

29. 'In one way' by reason of the mention of one; it is known by repetition.

अविकारो वा बहूनामेककर्मवत् ॥३०॥

30. On the other hand, it should remain unchanged like the performance of many acts by one.

सकृत्त्वं चैकध्यं स्यादेकत्वात्त्वचोऽनभिप्रेतं तत्प्रकृतित्वात्परेष्वभ्यासेन विवृद्धावभिधानं स्यात् ॥३१॥

31. On the other hand, the formula is to be repeated once by reason of the skin being one; by reason of its being a model, it is unsuitable; so in subsequent acts on the increase, the naming will be (by repetition).

मेधपतित्वं स्वामिदेवतस्य समवायात्सर्वत्र च प्रयुक्तत्वात्तस्या-चान्यायनिगदत्वात्सर्वत्रैवाविकारः स्यात् ॥३२॥

32. The word '*medhapati*' being connected with the master and the deity and being used everywhere and as it is said to be improper, it is to be used unaltered every where.

अपि वा द्विसमवायोऽर्थान्यत्वे यथासंख्यं प्रयोगः स्यात् ॥३३॥

33. On the other hand, there is connection with two and on the sense being different, the application shall be according it.

स्वामिनो वैकशब्द्यादुत्कर्षो देवतायां स्यात्पत्न्यां द्वितीयशब्दः स्यात् ॥३४॥

34. On the other hand the master being one word, there will be an importation of deity or the wife would be the second word.

देवता तु तदाशीष्ट्वात्सम्प्राप्तत्वात्स्वामिन्यनर्थिकास्यात् ॥३५॥

35. On the other hand, the god by reason of the object of the hopes and having parted with the ownership the word master becomes meaningless.

उत्सर्गाच्च भक्त्यातस्मिन्पतित्वं स्यात् ॥३६॥

36. By reason of relinquishment, the ownership is in him in a secondary sense.

उत्कृष्येतैकसंयुक्तो द्विदेवते सम्भवात् ॥३७॥

37. There is an importation in connection with one by reason of the possibility of two gods.

एकस्तु समवायात्तस्य तल्लक्षणत्वात् ॥३८॥

38. On the other hand, it is one by affinity because it has that characteristic.

संसर्गित्वाच्च तस्मात्तेन विकल्पः स्यात् ॥३९॥

39. By reason of jointness, there will then be option.

एकत्वेपि गुणानपायात् ॥४०॥

40. In unity also, by reason of the undesirability of the qualities.

नियमो बहुदेवते विकारः स्यात् ॥४१॥

41. There is a restrictive rule; in the case of many deities, the modified form.

विकल्पो वा प्रकृतिवत् ॥४२॥

42. On the other hand, there is an option like the model sacrifice.

अर्थान्तरे विकारः स्याद्देवतापृथक्त्ववादेकाभिसमवायात्स्यात् ॥४३॥

43. In a different object, there is modification by reason of the gods being different and one being sufficient for one.

END OF PĀDA 3

***

PĀDA 4

षड्विंशतिरभ्यासेन पशुगणे तत्प्रकृतित्वाद्गणस्य प्रविभक्तत्वादविकारे हि तासामकार्त्स्न्येनाभिसम्बन्धो विकारान्न समासः स्यादसंयोगाच्च सर्वाभिः ॥१॥

1. In a group of animals, there is a repetition of twentysix by reason of its being a model and the group being divided; because in the unmodified form, their relationship is with a part, and by reason of the modified form, there will be no aggregate because there is no connection with all.

अभ्यासेऽपि तथेति चेत् ॥२॥

2. "In repetition also the same" if you say.

न गुणादर्थकृतत्वाच्च ॥३॥

3. Not so, by reason of its being a quality and for a purpose.

समासेऽपि तथेति चेत् ॥४॥

4. "In the aggregates also the same" if you say.

नासम्भवात् ॥५॥

5. Not so, by reason of impossibility.

स्वाभिश्च वचनं प्रकृतौ तथेह स्यात् ॥६॥

6. And the formula in the model sacrifice is in its proper form and so is here.

वङ्क्रीणान्तु प्रधानत्त्वात्समासेनाभिधानं स्यात्प्राधान्यमध्रिगोस्तदर्थत्वात् ॥७॥

7. On the other hand, by reason of the ribs being principal the naming is by aggregate; the *adhrigu* priest is principal because he is for it.

तासां च कृत्स्नवचनात् ॥८॥

8. And by reason of their being covered by the whole sentence.

अपि त्व सन्निपातित्वात्पत्नीवदाम्नातेनाभिधानं स्यात् ॥९॥

9. On the other hand by reason of its being remote, like *patnīvat*, there will be naming by the direction.

विकारस्तु प्रदेशत्वाद्यजमानवत् ॥१०॥

10. On the other hand, there is modification by reason of transfer as in a *yajamāna* (sacrificer).

अपूर्वत्वात्तथा पत्न्याम् ॥११॥

11. And by reason of the *apūrva* nature in *patnīṃsannahya*.

अनाम्नातस्त्वविकारात्सङ्ख्यासु सर्वगामित्वात् ।१२॥

12. On the other hand, it is not laid down by reason of no modification, because in the number there is the applicability to all.

सङ्ख्या त्वेवं प्रधानं स्याद्वङ्क्रयः पुनः प्रधानम् ॥१३॥

13. On the other hand the number in this way is principal and the ribs are again principal.

अनाम्नातवचनमवचनेन हि वङ्क्रीणां स्यान्निर्देशः ॥१४॥

14. The formula is not laid down; because by an unsanctioned text, there is a direction as to ribs.

अभ्यासो वाऽविकारात्स्यात् ॥१५॥

15. On the other hand there is repetition by reason of no modification.

पशुस्त्वेवं प्रधानंस्यादभ्यासस्य तन्निमित्तत्वात्तस्मात्समासशब्दः स्यात् ॥१६॥

16. On the other hand, the animal is principal in this way; by reason of the repetition being for it, there would be, therefore, an aggregate word.

अश्वस्य चतुस्त्रिंशत्तस्य वचनाद्वैशेषिकम् ॥१७॥

17. There is speciality by reason of the text of 34 of the horse.

तत्प्रतिषिध्य प्रकृतिर्नियुज्यते सा चतुस्त्रिंशद्वाच्यत्वात् ॥१८॥

18. Prohibiting it, the formula of the model sacrifice fits in by reason of the text containing 34.

ऋग्वास्यादाम्नातत्वादविकल्पश्च न्याय्यः ॥१९॥

19. On the other hand, the *ṛk* verse by reason of its being laid down; it is proper not to have option.

तस्यां तु वचनादैरवत्पदविकार: स्यात् ॥२०॥

20. On the other hand, in it by reason of the text, there is a change of word as in *aira.*

सर्वप्रतिषेधो वाऽसंयोगात्पदेन स्यात् ॥२१॥

21. On the other hand, the whole is prohibited, by reason of there being no connection with the word.

वनिष्ठुसन्निधानादुरूकेण वपाभिधानम् ॥२२॥

22. By reason of being near the organ, by '*urūka*' is meant fat.

प्रशसाऽस्याभिधानम् ॥२३॥

23. The term '*praśasā*' means a sword.

बाहुप्रशंसा वा ॥२४॥

24. Or it may be in praise of the arms.

श्येन-शला-कश्यप-कवषस्त्रेकपर्णेष्वाकृतिवचनं प्रसिद्धसन्निधानात् ॥२५॥

25. In hawk, dart, tortoise, thorn and leaf of a tree there is the significance of the form by reason of the proximity of the well-known.

कार्त्स्न्यं वा स्यात्तथाभावात् ॥२६॥

26. On the other hand, in its entirety by reason of its being like it.

अध्रिगोश्च तदर्थत्वात् ॥२७॥

27. And the *adhrigu* priest is for that object.

प्रासङ्गिके प्रायश्चित्तं न विद्यते परार्थत्वात्तदर्थे हिविधीयते ॥२८॥

28. In the incidental there is no penance by reason of its being for another. It is laid down for it.

धारणे च परार्थत्वात् ॥२९॥

29. And in preservation by reason of its being for another:

क्रियार्थत्वादितरेषु कर्म स्यात् ॥३०॥

30. By reason of being for action in others, there is a ceremony.

न तूत्पन्ने यस्य चोदनाऽप्राप्तकालत्वात् ॥३१॥

31. On the other hand, the direction does not apply on its production (for another) by reason of there being no time for it.

प्रदानदर्शनं श्रपणे तद्धर्मभोजनार्थत्वात्संसर्गाच्च मधूदकवत् ॥३२॥

32. The gift is seen in boiling, by reason of its being for food and by mixture like honey and water.

संस्कारप्रतिषेधश्च तद्वत् ॥३३॥

33. Prohibition of purificatory rite is like it.

तत्प्रतिषेधे च तथाभूतस्य वर्जनात् ॥३४॥

34. And on its prohibition, anything in its form is also prohibited.

अधर्मत्वमप्रदानात्प्रणीतार्थे विधानादतुल्यत्वादसंसर्गः ॥३५॥

35. It is not its characteristic by reason of its being not given and by reason of its being for the purpose of cooking and because of inequality, there is no amalgamation.

परो नित्याऽनुवादः स्यात् ॥३६॥

36. The other is a permanent statement of facts.

विहितप्रतिषेधो वा ॥३७॥

37. Or it may be a prohibition of a sanctioned practice.

वर्जने गुणभावित्वात्तदुक्तप्रतिषेधात्स्यात्कारणात्केवलाशनम् ॥३८॥

38. In prohibition by reason of its being subordinate and by reason of the said prohibition; only (simple) diet by this reason (is allowed).

व्रतधर्माच्चलेपवत् ॥३९॥

39. And by reason of the observance of a vow like the (abstinence from certain kinds of) food.

रसप्रतिषेधौ वा पुरुषधर्मत्वात् ॥४०॥

40. On the other hand, the prohibition of the juice (of flesh) is by reason of its being the duty of a man.

अभ्युदये दोहापनयः स्वधर्मा स्यात्प्रवृत्तत्वात् ॥४१॥

41. In an *abhyudayeṣṭi*, when there is transference of milking, its own procedure applies, because it has been commenced.

शृतोपदेशाच्च ॥४२॥

42. And by reason of the direction of 'boiled'.

अपनयो वार्थान्तरे विधानाच्चरुपयोवत् ॥४३॥

43. On the other hand there is a transfer by reason of ordaining it for a different object like the boiled rice.

लक्षणार्था शृतश्रुतिः ॥४४॥

44. The word *ṛta* is for pointing out.

श्रयणानां त्वपूर्वत्वात्प्रदानार्थेविधानं स्यात् ॥४५॥

45. On the other hand, by reason of the extraordinary principle, the injunction relating to milk is for gift.

गुणो वा श्रयणार्थत्वात् ॥४६॥

46. On the other hand, it is subordinate by reason of its being for mixture.

अनिर्देशाच्च ॥४७॥

47. And by reason of there being no direction.

श्रुतेश्च तत्प्रधानत्वात् ॥४८॥

48. And that being the principal according to the Vedas.

अर्थवादश्च तदथवत् ॥४९॥

49. And the *arthavāda* is for that object.

संस्कारं प्रति भावाच्च तस्मादप्यप्रधानम् ॥५०॥

50. And being for the purificatory rite, it is, therefore, not principal.

पर्य्यग्निकृतानामुत्सर्गे तादर्थ्यमुपधानवत् ॥५१॥

51. In relinquishment of those that have been taken round the fire, they are for that object like placing near.

शेषप्रतिषेधो वाऽर्थाभावादिडान्तवत् ॥५२॥

52. On the other hand, it is a prohibition of the remaining act by reason of the want of purpose like the end of *iḍā*.

पूर्वत्त्वाच्च शब्दस्य संस्थापयतीति चोप्रबृत्तेनोपपद्यते ॥५३॥

53. And by reason of the word having commencement; 'he finishes' does not apply to an act which is not commenced.

प्रबृत्तेर्यज्ञहेतुत्वात्प्रतिषेधे संस्काराणामकर्म स्यात्तत्कारितत्वाद्यथा प्रयाजप्रतिषेधे ग्रहणमाज्यस्य ॥५४॥

54. Of the application being for the sacrifice, (and) on the prohibition of the purificatory rites, there is non-performance by reason of its being for it; as the taking of ghee on the prohibition of *prayāja*.

क्रिया वास्याद्वत्रचचथेदादकर्म सर्वहानं स्यात् ॥५५॥

55. On the other hand, there is an action by reason of the separation; there is non-performance of all subordinate acts, if there is non-performance of all subordinate acts, if there is non-performance of the principal act.

आज्यसंस्थाप्रतिनिधिः स्याद्द्रव्योत्सर्गात् ॥५६॥

56. The finishing with ghee is a substitute by reason of relinquishing the substance.

समाप्तिवचनात् ॥५७॥

57. By reason of the word 'completing'.

चोदना वा कर्मोत्सर्गादन्यैः स्यादविशिष्टत्वात् ॥५८॥

58. On the other hand, it is an injunction; by reason of the completion of the act, there is another separate act, because there is nothing special in it.

अनिज्यां च वनस्पतेः प्रसिद्धाऽन्तेन दर्शयति ॥५९॥

59. Of the herb, it is well-known that it is non-sacrifice; from it also, it appears.

संस्था तद्देवतत्वात्स्यात् ॥६०॥

60. The completion is by reason of the deity of the same.

END OF PĀDA 4

* * *

END OF ADHYĀYA IX

ADHYĀYA X

PĀDA 1

विधेः प्रकरणान्तरेऽतिदेशात्सर्वकर्म स्यात् ॥१॥

1. By reason of the transfer of the command in the other context, the whole action should be performed.

अपि वाऽभिधानसंस्कारद्रव्यमर्थे क्रियेत तादर्थ्यात् ॥२॥

2. On the other hand the mantras, purificatory rite and substance are with a purpose by reason of their being for it.

तेषामप्रत्यक्षविशिष्टत्वात् ॥३॥

3. By reason of their being specialised by the invisible effect.

इष्टिरारम्भसंयोगादङ्गभूतान्निवर्त्तेतारम्भस्य प्रधानसंयोगात् ॥४॥

4. The sacrifice by reason of the connection with the beginning and by reason of its being a part, is suspended because the beginning is connected with the principal.

प्रधानाच्चान्यसंयुक्तात्सर्वारम्भान्निवर्त्तेतानङ्गत्वात् ॥५॥

5. And being principal and connected with another and by reason of the beginning to all, they are suspended, because they have no parts.

तस्यां तु स्यात्प्रयाजवत् ॥६॥

6. On the other hand, there is in it like *prayāja.*

न वाङ्गभूतत्वात् ॥७॥

7. Not so, by reason of its being a part.

एकवाक्यत्वाच्च ॥८॥

8. And by reason of having a unity of sentence.

कर्म च द्रव्यसंयोगार्थमर्थाभावान्निवर्त्तेत तादर्थ्यं श्रुतिसंयोगात् ॥९॥

9. And the ceremony is with an object in connection with the substance and is suspended by reason of the failure of that object; it is for it by reason of the connection with the Vedic text.

स्थाणौ तु देशमात्रत्वादनिवृत्तिः प्रतीयेत ॥१०॥

10. On the other hand, in a pillar by reason of the restriction to the locality, it appears that there is no suspension.

अपि वा शेषभूतत्वात्संस्कारः प्रतीयेत ॥११॥

11. On the other hand, by reason of its being a subsidiary action, it appears to be a purificatory rite.

समाख्यानं च तद्वत् ॥१२॥

12. And the *samākhyā* is like it.

मन्त्रवर्णश्च तद्वत् ॥१३॥

13. And the inference from the text is like it.

प्रयाजे च तन्न्यायत्वात् ॥१४॥

14. And in *prayāja*, by reason of the same argument.

लिङ्गदर्शनाच्च ॥१५॥

15. And by seeing the *liṅga.*

तथाज्यभागाग्निरपीति चेत् ॥१६॥

16. "And in the same way the ghee offering to *agni* also", if you say.

व्यपदेशाद्देवतान्तरम् ॥१७॥

17. By reason of designation, the other deity.

समत्वाच्च ॥१८॥

18. By reason of equality.

पशावपीति चेत् ॥१९॥

19. "In animal also" if you say.

न तदभूतवचनात् ॥२०॥

20. Not so, by reason of the word being subject to it.

लिङ्गदर्शनाच्च ॥२१॥

21. And by seeing the *liṅga.*

गुणो वा स्यात्कपालवद्गुणभूतविकाराच्च ॥२२॥

22. On the other hand, he is subsidiary like a pan by reason of his being a modification of the subordinate act.

अपि वा शेषभूतत्वात्तत्संस्कारः प्रतीयेत स्वाहाकारवदङ्गानामर्थ-संयोगात् ॥२३॥

23. On the other hand, it appears to be a purificatory rite by reason of its being a subordinate act like *svāhākāra*, because the parts are connected with the object.

व्यद्धवचनञ्च विप्रतिपत्तौ तदर्थत्वात् ॥२४॥

24. And the text as regards accumulation in case of difference, is for its object.

गुणेपीति चेत् ॥२५॥

25. "In a subordinate act also" if you say.

नासंहानात्कपालवत् ॥२६॥

26. Not so, by reason of no loss, like an earthen pan.

गृहाणाञ्च सम्प्रतिपत्तौ तद्वचनं तदर्थत्वात् ॥२७॥

27. And in the harmony of the cups, that text is for that object.

गृहाभावे च तद्वचनम् ॥२८॥

28. And in the absence of the cups, that text.

देवतायाश्च हेतुत्वं प्रसिद्धं तेन दर्शयति ॥२९॥

29. And the reason of the deity is well-known; and from it, it is also shown.

अविरुद्धोपपत्तिरर्थापत्तेः श्रृतवद्भूतविकारः स्यात् ॥३०॥

30. There is the application of the procedure which is not contradictory by reason of the inference, like the boiled milk, though subordinate modification.

स द्व्यर्थः स्यादुभयोः श्रुतिभूतत्वाद्विप्रतिपत्तौ तादर्थ्याद्विकारत्वमुक्तं तस्यार्थवादत्वम् ॥३१॥

31. It has double object by reason of the Vedic text being for it; in this conflict; the modification is laid down for its object, and hence its nature of *arthavāda*.

विप्रतिपत्तौ तासामाख्याविकारः स्यात् ॥३२॥

32. On conflict, their name is modified.

अभ्यासो वा प्रयाजवदेकदेशोऽन्यदेवत्यः ॥३३॥

33. On the other hand, there will be repetition like *prayāja* offerings; the other deity belongs to a part.

चरुर्हविर्विकारः स्यादिज्यासंयोगात् ॥३४॥

34. The *caru* (rice) is modified form of offering by reason of its connection with the sacrifice.

प्रसिद्धगृहणत्वाच्च ॥३५॥

35. And by reason of accepting the well-known signification.

ओदनो वाऽन्नसंयोगात् ॥३६॥

36. On the other hand, the boiled rice by reason of its connection with the corn.

न द्व्यर्थत्वात् ॥३७॥

37. Not so, by reason of the double meaning.

कपालविकोरो वा विशयेऽर्थोपपत्तिभ्याम् ॥३८॥

38. Or in a case of doubt, it may mean a pan by reason of the purpose and the propriety.

गुणमुख्यविशेषाच्च ॥३९॥

39. And by reason of the difference of the principal and the subsidiary.

तच्छ्रुतौ चान्यहविष्ट्वात् ॥४०॥

40. And by reason of other offerings in that text.

लिङ्गदर्शनाच्च ॥४१॥

41. And by seeing the force of the text.

ओदनो वा प्रयुक्तत्वात् ॥४२॥

42. On the other hand, rice by the usage.

अपूर्वव्यपदेशाच्च ॥४३॥

43. And by reason of designating the extraordinary principle.

तथा च लिङ्गदर्शनम् ॥४४॥

44. And similarly the force of the text is visible.

स कपाले प्रकृत्या स्यादन्यस्य चाश्रुतित्वात् ॥४५॥

45. That in a pan by the model sacrifice, because any other is not heard of.

एकस्मिन्वाविप्रतिषेधात् ॥४६॥

46. In one, by reason of the contradiction.

न वाऽर्थान्तरसंयोगादपूपे पाकसंयुक्तं धारणार्थं चरौ भवति तत्रार्थात्पात्रलाभः स्यादनियमोऽविशेषात् ॥४७॥

47. Not so; by reason of the connection with another in the cake; in rice, there is (a vessel) to hold it for cooking; there is a vessel for

the object. So there is no rule by reason of there being nothing special.

चरौ वा लिङ्गदर्शनात् ॥४८॥

48. On the other hand, a pot by seeing the *liṅga*.

तस्मिन्पेषणमनर्थलोपात्स्यात् ॥४९॥

49. In it, there is grinding by reason of uselessness.

अक्रिया वा अपूपहेतुत्वात् ॥५०॥

50. On the other hand, it is not performed by reason of the cake.

पिण्डार्थत्वाच्च संयवनम् ॥५१॥

51. And mixing of water with flour is with the object of making balls.

संवपनञ्च तादर्थ्यात् ॥५२॥

52. And the putting of the flour in a vessel with a view to mix it with water by reason of its being for that object.

सन्तापनमधःश्रपणात् ॥५३॥

53. There is heating of the pans by placing the hot cinders underneath.

उपधानं च तादर्थ्यात् ॥५४॥

54. And placing of the pans on the hot cinders by reason of its being for its object.

पृथुश्लक्ष्णे वाऽनपूपत्वात् ॥५५॥

55. On the other hand, spreading and smoothing by reason of there being no cake.

अभ्यूहश्चोपरिपाकार्थत्वात् ॥५६॥

56. And covering of the cake with hot cinders, by reason of their being for baking.

तथावज्वलनम् ॥५७॥

57. Similarly kindling of the cinders on the cakes.

व्युद्धृत्यासादनं च प्रकृतावश्रुतित्वात् ॥५८॥

58. And separating of cakes from the pans and placing them on the *antarvedi* by reason of its non-mention in the model sacrifice.

END OF PĀDA 1

***

PĀDA 2

कृष्णलेष्वर्थलोपादपाकः स्यात् ॥१॥

1. There is no cooking in *kṛṣṇala* by reason of uselessness.

स्याद्वा प्रत्यक्षशिष्टत्वात्प्रदानवत् ॥२॥

2. On the other hand, it should be performed, by reason of its being laid down like the gift.

उपस्तरणाभिधारणयोरमृतार्थत्वादकर्म स्यात् ॥३॥

3. The quartering, spreading (of Puroḍāśa) and flushing it with ghee, by reason of their being for the nectar, should not be performed.

क्रियेत वाऽर्थदत्वात्तयोः संसर्गहेतुत्वात् ॥४॥

4. On the other hand, they should be performed by reason of *arthavāda* and their being the cause of contact.

अकर्म वा चतुर्भिराप्तिवचनात्सह पूर्णं पुनश्चतुरवत्तम् ॥५॥

5. On the other hand, they should not be performed by reason of the completion with the word four in the completion text where the four-fold nature finds ful realisation.

क्रिया वा मुख्यावदानपरिमाणात्सामान्यात्तद्गुणत्वम् ॥६॥

6. On the other hand, they should be performed by reason of the measure of the principal offering; in common it is its subordinate.

तेषां चैकावदानत्वात् ॥७॥

7. And by reason of their one gift.

आप्तिः संख्यासमानत्वात् ॥८॥

8. Completion, by reason of the number being the same.

सतोस्त्वाप्तिवचनं व्यर्थम् ॥९॥

9. On the other hand, the completion sentence of the existent, is useless.

विकल्पस्त्वेकावदानत्वात् ॥१०॥

10. On the other hand, there is alternative by reason of one gift.

सर्वविकारे त्वभ्यसानर्थक्यं हविषो हीतरस्य स्यादपि वा स्विष्टकृतः स्यादितरस्यान्याय्यत्वात् ॥११॥

11. On the other hand, on the offering of the whole, the repetition of the other offering is useless, by reason of the other *sviṣṭakṛt* offering being unreasonable.

अकर्म वा संसर्गार्थनिवृत्तत्वात्तस्मादाप्तिसमर्थत्वं ॥१२॥

12. On the other hand, they are not to be performed by reason of the object of removal of the thing stuck; the completion text is, therefore, proper.

भक्षाणां तु प्रीत्यर्थत्वादकर्म स्यात् ॥१३॥

13. On the other hand by reason of eating (of food) being for satisfaction, it should not be done.

स्याद्वा निर्द्धानदर्शनात् ॥१४॥

14. On the other hand, by seeing the term 'sucking'.

वचनं वाज्यभक्षस्य प्रकृतौ स्यादभागित्वात् ॥१५॥

15. On the other hand, the text is in connection with eating of ghee, in the model sacrifice by reason of its indivisiblity.

वचनं वा हिरण्यस्य प्रदानवदाज्यस्य गुणभूतत्वात् ॥१६॥

16. On the other hand, the text is in connection with gold like the gift, the ghee being subsidiary.

एकधोपहारे सहत्वं ब्रह्मभक्षाणां प्रकृतौ विहितत्वात् ॥१७॥

17. In one offer for eating, there is simultaniety of the eating of the portions set apart for the *Brahmā* priest, by reason of its being ordained in the model sacrifice.

सर्वत्वं च तेषामधिकारात्स्यात् ॥१८॥

18. And the whole, by reason of the right in them.

पुरुषापनयो वा तेषामवाच्यत्वात् ॥१९॥

19. On the other hand, the removal of other priests; their taking of it is not sanctioned.

पुरुषापनयात्स्वकालत्वम् ॥२०॥

20. By reason of removal of other priests, there is appointed time.

एकार्थत्वादविभागः स्यात् ॥२१॥

21. By reason of one object, there is no division.

ऋत्विग्दानं धर्ममात्रार्थं स्याद्ददातिसामर्थ्यात् ॥२२॥

22. A gift to *ṛtvik* priests is with a view to religious fruit, by force of the word *dadāti.*

परिक्रयार्थं वा कर्मसंयोगाल्लोकवत् ॥२३॥

23. Or for securing the services, by reason of its connection with the work done as in ordinary life.

दक्षिणायुक्तवचनाच्च ॥२४॥

24. By reason of the text "engaged on fee".

नयाऽन्येनानम्येत परिक्रीयात्कर्मणः परार्थत्वात् ॥२५॥

25. And nor can service be secured by any other means; because hiring for the work is for the purpose of another.

परिक्रीतवचनाच्च ॥२६॥

26. And by reason of the text 'hired'.

सनिवन्येव भृति वचनात् ॥२७॥

27. By reason of the word 'wages' in connection with alms.

नैष्कर्तृकेण संस्तवाच्च ॥२८॥

28. By reason of the praise of the carrier of fuel.

शेषभक्षाश्च तद्वत् ॥२९॥

29. And similarly the remnants of the food.

संस्कारो वा द्रव्यस्य परार्थत्वात् ॥३०॥

30. On the other hand, it is a purificatory rite by reason of the substance being for another.

शेषे च समत्वात् ॥३१॥

31. And by reason of equality in the remnants.

स्वामिनि च दर्शनात्तत्सामान्यादितरेषांतथात्वम् ॥३२॥

32. And by seeing in the master; by reason of its being common, the same with others.

तथा चान्यार्थदर्शनम् ॥३३॥

33. And similarly there are other proofs.

वरणमृत्विजामानमनार्थत्वात्सत्रे न स्यात्स्वकर्मत्वात् ॥३४॥

34. The appointment of the *ṛtvik* is to secure his services; it is not in a sacrificial session being one's own act.

परिक्रयश्च तादर्थ्यात् ॥३५॥

35. And hiring by reason of its being for it.

प्रतिषेधश्च कर्मवत् ॥३६॥

36. And the prohibition is like the act.

स्याद्वाप्रासर्पिकस्य धर्ममात्रत्वात् ॥३७॥

37. On the other hand it may be by reason of the gift being out of religious motives.

न दक्षिणाशब्दात्तस्मान्नित्यानुवादः स्यात् ॥३८॥

38. Not so, by reason of the word 'fee'; it is, therefore, a permanent restatement.

उदवसानीयः सत्रधर्मा स्यात्तदङ्गत्वात्तत्र दानं धर्ममात्रं स्यात् ॥३९॥

39. The *udavasānīya* partakes the quality of a *satra* by reason of its being a part of it. There the gift is out of charity (religious motive).

न त्वेतत्प्रकृतित्वाद्विभक्तचोदितत्वाच्च ॥४०॥

40. On the other hand, it is not so by reason of its being a model and by its being separately laid down.

तेषां तु वचनाद्द्वियज्ञवत्सहप्रयोगः स्यात् ॥४१॥

41. On the other hand, their joint participation by reason of the text, like the sacrifice in which two sacrificers take part.

तत्रान्यानृत्विजो वृणीरन् ॥४२॥

42. There, other preists should be appointed.

एकैकशस्त्वविप्रतिषेधात्प्रकृतेश्चैकसंयोगात् ॥४३॥

43. On the other hand, one by one by reason of no prohibition and because in the model sacrifice there is connection with one.

कामेष्टौ च दानशब्दात् ॥४४॥

44. And in the *kāmeṣṭi* by reason of the word gift.

वचनं वा सत्रत्वात् ॥४५॥

45. On the other hand, it is a command by reason of the *satra*.

द्वेष्ये च चोदनाद्दक्षिणापनयात् ॥४६॥

46. And there is a non-application of fee in an enemy, by reason of there being no command.

अस्थियज्ञोऽविप्रतिषेधादितरेषां स्याद्विप्रतिषेधादस्थनाम् ॥४७॥

47. The *asthiyajña* by reason of no prohibition, is of the others because of the prohibition of the bones.

यावदुक्तमुपयोगः स्थात् ॥४८॥

48. As much said, is applicable.

यदि तु वचनात्तेषां जपसंस्कारमर्थलुप्तं सेष्टि तदर्थत्वात् ॥४९॥

49. On the other hand, if it is under a text, the muttering of the prayer and shaving are not to be performed being for no purpose; the *iṣṭi* is much more so, by reason of its being for him.

क्रत्वर्थं तु क्रियेत गुणभूतत्वात् ॥

On the other hand, they should be done for the sacrifice, he being subordinate.

काम्यानि तु न विद्यन्ते कामा ज्ञानाद्यथेतरस्यानुच्यमानानि ॥५०॥

50. On the other hand, desire-accomplishing acts do not exist by reason of no knowledge of the desire, just like the desire of the other not expressed.

ईहार्थाश्चाभावात्सूक्तवाकवत् ॥५१॥

51. And they are with the objects of activity; by reason of the absence, (they should not be performed) being fit in the *sūktavāka* (praises).

स्युर्वाऽर्थवादत्वात् ॥५२॥

52. On the other hand, it should be repeated being a praise.

नेच्छाभिधानात्तदभावादितरस्मिन् ॥५३॥

53. Not so, by reason of the mention of the desire and that is absent in the other.

स्युर्वा होतृकामाः ॥५४॥

54. On the other hand, there is the desire of the Hotā.

न तदाषीष्ट्वात् ॥५५॥

55. Not so, by reason of their being desires.

सर्वस्वारस्यदिष्टगतौ समापनं न विद्यते कर्मणो जीवसंयोगात् ॥५६॥

56. On the death, the completion of the *sarvasvāra* does not exist, because the action is connected with life.

स्याद्वोभयोः प्रत्यक्षशिष्टत्वात् ॥५७॥

57. On the other hand, of both by reason of the direct command.

गते कर्मास्थियज्ञवत् ॥५८॥

58. On death, the sacrifice is like *asthiyajña.*

जीवत्यवचनमायुराशिषस्तदर्थत्वात् ॥५९॥

59. In the living, the benediction for life should not be pronounced, because that is for its objec·.

वचनं वा भागित्वात्प्राग्यथोक्तात् ॥६०॥

60. The formula should be uttered by reason of his sharing it before the utterance as said.

क्रिया स्याद्धर्ममात्राणाम् ॥६१॥

61. Procedure of the invisible purpose should be performed.

गुणलोपे च मुख्यस्य ॥६२॥

62. And on the omission of the subordinate, the principal is omitted.

मुष्टिलोपात्तु संख्यालोपस्तद्गुणत्वात्स्यात् ॥६३॥

63. On the other hand, it is better to drop the number than the handful, because it is subordinate.

न निर्वापशेषत्वात् ॥६४॥

64. Not so, by reason of being subordinate to the offering.

संख्या तु चोदनां प्रति सामान्यात्तद्विकारः संयोगाच्च परं मुष्टेः ॥६५॥

65. On the other hand, the number being common with the injunction, is dropped and by connection, further the handfuls.

न चोदनाभिसम्बन्धात्प्रक्रतौ संस्कारयोगात् ॥६६॥

66. Not so, by reason of the connection with the injunction and by the connection with purificatory rite in the model sacrifice.

औत्पत्तिके तु द्रव्यतो विकारः स्यादकार्यात्वात् ॥६७॥

67. On the other hand, when the word is applicable to the whole class is its origin, the substance is suspended by reason of its being of no use.

नैमित्तिके तु कार्य्यत्वात्प्रकृतेः स्यात्तदापत्तेः ॥६८॥

68. On the other hand, in the accidental being of use, because the model sacrifice is complied with.

विप्रतिषेधे तद्वचनात्प्राकृतगुणलोपः स्यात्तेनच कर्मसंयोगात् ॥६९॥

69. On conflict, by reason of its text the quality of the model sacrifice is omitted, because it is connected with the act.

परेषां प्रतिषेधः स्यात् ॥७०॥

70. There is a prohibition of others.

प्रतिषेधाच्च ॥७१॥

71. And by reason of prohibition.

अर्थाभावे संस्कारत्वं स्यात् ॥७२॥

72. If there be no visible effect to be produced in it, the rite should be performed.

अर्थेन च विपर्य्यासे तादर्थ्यात्तत्त्वमेव स्यात् ॥७३॥

73. And on the transposition of the object, the existence is not destroyed by reason of that being for it.

END OF PĀDA 2

***

PĀDA 3

विकृतौ शब्दवत्त्वात्प्रधानस्य गुणानामधिकोत्पत्तिः सन्निधानात् ॥१॥

1. In the modified sacrifice, by reason of the word of the principal, the subordinate acts will multiply because it is near it.

प्रकृतिवत्तस्य चानुपरोधः ॥२॥

2. And like the model sacrifice, there will be no obstruction of it.

चोदनाप्रभुत्वाच्च ॥३॥

3. And by reason of the power of the command.

प्रधानं त्वङ्गसंयुक्तं तथाभूतमपूर्वं स्यात्तस्य विध्युपलक्षणात्सर्वो हि पूर्ववान्विधिरविशेषात्प्रवर्तितः ॥४॥

4. The principal consists of its subsidiary acts; in this state, it produces an invisible effect; by reason of its transfer to the modified sacrifice, everyone of it has a model, because it applies without any distinction.

न चाङ्गविधिरनङ्गे स्यात् ॥५॥

5. And there cannot be any *aṅgavidhi* in a sacrifice which has no parts.

कर्मणश्चैकशब्द्यात्सन्निधाने विधेराख्यासंयोगो गुणेन तद्विकारःस्याच्छब्दस्य विधिगामित्वाद्गुणस्य चोपदेश्यत्वात् ॥६॥

6. And the act (consisting of the principal and subordinate) by reason of one word; being close to the principal *vidhi*, the *guṇavidhi* is

connected with it under a name; by this subordination, there is a modification because the word applies to the *vidhi* and the subordinate acts are ordained.

अकार्य्यत्वाच्च नाम्नः ॥७॥

7. And by reason of the word being for no purpose.

तुल्याच प्रभुता गुणे ॥८॥

8. And they are equally capable of conveying the subordinate (act).

सर्वमेवंप्रधानमिति चेत् ॥९॥

9. If you say "all are principal".

तथाभूतेनसंयोगाद्यथार्थविधयः स्युः ॥१०॥

10. By reason of the connection with that state, the *vidhis* will be in the proper sense of the term.

विधित्वं चाविशिष्ठ मेवं प्राकृतानां वैकृतैः कर्मणायोगात्तस्मात्सर्वं प्रधानार्थम् ॥११॥

11. And there is no difference of the injunction of the model sacrifice by reason of the connection of the act with the modified sacrifice; therefore all is for the principal.

समत्वाच्च तदुत्पत्तेः संस्कारैरधिकारः स्यात् ॥१२॥

12. And by reason of the equality of their origin with the rites, the procedure is (regulated).

हिरण्यगर्भः पूर्वस्य मन्त्रलिङ्गात् ॥१३॥

13. *Hiraṇyagarbha* of the first part, by the sign of the *mantra*.

प्रकृत्यनुपरोधाच्च ॥१४॥

14. And by reason of no obstruction of the model sacrifice.

उत्तरस्य वा मन्त्रार्थित्वात् ॥१५॥

15. On the other hand, the latter part by reason of the *mantra* being for the purpose as it is done without a *mantra ādhāra*.

विध्यतिदेशात्तच्छ्रुतौ विकारः स्याद्गुणानामुपदेश्यत्वात् ॥१६॥

16. By reason of the transfer of the injunction, there is a modification in that which is laid down; because the subordinate acts have been laid down.

पूर्वस्मिंश्चामन्त्रत्वदर्शनात् ॥१७॥

17. And by seeing the absence of mantra in the first part.

संस्कारे तु क्रियान्तर तस्य विधायकत्वात् ॥१८॥

18. On the other hand, in the purificatory rites, there is a separate action by reason of its being commanded.

प्रकृत्यनुपरोधाच्च ॥१९॥

19. And by reason of the model sacrifice being not obstructed.

विधेस्तु तत्र भावात्सन्देहे यस्य शब्दस्तदर्थः स्यात् ॥२०॥

20. On the other hand, the command being there by transfer, on doubt the word conveys the meaning in which it is used.

संस्कारसामर्थ्याद्गुणसंयोगाच्च ॥२१॥

21. By reason by the power of the ceremony and by reason of the connection with the quality.

विप्रतिषेधात्क्रियाप्रकरणे स्यात् ॥२२॥

22. And by reason of the prohibition in the context of the procedure.

षड्भिर्दीक्षयतीति तासां मन्त्रविकारः श्रुतिसंयोगात् ॥२३॥

23. In the text "he initiates with six", the mantras are modified by reason of the connection with the text.

अभ्यासात्तु प्रधानस्य ॥२४॥

24. On the other hand, by reason of the repetition of the principal.

आवृत्त्या मन्त्रकर्म स्यात् ॥२५॥

25. By repetition, the act of uttering the *mantra* is done.

अपिवा प्रतिमन्त्रत्वात्प्राकृतानामहानिः स्यादन्यायश्च कृतेऽभ्यासः ॥२६॥

26. On the other hand, by reason of each *mantra*, there is no suspension of the *mantras* of the model sacrifice; on once pronouncing the mantra of the modified sacrifice, the repetition of the same is improper.

पौर्वापर्य्यञ्चाभ्यासे नोपपद्यते नैमित्तिकत्वात् ॥२७॥

27. And the priority and posteriority do not arise in the case of repetition by reason of their being correlative.

तत्प्रथक्त्वं च दर्शयति ॥२८॥

28. And their separation shows.

न चाविशेषाद्व्यपदेशः स्यात् ॥२९॥

29. And there can be no denomination, by reason of there being nothing special.

अग्न्याधेयस्य नैमित्तिके गुणविकारे दक्षिणादानमधिकं स्याद्वाक्य-संयोगात् ॥३०॥

30. On the establishment of fire being the cause and on the modification of the subordinate act, the payment of fee will be in addition by reason of the connection with the sentence.

शिष्टत्वाच्चेतरासां यथास्थानम् ॥३१॥

31. And by reason of the text, there will be an aggregate of the other in order.

विकारस्त्वप्रकरणे हि काम्यानि ॥३२॥

32. On the other hand, there is suspension; there it is not in the context, because they are desire-accomplishing.

शङ्कते च निवृत्तेरुभयत्वंहिश्रूयते ॥३३॥

33. And the suspension is inferred because both are mentioned.

वासो वत्सश्च सामान्यात् ॥३४॥

34. And cloth and calf, by reason of being common.

अर्थापत्तेस्तद्धर्मा: स्यान्निमित्ताख्याभिसंयोगात् ॥३५॥

35. By reason of serving the purpose, they partake of its quality, because they are connected with the name of the cause.

दाने पाकोऽर्थलक्षणः ॥३६॥

36. In the gift, the cooking which is the mark of the gift.

पाकस्य चान्नकारित्त्वात् ॥३७॥

37. And of the cooking by reason of the food.

तथाभिधारणस्य ॥३८॥

38. And similarly of the sprinkling of ghee.

द्रव्यविधिसन्निधौ सङ्ख्या तेषां गुणत्वात्स्यात् ॥३९॥

39. In proximity with the injunction relating to the substance, the number thereof is by reason of the subordinate.

समत्वात्तु गुणानामेकस्यश्रुतिसंयोगात् ॥४०॥

40. On the other hand, by reason of the equality of the subordinate acts, it applies to one because of the mention in the text.

यस्य वा सन्निधाने स्याद्वाक्यतोह्यभिसम्बन्धः ॥४१॥

41. On the other hand, it will apply to that which is near because it is syntactically connected.

असंयुक्तास्तु तुल्यवदितराभिर्विधीयन्ते तस्मात्सर्वाधिकारः स्यात् ॥४२॥

42. On the other hand, being unconnected, like equal it is connected with others; therefore it applies to all collectively.

असंयोगाद्विधिश्रुतावेकजाताधिकारः स्याच्छ्रुत्याकोपात्क्रतोः ॥४३॥

43. By reason of want of connection in the scriptural injunction, it applies to one class only and to avoid contradiction with the scriptural text, it applies to the sacrifice.

शब्दार्थश्चापि लोकवत् ॥४४॥

44. And the signification of the word is like the word in common language.

सापशूनामुत्पत्तितो विभागात् ॥४५॥

45. That applies to animals by reason of the division by virtue of the significant power.

अनियमोऽविशेषात् ॥४६॥

46. (On the other hand), there is no rule by reason of there being nothing special.

भागिवाद्वा गवां स्यात् ॥४७॥

47. On the other hand, of the cows by reason of great usefulness.

प्रत्ययात् ॥४८॥

48. By the practice.

लिङ्गदर्शनाच्च ॥४९॥

49. And by seeing the indicative mark.

तत्र दानं विभागेन प्रदानानां पृथक्त्वात् ॥५०॥

50. There the gift is by division, by reason of the gift being separate.

परिक्रयाच्च लोकवत् ॥५१॥

51. And by reason of hiring, just as in common life.

विभागं चापि दर्शयति ॥५२॥

52. And the division is shown.

समं स्यादश्रुतित्वात् ॥५३॥

53. Equal by reason of its being not sanctioned by the Veda.

अपि वा कर्मवैषम्यात् ॥५४॥

54. On the other hand, by reason of the inequality of the work done.

अतुल्याः स्युः परिक्रये विषमाख्या विधिश्रुतौ परिक्रयान्न कर्मण्युपपद्यते दर्शनाद्विशेषस्य तथाभ्युदये ॥५५॥

55. There is inequality in hiring; the inequality arises under an injunction of the text but not by the inequality of the work done; because there is seen a special text in connection with future reward.

तस्य धेनुरिति गवां प्रकृतौ विभक्तचोदितत्वात्सामान्यात्तद्विकारः स्याद्यथेष्टिर्गुणशब्देन ॥५६॥

56. The text "his cow" sets aside as a rule the 'cow' in the model sacrifice by reason of the separate command, just as the *iṣṭi* by the word indicating the quality.

सर्वस्य वा क्रतुसंयोगादेकत्वं दक्षिणार्थस्य गुणानां कार्य्यैत्वादर्थे विकृतौ श्रुतिभूतं स्यात्तस्मात् समवायाद्धिकर्मभिः ॥५७॥

57. On the other hand, of all by reason of the connection with the sacrifice; the onness of the object of the fee by reason of the oneness of the action; of the subordinate acts in the modified sacrifice, the object of the model sacrifice, is governed by the text; therefore by reason of the connection with the action.

चोदनानामनाश्रयाल्लिङ्गेन नियमः स्यात् ॥५८॥

58. By reason of the command being without support, the rule is by the force of the text.

एका पञ्चेति धेनुवत् ॥५९॥

59. 'One and five' like a cow.

त्रिवत्सश्च ॥६०॥

60. And 3 year-old-heifer.

तथा च लिङ्गदर्शनम् ॥६१॥

61. Similarly the *liṅga* is seen.

एके तु श्रुतिभूतत्वात्सङ्ख्यया गवां लिङ्गविशेषेण ॥६२॥

62. On the other hand, in one by reason of the text with the number of the cows, by the special *liṅga.*

प्रकाशौ तथेति चेत् ॥६३॥

63. And similarly 'candlestick', if you say.

अपि त्ववयवार्थत्वाद्विभक्तप्रकृतित्वाद्गुणेदन्ताविकारः स्यात् ॥६४॥

64. On the other hand, being for the purpose of a part and being separate in the model sacrifice, there is a modification in the extent of the subordinate act.

धेनुवच्चाश्वदक्षिणा स ब्रह्मण इति पुरुषापनयो यथा हिरण्यस्य ॥६५॥

65. And like 'cow' the fee of the horse; that to Brāhmaṇa priests; the deprivation of other priests just as in the case of the gold.

एके तु कर्तृसंयोगात्स्रग्वत्तस्य लिङ्गविशेषेण ॥६६॥

66. On the other hand, it suspends only one portion by reason of the mention of the agent; like a garland, by special *liṅga.*

अपि वा तदधिकाराद्धिरण्यवद्विकारः स्यात् ॥६७॥

67. On the other hand, by reason of its being under that topic, the modification is like the gold.

तथा च सोमचमसः ॥६८॥

68. And similarly the soma chamas (Soma cup).

सर्वविकारो वा क्रत्वर्थे प्रतिषेधात् पशूनां ॥६९॥

69. On the other hand, the modification of all, because for the purpose of sacrifice the animals are prohibited.

ब्रह्मदानेऽविशिष्टमिति चेत् ॥७०॥

70. 'It is not particular with the gift to *Brahmā*', if you say.

उत्सर्गस्य क्रत्वर्थत्वात्प्रतिषिद्धस्य कर्मस्यान्न च गौणः प्रयोजनमर्थः स दक्षिणानां स्यात् ॥७१॥

71. The gift being for the sacrifice, there is no action of the prohibited; nor is the purpose with the subordinate acts; that object is with the fee.

यदि तु ब्रह्मणस्तदूनं तद्विकारः स्यात् ॥७२॥

72. On the other hand, if to the *Brahmā,* without it there is a modification.

सर्वं वा पुरुषापनयात्तासां क्रतुप्रधानत्वात् ॥७३॥

73. On the other hand, the entire by reason of the deprivation of the other priests and by reason of the sacrifice being principal.

यजुर्युक्तेऽध्वर्य्योर्दक्षिणा विकारः स्यात् ॥७४॥

74. On the other hand, in the chariot yoked with *yajumantra*, there is the suspension of the fee of *adhvaryu*.

अपि वा श्रुतिभूतत्वात्सर्वासां तस्य भागो नियम्यते ॥७५॥

75. On the other hand, by reason of the text, of all gifts, his share is demarcated.

END OF PĀDA 3

***

PĀDA 4

प्रकृतिलिङ्गासंयोगात्कर्मसंस्कारंविकृतावधिकं स्यात् ॥१॥

1. By reason of there being no connection with the mark of the model sacrifice, the purificatory rite in the modified sacrifice will be in addition.

चोदनालिङ्गसंयोगे तद्विकारः प्रतीयेत प्रकृतिसन्निधानात् ॥२॥

2. In connection with the mark of the *codanā*, its modification is inferred by reason of the proximity of the model sacrifice.

सर्वत्र तु ग्रहाम्नानमधिकं स्यात्प्रकृतिवत् ॥३॥

3. On the other hand, every where the ordaining of the cups is for increase, just as in the model sacrifice.

अधिकैश्चैकवाक्यत्वात् ॥४॥

4. And with the combination, by reason of the unity of the sentence.

लिङ्गदर्शनाच्च ॥५॥

5. And by seeing the force of the text.

प्राजापत्येषु चाम्नानात् ॥६॥

6. And in *prājāpatya*, by reason of laying down.

आमने लिङ्गदर्शनात् ॥७॥

7. And in *āmanahoma* by seeing the *liṅga*.

उपगेषु शरवत्स्यात्प्रकृतिलिङ्गसंयोगात् ॥८॥

8. In the musicians, like the reed by reason of the mention of the sign of the model sacrifice.

आनर्थक्यात्त्वधिकं स्यात् ॥९॥

9. On the other hand, by reason of meaninglessness, there will be a combination.

संस्कारे चान्यसंयोगात् ॥१०॥

10. And in a purificatory rite, by reason of the mention of another time.

प्रयाजवदिति चेत् ॥११॥

11. If you say "like *prayāja*".

नार्थान्यत्वात् ।१२॥

12. Not so, by reason of the object being different.

आच्छादने त्वैकार्थ्यात्प्राकृतस्य विकारः स्यात् ॥१३॥

13. On the other hand, in covering by reason of one object; the garment of the model sacrifice is set aside.

अधिकं वान्यार्थत्वात् ॥१४॥

14. On the other hand, an addition by reason of the object being different.

समुच्चयं च दर्शयति ॥१५॥

15. And combination is shown.

सामस्वर्थान्तरश्रुतेरविकारः प्रतीयेत ॥१६॥

16. In songs by reason of the text for a different object, it appears that there is a combination.

अर्थे त्वश्रूयमाणे शेषत्वात्प्राकृतस्य विकारः स्यात् ॥१७॥

17. On the other hand, the object being not laid down and being a subsidiary act it suspends the song of the model sacrifice.

सर्वेषामविशेषात् ॥१८॥

18. Of all, by reason of there being nothing special.

एकस्य वा श्रुतिसामर्थ्यात्प्रकृतेश्चाविकारात् ॥१९॥

19. On the other hand, of one by the force of the text and by reason of the model sacrifice.

स्तोमविवृद्धौ त्वधिकं स्यादविवृद्धौ द्रव्यविकारः स्यादितरस्याश्रुतित्वाच्च ॥२०॥

20. On the increase of the songs, there is combination and on the decrease there is annulment, because the other is not heard of.

पवमाने स्यातां तस्मिन्नावापोद्वापदर्शनात् ॥२१॥

21. Both are in *pavamāna*, by reason of seeing *āvāpa* and *udvāpa.*

वचनानित्वपूर्वत्वात् ॥२२॥

22. On the other hand, text by reason of its being extraordinary.

विधिशब्दस्य मन्त्रत्वे भावः स्यात्तेन चोदना ॥२३॥

23. In the nature of the *mantra*, there is an existence of the word indicating command; hence there is injunction.

शेषाणां वा चोदनैकत्वात्तस्मात्सर्वत्र श्रूयते ॥२४॥

24. And the subsidiary acts being governed by one command, therefore, it is every where so laid down.

तथोत्तरस्यांततौ तत्प्रकृतित्वात् ॥२५॥

25. Similarly in the subsequent ceremony by reason of its having a model sacrifice.

प्राकृतस्य गुणश्रुतौ सगुणेनाभिधानं स्यात् ॥२६॥

26. Of the model sacrifice by reason of the text about the quality, the address is with its quality.

अविकारो वाऽर्थशब्दानपायात्स्याद्द्रव्यवत् ॥२७॥

27. On the other hand, unaltered by reason of not giving up the significant word, like the substance.

तथारम्भासमवायाद्वा चोदितेनाभिधानं स्यादर्थस्य श्रुतिसमवायित्वादवचने च गुणशास्त्रमनर्थकंस्यात् ॥२८॥

28. On the other hand, by reason of its being not connected with the origin, the address is by what has been laid down; the meaning being connected with the text, on not pronouncing (the attribute) the text as to the attribute will be meaningless.

द्रव्येष्वारम्भगामित्वादर्थे विकारः सामर्थ्यात् ॥२९॥

29. In the substances, in the meaning of the word being connected with the origin, there is modification by reason of the power.

बुधन्वान्पवमानवद्विशेषनिर्देशात् ॥३०॥

30. '*Budhanvān*' like *pavamāna*, by reason of the mention of the particular.

मन्त्रविशेषनिर्देशान्न देवताविकारः स्यात् ॥३१॥

31. There is no modification of the deity, by reason of pointing out a special *mantra.*

विधिनिगमभेदात्प्रकृतौ तत्प्रकृतित्वाद्विकृतावपिभेदः स्यात् ॥३२॥

32. By reason of the difference between the injunction and the mantra in the model sacrifice there will be a difference in the modified sacrifice because that is its model.

यथोक्तं वा विप्रतिपत्तेर्न चोदना ॥३३॥

33. On the other hand, just as directed; but the difference is not an injunction.

स्विष्टकृद्देवतान्यत्वे तच्छब्दत्वान्निवर्त्तेत ॥३४॥

34. In the diety of *sviṣṭakṛt* being different, by reason of that word, it is suspended.

संयोगो वाऽर्थापत्तेरभिधानस्य कर्मजत्वात् ॥३५॥

35. It is a compound word, by reason of the significance of the word, because the address depends on the action.

सगुणस्य गुणलोपे निगमेषु यावदुक्तं स्यात् ॥३६॥

36. Of one who is with the attribute, on the deprivation of the attribute in the mantra, the application is restricted to that only.

सर्वस्य वैककर्म्यात् ॥३७॥

37. Of all, by reason of the unity of the action.

स्विष्टकृदावापिकोऽनुयाजे स्यात्प्रयोजनवदङ्गानामर्थसंयोगात् ॥३८॥

38. The *sviṣṭakṛt* in *anuyāja* pertains to *āvāpa*, being for a purpose because the parts are connected with the purpose.

अन्वाहेति च शस्त्रवत्कर्म स्याच्चोदनान्तरात् ॥३९॥

39. And *anvāha* like *śaṃsati* is the principal act, by reason of a separate injunction.

संस्कारो वा चोदितस्य शब्दस्य वचनार्थत्वात् ॥४०॥

40. On the other hand, it is a subordinate act because there is the purpose of the word of the injunction.

स्याद्गुणार्थत्वात् ॥४१॥

41. It may be, by reason of its being for a subordinate act.

मनोतायां तु वचनादविकारः स्यात् ॥४२॥

42. On the other hand, in *manotā*, there is no modification by reason of the text.

पृष्ठार्थेऽन्यद्रथन्तरात्तद्योनिपूर्वत्वादृचां प्रविभक्तत्वात् ॥४३॥

43. In the object of *pṛṣṭha*, other than *rathantara* (should be sung,) by reason of that being the *yoni* in the model sacrifice and by reason of the *ṛk* verses being divided.

स्वयोनौ वा सर्वाख्यत्वात् ॥४४॥

44. On the other hand, in its own *yoni* by reason of its having the name of all.

यूपवदिति चेत् ॥४५॥

45. If you say "like a sacrificial post".

न कर्मसंयोगात् ॥४६॥

46. Not so, by reason of its connection with the action.

कार्य्यत्वादुत्तरयोर्यथाप्रकृति ॥४७॥

47. By reason of the action, in the *uttarā* just as it is in the model sacrifice.

समानदेवते वा तृचस्याविभागात् ॥४८॥

48. On the other hand, in the song which has a common deity, by reason of indivisibility of *tṛca*.

ग्रहाणां देवतान्यत्वे स्तुतशस्त्रयोः कर्मत्वादविकारः स्यात् ॥४९॥

49. On the deities of the cups being different, the *stuti* and *śastra* praises by reason of their being principal, are to be applied unmodified.

उभयपानात्पृषदाज्ये दध्नःस्यादुपलक्षणं निगमेषु पातव्यस्योपलक्षणात् ॥५०॥

50. By reason of drinking both, there is an addition of curd in the mixture called *pṛṣadājya* because in the model sacrifice the substance to be drunk is pointed out.

न वा परार्थत्वाद्यज्ञपतिवत् ॥५१॥

51. On the other hand not so, by reason of its being for another like *yajñapati*.

स्याद्वा आवाहनस्य तादर्थ्यात् ॥५२॥

52. On the other hand, it should be done, because it is with the object of invocation.

न वा संस्कारशब्दत्वात् ॥५३॥

53. On the other hand, not so, by reason of the word indicating purificatory rite.

स्याद्वाद्रव्याभिधानात् ॥५४॥

54. On the other hand, there should be an addition by reason of naming of the substance.

दध्नस्तुगुणभूतत्वादाज्यपानिगमाः स्युर्गुणत्वं श्रुतेराज्यप्रधानत्वात् ॥५५॥

55. On the other hand, the curd being subordinate, the '*ājyapā*' is to be pronounced; it is subordinate because in the text the '*ājya*' is principal.

दधिवा स्यात्प्रधानमाज्ये प्रथमान्त्यसंयोगात् ॥५६॥

56. On the other hand, the curd is principal; because in ghee, the first and the last are connected.

अपिवाज्यप्रधानत्वाद्गुणार्थे व्यपदेशे भक्त्या संस्कारशब्दः स्यात् ॥५७॥

57. On the other hand, by reason of ghee being principal, in the denomination in the object of the subordinate act, the word denoting purificatory rite is in the secondary sense.

अपि वाख्याविकारत्वात्तेन स्यादुपलक्षणम् ॥५८॥

58. On the other hand, by reason of the modification in the name, the pointing out should be by that.

न वा स्याद्गुणशास्त्रत्वात् ॥५९॥

59. Not so by reason of laying down the quality.

END OF PĀDA 4

* * *

PĀDA 5

आनुपूर्व्यवतामेकदेशग्रहणेष्वागमवदन्त्यलोपः स्यात् ॥१॥

1. On transference of a portion of those that come in order, the last one is omitted like the incomers.

लिङ्गदर्शनाच्च ॥२॥

2. And by reason of the indicative mark.

विकल्पो वा समत्वात् ॥३॥

3. On the other hand, there is option by reason of equality.

क्रमादुपजनोऽन्त्येस्यात् ॥४॥

4. On coming in order, the last.

लिङ्गमविशिष्टं सङ्ख्याया हि तद्वचनम् ॥५॥

5. The *liṅga* is general, because that word relates to the number.

आदितो वा प्रवृत्तिः स्यादारम्भस्य तदादित्वाद्वचनादन्त्यविधिः स्यात् ॥६॥

6. On the other hand, the application is from the beginning; of the commencement being the first by reason of the text, the last is to be omitted.

एकत्रिके तृचादिषु माध्यन्दिनेछन्दसां श्रुतिभूतत्वात् ॥७॥

7. In the sacrifice in one *trika* and *mādhyandinapavamāna* the first of each *tṛca*, by reason of the mantra being dependent on the text.

आदितो वा तन्न्यायत्वादितरस्यानुमानिकत्वात् ॥८॥

8. On the other hand, from the first by reason of that rule and by reason of the other based on an inference.

यथानिवेशश्च प्रकृतिवत्सङ्ख्यामात्रविकारत्वात् ॥९॥

9. And introducing the *ṛk* according to the model sacrifice is by reason of the modification of the number only.

त्रिकस्तृचे धुर्य्ये स्यात् ॥१०॥

10. The *trika* which is in *dhū* song, is to be sung in *tṛca*.

एकस्यां वा स्तोमस्यावृत्तिधर्मत्वात् ॥११॥

11. On the other hand, in one verse by reason of the characteristic of the song to be repeated.

चोदनासु त्वपूर्वत्वाल्लिङ्गेन धर्मनियमः स्यात् ॥१२॥

12. On the other hand, in the command, there being extraordinary principle, the rule as to procedure is by the inference from the text.

प्राप्तिस्तु रात्रिशब्दसम्बन्धात् ॥१३॥

13. On the other hand, the transference by reason of the connection of the word 'night'.

अपूर्वासु तु सङ्ख्यासु विकल्पः स्यात्सर्वासामर्थवत्त्वात् ॥१४॥

14. There is option in the numbers which have been ordained, because all are for a purpose.

स्तोमविवृद्धौ प्राकृतानामभ्यासेन सङ्ख्यापूरणमविकारात्सङ्ख्यायां गुणशब्दत्वादन्यस्य चाश्रुतित्वात् ॥१५॥

15. In the case where the songs preponderate, the number is to be completed by repeating the songs of the model sacrifice by reason of no change and the number being subordinate and importing of others being non-Vedic.

आगमेन वाऽभ्यासस्याश्रुतित्वात् ॥१६॥

16. On the other hand by importation, because the repetition is un-Vedic.

सङ्ख्यायाश्च पृथक्तवनिवेशात् ॥१७॥

17. And of the number being applicable to several objects.

पराक्शब्दत्वात् ॥१८॥

18. By reason of the word 'reverse'.

उक्ताविकाराच्च ॥१९॥

19. By reason of the non-modification of that which is uttered.

अश्रुतित्वान्नेति चेत् ॥२०॥

20. If you say "it should not be done by its being not ordained".

स्यादर्थचोदितानां परिमाणशास्त्रम् ॥२१॥

21. It should be done, because the laying down of quantity is the object of the text.

आवापवचनं चाभ्यासे नोपपद्यते ॥२२॥

22. And the *āvāpa* text is not applicable to repetition.

साम्नांचोत्पत्तिसामर्थ्यात् ॥२३॥

23. And by reason of the force of the origin of the songs.

धूर्येष्वपीति चेत् ॥२४॥

24. If you say that in *dhū* also.

नावृत्तिधर्म्मत्वात् ॥२५॥

25. Not so, by reason of the characteristics of the repetition.

वहिष्पवमाने न ऋगागमः सामैकत्वात् ॥२६॥

26. On the other hand, in *vahiṣpavamāna*, the *ṛk* is to be brought in, by reason of the unity of the psalm.

अभ्यासेन तु संख्यापूरणं सामधेनीष्वभ्यासप्रकृतित्वात् ॥२७॥

27. On the other hand, in *sāmadhenīs* the number is to be completed by repetition, because there is repetition in the model sacrifice.

अविशेषान्नेति चेत् ॥२८॥

28. "By reason of there being nothing special" if you say.

स्यात्तद्धर्मत्वात् प्रकृतिवदभ्यस्येताऽऽसङ्ख्यापूरणात् ॥२९॥

29. It should be so, by reason of the characteristic of the model sacrifice; it should be repeated just as in the model sacrifice, by reason of completing the number limited.

यावदुक्तं वा कृतपरिमाणत्वात् ॥३०॥

30. On the other hand, there is repetition up to what has been ordained by reason of having fixed the quantity.

अधिकानाञ्च दर्शनात् ॥३१॥

31. And by seeing excess.

कर्मस्वपीति चेत् ॥३२॥

32. If you say "that it should also be in the sacrifice".

न चोदितत्वात् ॥३३॥

33. Not so, by reason of there being directed.

षोडशिनो वैकृतत्वं तत्र कृत्स्नविधानात् ॥३४॥

34. The *ṣoḍaśī* partakes of the nature of the modified sacrifice, because there the entire procedure is laid down.

प्रकृतौ चाऽभावदर्शनात् ॥३५॥

35. And by seeing its absence in the model sacrifice.

अयज्ञवचनाच्च ॥३६॥

36. And by reason of non-sacrificial text.

प्रकृतौ वा शिष्टत्वात् ॥३७॥

37. On the other hand, in the model sacrifice, by reason of its being so ordained.

प्रकृतिदर्शनाच्च ॥३८॥

38. And by seeing the model sacrifice.

आम्नातंपरिसङ्ख्यार्थम् ॥३९॥

39. Laying down is with an object of *parisaṃkhyā.*

उक्तमभावदर्शनम् ॥४०॥

40. Its absence is said.

गुणादयज्ञत्वम् ॥४१॥

41. By reason of the praise, it is non-sacrificial.

तस्याग्रयणाद्ग्रहणम् ॥४२॥

42. It is taken from *āgrayaṇa.*

उक्थ्याच्च वचनात् ॥४३॥

43. And from *ukthya* under a text.

तृतीयसवने वचनात्स्यात् ॥४४॥

44. At the time of the third *savana* under the text.

अनभ्यासे पराक्शब्दस्य तादर्थ्यात् ॥४५॥

45. In the sense of no repetition, because the word *parāk* is used in that sense.

उक्थ्यविच्छेदवचनत्वाच्च ॥४६॥

46. By reason of the text about separation from the *uktyha.*

आग्रयणाद्वा पराक्शब्दस्य देशवाचित्वात्पुनराधेयवत् ॥४७॥

47. On the other hand, from *āgrayaṇa* because the word '*parāk*' denotes space, just as in re-establishment of fire.

विच्छेदः स्तोमसामान्यात् ॥४८॥

48. The separation, by reason, of the unity of the song.

उक्थ्याऽग्निष्टोमसंयोगादस्तुतशस्त्रः स्यात्सतिहि संस्थान्यत्वम् ॥४९॥

49. *Ukthya* being connected with *agniṣṭoma*, it is without praise songs, because if it be with them, then there would be different series of songs.

संस्तुतशस्त्रो वा तदङ्गत्वात् ॥५०॥

50. On the other hand, with the praise songs by reason of their being the parts.

लिङ्गदर्शनाच्च ॥५१॥

51. And by seeing the *liṅga*.

वचनात्संस्थान्यत्वम् ॥५२॥

52. Under a text, it would come under a different *saṃsthā*.

अभावादतिरात्रेषुगृह्यते ॥५३॥

53. By reason of the absence, it is taken in *atirātra*.

अन्वयो वानारभ्य विधानात् ॥५४॥

54. On the other hand, it is connected by reason of its being an *anārabhyavidhi* (belonging to no particular context.)

चतुर्थेचतुर्थेऽहन्यहीनस्य गृह्यतइत्यभ्यासेनप्रतीयेत भोजनवत् ॥५५॥

55. "Of the sacrifice that lasts for more than a day, it is taken on the 4th day, 4th day"; it appears to be so from repetition like the food.

अपि वा सङ्ख्यावत्त्वान्नानाहीनेषु गृह्यते पक्षवदेक स्मिन्संख्यार्थभावात् ॥५६॥

56. On the other hand, in several *ahīna* sacrifices it is to be taken by reason of the number like a fortnight; because in one there cannot be the same object of the number.

भोजने तत्सङ्ख्यं स्यात् ॥५७॥

57. In the case of food, that number is proper.

जगत्साम्नि सामाभावादृक्तः सामतदाख्यं स्यात् ॥५८॥

58. In a *jagat* song; it being nowhere in the songs, is a song after the *ṛk* and is socalled.

उभयसाम्नि नैमित्तिकं विकल्पेन समत्वात्स्यात् ॥५९॥

59. In a sacrifice which has double songs, there is a cause by option because of the equality.

मुख्येन वा नियम्येत ॥६०॥

60. On the other hand, it may be regulated by the principal.

निमित्तविघाताद्वा क्रतुयुक्तस्य कर्म स्यात् ॥६१॥

61. On the other hand, by reason of the disappearance of the cause, the action is of the sacrifice.

ऐन्द्रवायवस्याग्रवचनादादितः प्रतिकर्षः स्यात् ॥६२॥

62. Under the text that *aindravāyava* cups are first, they should be displaced and taken first of all.

अपि वा धर्माविशेषात्तद्धर्माणां स्वस्थाने प्रकरणादग्रत्वमुच्यते ॥६३॥

63. On the other hand, by reason of the procedure being general, the procedure of that will be at its own place; by reason of the context, it is called first.

धारासंयोगाच्च ॥६४॥

64. And by reason of the connection with '*dhārā*'.

कामसंयोगे तु वचनादादितः प्रतिकर्षः स्यात् ॥६५॥

65. On the other hand, when desire is connected under the text, they will be displaced and brought first.

तद्देशानां वाऽग्रसंयोगात्तद्युक्तं कामशास्त्रं स्यान्नित्यसंयोगात् ॥६६॥

66. On the other hand, by reason of being the first in their order, the text laying down the desire is along with it; because it is permanently connected.

परेषु चाग्रशब्दः पूर्ववत्स्यात्तदादिषु ॥६७॥

67. And the word 'first' in the subsequent ones, like the preceding (*adhikaraṇa*) in that &c.

प्रतिकर्षो वा नित्यार्थेनाग्रस्य तदसंयोगात् ॥६८॥

68. On the other hand, there is displacement; the object is permanently connected with the 'first', by reason of that being unconnected.

प्रतिकर्षञ्च दर्शयति ॥६९॥

69. And the displacement is shown.

पुरस्तादैन्द्रवायवस्याग्रस्य कृतदेशत्वात् ॥७०॥

70. Before *aindravāyava*, by reason of making the first as the place.

तुल्यधर्मत्वाच्च ॥७१॥

71. By reason of having the equal characteristics.

तथा च लिङ्गदर्शनम् ॥७२॥

72. And similarly there is an indicative mark.

सादनं चापि शेषत्वात् ॥७३॥

73. And the remnants also by reason of being the *śeṣa*.

लिङ्ग दर्शनाच्च ॥७४॥

74. And by seeing the force of the text.

प्रदानं चापि सादनवत् ॥७५॥

75. And the gift is also like the remnants.

न वा प्रधानत्वाच्छेषत्वात्सादनंतथा ॥७६॥

76. Not so; by reason of being the principal and by reason of the subordinate, the remnants are transposed.

त्र्यनीकायां न्यायोक्तेष्वाम्नानं गुणार्थं स्यात् ॥७७॥

77. In *tryanīkā* when it is properly ordained, it is by way of description of quality.

अपि वा वाऽहर्गणेष्वग्निवत्समानविधानं स्यात् ॥७८॥

78. On the other hand in the sacrifice lasting for days like the establishment of fire, it is of equal command.

द्वादशाहस्य व्यूढसमूढत्वं पृष्ठवत्समानविधानं स्यात् ॥७९॥

79. The *vyūḍha* and *samūḍha* of *dvādaśāha* are of equal commands, like the *pṛṣṭha* songs.

व्यूढो वा लिङ्गदर्शनात्समूढविकारः स्यात् ॥८०॥

80. On the other hand *vyūḍha* is the modified form of *samūḍha*, by seeing the *liṅga*.

कामसंयोगात् ॥८१॥

81. By reason of the connection with the desire.

तस्योभयथा प्रवृत्तिरैककर्म्यात् ॥८२॥

82. Its application is in both ways, because being one act.

एकादशिनीवत् त्र्यनीका परिवृत्तिः स्यात् ॥८३॥

83. Like *ekādaśinī*, *tryanīkā* is to be repeated.

स्वस्थानविवृद्धिर्वाऽह्नामप्रत्यक्षसङ्ख्यत्वात् ॥८४॥

84. On the other hand, they should be done on the *svasthānavivṛddhi* principle, because the number of the days have not been laid down.

पृष्ठ्यावृतौ चाग्रयणस्य दर्शनात् त्रयस्त्रिंशे परिवृत्तौ पुनरैन्द्रवायवः स्यात् ॥८५॥

85. On the other repetition of the songs, by reason of seeing the *āgrayaṇa* and on reversal of 33 again, there are *indravāyava* cups.

वचनात्परिवृत्तिरैकादशिनेषु ॥८६॥

86. There is a repetition in *ekādaśinī* under a text.

लिङ्गदर्शनाच्च ॥८७॥

87. And by seeing the *liṅga.*

छन्दोव्यतिक्रमाद्व्यूढे भक्षपवमानपरिधिकपालस्यमन्त्राणां यथोत्पत्ति-वचनमूहवत्स्यात् ॥८८॥

88. By reason of the change of metre in *vyūḍha* , the mantras belonging to *bhakṣa, pavamāna, paridhi* and *kapāla* should be read as original, like *ūha.*

End of Pāda 5

***

PĀDA 6

एकर्चस्थानि यज्ञे स्युः स्वाध्यायवत् ॥१॥

1. In a sacrifice in one *ṛk* verse, just as in reading.

तृचे वा लिङ्गदर्शनात् ॥२॥

2. On the other hand, in a group of 3 *ṛk* verses, by reason of seeing the force of the text.

स्वर्दृशं प्रतिवीक्षणं कालमात्रं परार्थत्वात् ॥३॥

3. Waiting for *svardṛśa*; it is a time limit by reason of its being for the object of another.

पृष्ठ्यस्य युगपद्विधेरेकाहवद्द्विसामत्वम् ॥४॥

4. By reason of simultaneous *vidhi* in connection with *pṛṣṭhya*, it has double simultaneous song like *ekāha.*

विभक्ते वा समस्तविधानात्तद्विभागेविप्रतिषिद्धिम् ॥५॥

5. On the other hand, in division by reason of laying down the entirety; in that division there is a prohibition.

समासस्त्वेकादशिनेषु तत्प्रकृतित्वात् ॥६॥

6. On the other hand, collectively in *ekādaśinī*, by reason of that being in the model sacrifice.

विहारप्रतिषेधाच्च ॥७॥

7. And by reason of the prohibition of sacrificing an animal on each day.

श्रुतितो वा लोकवद्विभागः स्यात् ॥८॥

8. On the other hand, by reason of the text, there is a division just as in the ordinary life.

विहारप्रकृतित्वाच्च ॥९॥

9. And by reason of the sacrifice of each animal on each day in the model sacrifice.

विशये च तदासत्तेः ॥१०॥

10. And in a doubt, by reason of the compliance with that.

त्रयस्तथेति चेत् ॥११॥

11. If you say, "three similarly".

न समत्वात्प्रयाजवत् ॥१२॥

12. Not so, by reason of equality as in *prayāja* offering.

सर्वपृष्ठे पृष्ठशब्दात्तेषां स्यादेकदेशत्वं पृष्ठस्य कृतदेशत्वात् ॥१३॥

13. By reason of the word '*pṛṣṭha*' in all *pṛṣṭha*, they are to be in one place of the *pṛṣṭha* because it is so directed.

विधेस्तु विप्रकर्षः स्यात् ॥१४॥

14. On the other hand, there will be separation of space by reason of the command.

वैरूपसामा क्रतुसंयोगात् त्रिवृद्वदेकसामा स्यात् ॥१५॥

15. The *vairūpa* song pertains to the whole sacrifice, just as *trivṛt* belongs to the sacrifice.

पृष्ठार्थे वा प्रकृतिलिङ्गसंयोगात् ॥१६॥

16. On the other hand, it is for the *pṛṣṭha*, by reason of the connection with the indicative power of the model sacrifice.

त्रिवृद्विदिति चेत् ॥१७॥

17. If you say, "like *trivṛt*."

न प्रकृतावकृत्स्नसंयोगात् ॥१८॥

18. Not so; by reason of their being not connected with the whole in the model sacrifice.

विधित्वान्नेति चेत् ॥१९॥

19. If you say "not so, by reason of its being a command".

स्याद्विशये तन्न्यायत्वात्कर्माविभागात् ॥२०॥

20. It is so in a case of doubt, by reason of its being proper and the unity of the action.

प्रकृतेश्चाविकारात् ॥२१॥

21. And by reason of the model sacrifice being not changed.

त्रिवृतिसङ्ख्यात्वेन सर्वसंख्याविकारः स्यात् ॥२२॥

22. In *trivṛt* with the number, the modification of the whole is meant.

स्तोमस्य वा तल्लिङ्गत्वात् ॥२३॥

23. On the other hand, of the song by reason of the inference from the text.

उभयसाम्नि विश्वजिद्वद्विभागः स्यात् ॥२४॥

24. In double songs, like *viśvajit* there is a separation.

पृष्ठार्थे वाऽतदर्थत्वात् ॥२५॥

25. On the other hand, in the object of the *pṛṣṭha* by reason of its being not for it.

लिङ्गदर्शनाच्च ॥२६॥

26. And by seeing the *liṅga*.

पृष्ठे रसभोजनमावृत्ते संस्थिते त्रयस्त्रिंशेऽहनि स्यात्तदानन्तर्य्यात्प्रकृतिवत् ॥२७॥

27. In a *pṛṣṭha* when there is a repetition of the eating of the liquid, it is to be done on the day of thirty-three by reason of that being at the end of it as in the model sacrifice.

अन्ते वा कृतकालत्वात् ॥२८॥

28. On the other hand, at the end, by reason of the time (of the tune).

अभ्यासे च तदभ्यासः कर्मणः पुनः प्रयोगात् ॥२९॥

29. And on repetition, there is its repetition by reason of the application of the act again.

अन्ते वा कृतकालत्वात् ॥३०॥

30. At the end, by reason of the time limit.

आवृत्तिस्तु व्यवाये कालभेदात् स्यात् ॥३१॥

31. On the other hand, there is repetition in an interval by reason of the separaton of time.

मधु न दीक्षिता ब्रह्मचारित्वात् ॥३२॥

32. The initiated ones do not partake of honey by reason of celibacy.

प्राश्येत यज्ञार्थत्वात् ॥३३॥

33. He should eat, by reason of its being for the sacrifice.

मानसमहरन्तरं स्याद्भेदव्यपदेशात् ॥३४॥

34. *Mānasa* is a separate day, by reason of marking the difference.

तेन च संस्तवात् ॥३५॥

35. And by reason of the praise by it.

अहरन्ताच्च परेण चोदना ॥३६॥

36. And the command is further from the last day.

पक्षे सङ्ख्या सहस्रवत् ॥३७॥

37. In that view, the number is like the thousand.

अहरङ्गं वांशुवच्चोदनाभावात् ॥३८॥

38. It is a part of the day like *aṅśu*, by reason of there being no command.

दशमविसर्गवचनाच्च ॥३९॥

39. And by reason of the completing sentence of the 10th day.

दशमेऽहनीति च तद्गुणशास्त्रात् ॥४०॥

40. And in the 10th, there is day by reason of that being ordained as subordinate.

सङ्ख्यासामञ्जस्यात् ॥४१॥

41. And by reason of the fitness of the number.

पश्वतिरेके चैकस्य भावात् ॥४२॥

42. And in the increase of animals, by reason of the increase of one.

स्तुतिव्यपदेशमङ्गेनविप्रतिषिद्धं व्रतवत् ॥४३॥

43. Differentiation based on the praise by the praise of the part is prohibited, just as in the *mahāvrata.*

वचनादतदन्तत्वम् ॥४४॥

44. By reason of the text, it is not its end.

सत्रमेकः प्रकृतिवत् ॥४५॥

45. One should perform a *satra* just as in *prakṛti.*

वचनात्तु बहूनां स्यात् ॥४६॥

46. By reason of the text, it is of many.

अपदेशः स्यादिति चेत् ॥४७॥

47. 'It is naming' if you say.

नैकव्यपदेशात् ॥४८॥

48. Not so, by reason of naming one.

सन्निवापञ्च दर्शयति ॥४९॥

49. And collection of fire at one place shows.

बहूनामिति चैकस्मिन्विशेषवचनं व्यर्थम् ॥५०॥

50. And the special text 'of many' in one, will be meaningless.

अन्ये स्युर्ऋत्विजःप्रकृतिवत् ॥५१॥

51. Others should be the priests just as in the model sacrifice.

अपि वा यजमानाः स्युर्ऋत्विजामभिधानसंयोगात्तेषां स्याद्यजमानत्वम् ॥५२॥

52. On the other hand, the sacrificers shall act by reason of the priests' name being connected. Theirs is the position of the sacrificers.

कर्तृसंस्कारो वचनादाधातृवदिति चेत् ॥५३॥

53. "It is a purificatory rite of the agent under a text just like one in the establishment of fire" if you say.

स्याद्विशये तन्नयायत्वात्प्रकृतिवत् ॥५४॥

54. It may be in a doubt by reason of its being proper, just as in the model sacrifice.

स्वाम्याख्याः स्युर्गृहपतिवदिति चेत् ॥५५॥

55. "If they mean masters like *gṛhapati*" if you say.

न प्रसिद्धग्रहणत्वादसंयुक्तस्य तद्धर्मेण ॥५६॥

56. Not so, by reason of the well-known signification; it is not associated with the duties of that.

दीक्षिताऽदीक्षितव्यपदेशश्च नोपपद्यतेऽर्थयोर्नित्यभावित्वात् ॥५७॥

57. And the distinction of the initiated and the uninitiated does not arise by reason of the objects being permanently in existence.

अदक्षिणत्वाच्च ॥५८॥

58. And by reason of the absence of fee.

द्वादशाहस्य सत्रत्वमासनोपायिचोदनेन यजमानबहुत्वेन च सत्रशब्दाभिसंयोगात् ॥५९॥

59. The *dvādaśāha* is a *satra* with the text containing *āsana* and *upāyi* and with many sacrificers by reason of their being connected with the word *satra.*

यजतिचोदनादहीनत्वं स्वामिनां चाऽस्थितपरिमाणत्वात् ॥६०॥

60. The *ahīna* is so-called by reason of the text containing *yajati* and by reason of the numberless sacrificers.

अहीने दक्षिणाशास्त्रं गुणत्वात्प्रत्यहं कर्मभेदः स्यात् ॥६१॥

61. In an *ahīna*, the rule as to payment of fee is daily, by reason of its being subordinate, because the action varies everyday.

सर्वस्य वैककर्म्यात् ॥६२॥

62. On the other hand, of the whole by reason of the unity of the act.

पृषदाज्यवद्वाऽह्नां गुणशास्त्रं स्यात् ॥६३॥

63. On the other hand, like *pṛṣadājya*, the days are subordinate.

ज्यौतिष्टोम्यस्तु दक्षिणाः सर्वासामेककर्मत्वात्प्रकृतिवत्तस्मान्नासां विकारः स्यात् ॥६४॥

64. On the other hand, the fee of the *jyotiṣṭoma* is of the whole by reason of the unity of the act, just as in the model sacrifice; therefore there modification is not (allowed).

द्वादशाहे तु वचनात्प्रत्यहं दक्षिणाभेदस्तत्प्रकृतित्वात्परेषु तासां संख्याविकारः स्यात् ॥६५॥

65. In a *dvādaśāha* under a text, there is a daily variation of fee, by reason of that being the model of it; in others, there number is modified.

परिक्रयाविभागाद्वा समस्तस्य विकारः स्यात् ॥६६॥

66. On the other hand, by reason of the indivisibility of the hiring, the whole is a modification.

भेदस्तु गुणसंयोगात् ॥६७॥

67. And the variation by reason of the connection with the subordinate.

प्रत्यहं सर्वसंस्कारः प्रकृतिवत्सर्वासां सर्वशेषत्वात् ॥६८॥

68. Every day, the purificatory rite on all just as in the model sacrifice by reason of all being the remainder.

एकार्थत्वान्नेति चेत् ॥६९॥

69. "Not so, by reason of the unity of the object; if you say".

स्यादुत्पत्तौ कालभेदात् ॥७०॥

70. In the origin it is divided, by reason of the difference of time.

विभज्य तु संस्कारवचनाद्द्वादशाहवत् ॥७१॥

71. On the other hand, after division by reason of the text relating to the purificatory rite like *dvādaśāha*.

लिङ्गेन द्रव्यनिर्देशे सर्वत्र प्रत्ययः स्याल्लिङ्गस्य सर्वगामित्वादाग्नेयवत् ॥७२॥

72. When a substance has been pointed out by a mark, it is to be recognised by it because the mark points it out every where as in the establishment of fire.

यावदर्थंवार्थ शेषत्वादल्पेन परिमाणं स्यात्तस्मिंश्च लिङ्गसामर्थ्यम् ॥७३॥

73. On the other hand, in proportion to the object by reason of the accomplishment of the object; there is a limit with the short number; in it, is the power of the mark.

आग्नेये कृत्स्नविधिः ॥७४॥

74. In the *āgneya*, the whole is enjoined.

ऋजीषस्य प्रधानत्वादहर्गणे सर्वस्य प्रतिपत्तिः स्यात् ॥७५॥

75. The soma dregs being principal in the sacrifice lasting for days, the whole is to be used as their final disposal.

वाससि मानोपावहरणे प्रकृतौ सोमस्य वचनात् ॥७६॥

76. By reason of the text about soma in the model sacrifice, the measurement and carrying of it, is in a cloth.

तत्राहर्गणेऽर्थाद्वासःप्रकृतिः स्यात् ॥७७॥

77. In the *ahargaṇa* by reason of the object, there is a different cloth (in compliance with) the model sacrifice.

मानं प्रत्युत्पादयेत्प्रकृतौ तेन दर्शनादुपावहरणस्य ॥७८॥

78. In the model sacrifice, the cloth is procured for measuring the soma creeper; by seeing the same used in carrying it to the sacrificial ground.

हरणे वा श्रुत्यसंयोगादर्थाद्विकृतौ तेन ॥७९॥

79. On the other hand, at the time of carrying it to the sacrificial ground, by reason of there being no mention of it in the text; by reason of the object with it in the modified sacrifice.

END OF PĀDA 6

***

PĀDA 7

पशोरेकहविष्ट्वं समस्तचोदितत्वात् ॥१॥

1. There is one entire offering of the animal by reason of the whole being ordered.

प्रत्यङ्गं वा ग्रहवदङ्गानां पृथक्कल्पनत्वात् ॥२॥

2. On the other hand, every part like the cup by reason of the separate dedication of the parts.

हविर्भेदात्कर्मणोऽभ्यासस्तस्मात्तेभ्योऽवदानं स्यात् ॥३॥

3. By reason of the different offerings there is the repetition of the sacrifice, therefore from them also there must be a cutting off.

आज्यभागवद्वा निर्देशात्परिसंख्यास्यात् ॥४॥

4. On the other hand, like ghee offering by reason of the pointing out, there is an implied prohibition.

तेषां वाद्व्यवदानत्वं विवक्षन्नभिनिर्दिशेत्पशोः पञ्चावदानत्वात् ॥५॥

5. On the other hand, the text appears to be laid down about their double cutting; because the animal is to be cut off into five parts.

अंसशिरोनूकसक्थिप्रतिषेधश्च तदन्यपरिसङ्ख्यानेऽनर्थकः स्यात्प्रदानत्वात्तेषां निरवदानप्रतिषेधः स्यात् ॥६॥

6. If the other parts are impliedly prohibited, the prohibition relating to shoulder, head, vertebral column and thigh is meaningless; by being the objects of gifts, their cutting off is prohibited.

अपि वा परिसङ्ख्या स्यादनवदानीयशब्दत्वात् ॥७॥

7. On the other hand, it is *parisaṃkhyā* by reason of the word 'not to be cut off'.

अब्राह्मणे च दर्शनात् ॥८॥

8. And by seeing in non-Brāhmaṇas.

श्रुताश्रुतोपदेशाच्च तेषामुत्सर्गवदयज्ञशेषत्वं ॥९॥

9. And by reason of laying down 'boiled' and 'unboiled'; there will be nothing left in the sacrifice like the *pātnīvata* offering.

इज्याशेषात्स्विष्टकृदिज्येत प्रकृतिवत् ॥१०॥

10. From the parts ordained for the sacrifice, the *sviṣṭakṛt* offering should be made as in the model sacrifice.

त्र्यङ्गैर्वा शरवद्विकारः स्यात् ॥११॥

11. On the other hand, there will be a modification with three parts just like reed.

अध्यूध्नी होतुस्त्र्यङ्गवदिडाभक्षविकारः स्यात् ॥१२॥

12. The *adhyūdhnī* is the modification of *iḍā* food of the Hotā priest.

शेषे वासमवैति तस्माद्रथवन्नियमः स्यात् ॥१३॥

13. On the other hand, it is united in the subordinate; therefore the rule is like that relating to the chariot.

अशास्त्रत्वात्तु नैवं स्यात् ॥१४॥

14. On the other hand, it cannot be so, by reason of there being no prescribed rule.

अपि वा दानमात्रं स्याद्भक्षशब्दानभिसम्बन्धात् ॥१५॥

15. On the other hand, it may be a donation because there is no connection with the word 'food'.

दातुस्त्वविद्यमानत्वादिडाभक्षविकारः स्याच्छेषं प्रत्यविशिष्टत्वात् ॥१६॥

16. On the other hand, by reason of the absence of the donor, it is in lieu of *iḍā* food because in the remnants, there is no speciality.

अग्नीधश्च वनिष्ठुरध्यूध्नीवत् ॥१७॥

17. And *vaniṣṭu* is of *agnīdha* like *adhyudhnī.*

अप्राकृतत्वान्मैत्रावरुणस्याभक्षत्वम् ॥१८॥

18. There is no food for *maitrāvaruṇa* by reason of its being absent in the model sacrifice.

स्याद्वा होत्रध्वर्य्युविकारत्वात्तयो कर्माभिसम्बन्धात् ॥१९॥

19. On the other hand there is, by reason of his being an assistant of *hotā* and *adhvaryu,* because they are connected with the act.

द्विभागः स्याद्द्विकर्मत्वात् ॥२०॥

20. There are two shares, by reason of there being double work.

एकत्वाद्वैकभागः स्याद्भागस्याश्रुतिभूतत्वात् ॥२१॥

21. On the other hand, being one he is entitled to one share, there being no text for assigning his shares.

प्रतिप्रस्थातुश्च वपाश्रपणात् ॥२२॥

22. And of the *pratiprasthātā* by reason of boiling the fat.

अभक्षो वा कर्मभेदात्तस्याः सर्वप्रदानत्वात् ॥२३॥

23. On the other hand, he has no share in the food by reason of his separate work and of there being no residue.

विकृतौ प्राकृतस्य विधेर्ग्रहणात्पुनः श्रुतिरनर्थिका स्यात् ॥२४॥

24. In the modified sacrifice, by reason of the command of the model sacrifice, the repetition is a tautology (meaningless).

अपि वाऽऽग्नेयवद्द्विशब्दत्वं स्यात् ॥२५॥

25. On the other hand, it is like the establishment of fire by reason of the double repetition.

न वा शब्दपृथक्त्वात् ॥२६॥

26. On the other hand, it is not so by reason of the difference of the text.

अधिकं वार्थवत्त्वात्स्यादर्थवादगुणाभावेवचनादविकारे तेषु हि तादर्थ्यं स्यादपूर्वत्वात् ॥२७॥

27. On the other hand, it is an additional sacrifice by reason of its being for the purpose; there being no statement of facts and praise, by reason of the text it remains unchanged: in this state, by reason of its being extraordinary.

प्रतिषेधः स्यादिति चेत् ॥२८॥

28. "It is a prohibition" if you say.

नाश्रुतत्वात् ॥२९॥

29. Not so, by reason of its being not ordained.

अग्रहणादिति चेत् ॥३०॥

30. 'By not accepting' if you say.

न तुल्यत्वात् ॥३१॥

31. Not so, by reason of the equality.

तथा तद्ग्रहणे स्यात् ॥३२॥

32. Similarly it will be in the acceptance thereof.

अपूर्वतां तु दर्शयेद्ग्रहणस्यार्थवत्त्वात् ॥३३॥

33. On the other hand, it may show an extraordinary principle; by reason of the acceptance being for the purpose.

ततोऽपि यावदुक्तं स्यात् ॥३४॥

34. Therefore, there are as many as are mentioned.

स्विष्टकृद्भक्षप्रतिषेधः स्यात्तुल्यकारणत्वात् ॥३५॥

35. There is a prohibition of the eating of the *sviṣṭakṛt* remnants, by reason of the equal causes.

अप्रतिषेधो वा दर्शनादिडायां स्यात् ॥३६॥

36. On the other hand, there is no prohibition, by seeing it in the case of *iḍā*.

प्रतिषेधो वा विधिपूर्वस्य दर्शनात् ॥३७॥

37. On the other hand, it is a prohibition by seeing the previous injunction.

शंय्विडान्तत्वे विकल्पः स्यात्परेषु पत्न्यनुयाजप्रतिषेधोऽनर्थकः स्यात् ॥३८॥

38. There is an option in the end of *śaṃyu* and *iḍā*; in the latter part, the prohibition as to *patnī* and *anuyāja* will be meaningless.

नित्यानुवादो वा कर्मणः स्यादशब्दत्वात् ॥३९॥

39. On the other hand, it is a permanent statement of facts, because the action (subsequent to *śaṃyuvāka*) is nowhere ordained.

प्रतिषेधार्थवत्त्वाच्चोत्तरस्य परस्तात्प्रतिषेधः स्यात् ॥४०॥

40. By reason of the prohibition being for a purpose, subsequent acts of the second are prohibited.

प्राप्तेर्वा पूर्वस्य वचनादतिक्रमः स्यात् ॥४१॥

41. On the other hand, the first is meant under the text, (otherwise) there will be a transgression.

प्रतिषेधस्य त्वरायुक्तत्वात्तस्य च नान्यदेशत्वम् ॥४२॥

42. The prohibition being connected with *tvarā* (quick), it has no other place for it.

उपसत्सु यावदुक्तमकर्म स्यात् ॥४३॥

43. In *upasats*, as much said should not be done.

स्रोवेण वाऽगुणत्वाच्छेपप्रतिषेधः स्यात् ॥४४॥

44. On the other hand, with the text pertaining to a ladle by reason of its being subordinate, the rest is prohibited.

अप्रतिषेधं वा प्रतिषिध्यप्रतिप्रसवात् ॥४५॥

45. On the other hand, not prohibited, after prohibiting, by reason of the counter-command.

अनिज्या वा शेषस्य मुख्यदेवतानभीज्यत्वात् ॥४६॥

46. On the other hand, the rest is not to be performed because there is no offering of ghee to the principal deities.

अवभृथे बर्हिषः प्रतिषेधाच्छेषकर्म स्यात् ॥४७॥

47. In the sacrifice by reason of the prohibition of *barhi*, the rest of the action is to be performed.

आज्यभागयोर्वा गुणत्वाच्छेषप्रतिषेधः स्यात् ॥४८॥

48. By reason of the ghee offerings being subordinate, the rest is prohibited.

प्रयाजानां त्वेकदेशप्रतिषेधाद्वाक्यशेषत्वं तस्मान्नित्यानुवादः स्यात् ॥४९॥

49. By reason of the prohibition of a part of the *prayāja* offerings, there is subordination of sentences; it is, therefore, a permanent statement of facts.

आज्यभागयोर्ग्रहणं नित्यानुवादो वा गृहमेधीयवत्स्यात् ॥५०॥

50. The acceptance of the ghee offering is by way of statement of facts like a *gṛhamedhīya.*

विरोधिनामेकश्रुतौ नियमः स्याद्ग्रहणस्यार्थवत्त्वाच्छरवच्च श्रुतितो विशिष्टत्वात् ॥५१॥

51. When there are two contradictories in one text, it is a restrictive rule, by reason of the transference being for a purpose like the reed and by reason of the special feature of the text.

उभयप्रदेशान्नेतिचेत् ॥५२॥

52. "Not so, by reason of the transfer of both" if you say.

शरेष्वपीति चेत् ॥५३॥

53. "In the reeds also" if you say.

विरोध्यग्रहणात्तथा शरेष्विति चेत् ॥५४॥

54. "By reason of not accepting the contradictories, the same is the case with the *śara*" if you say.

तथेतरस्मिन् ॥५५॥

55. Similarly in the others.

श्रुत्यानर्थक्यमिति चेत् ॥५६॥

56. "The text is meaningless" if you say.

ग्रहणस्यार्थवत्त्वादुभयोरप्रतिपत्तिः स्यात् ॥५७॥

57. By reason of the acceptance being for the purpose, there cannot be an application of both.

सर्वासाञ्च गुणानामर्थवत्त्वादग्रहणमप्रवृत्ते स्यात् ॥५८॥

58. And by acceptance of all, by reason of the significance of the subordinate acts there is no application.

अधिकं स्यादिति चेत् ॥५९॥

59. "There is a combination" if you say.

नार्थाभावात् ॥६०॥

60. Not so, by reason of the want of purpose.

तथैकार्थविकारे प्राकृतस्याप्रवृत्तिः प्रवृत्तौ हि विकल्पः स्यात् ॥६१॥

61. Similarly where one object is modified, the thing of the model sacrifice is suspended; because in its application, there is a dilemma.

यावच्छ्रुतीति चेत् ॥६२॥

62. 'Just as much laid down' if you say.

न प्रकृतावशब्दत्वात् ॥६३॥

63. Not so, by reason of there being no such direction in the model sacrifice.

विकृतौ त्वनियमः स्यात्पृषदाज्यवद्ग्रहणस्य गुणार्थत्वादुभयोश्चप्रदिष्टत्वाद्गुणशास्त्रं यदेति स्यात् ॥६४॥

64. On the other hand, in the modified sacrifice there is no rule like the mixture of curd and ghee by reason of the acceptance being for the purpose of the quality and by reason of both being laid down: when the laying down the quality of the subordinate act is (set aside).

ऐकार्थ्याद्वा नियम्येत श्रुतितो विशिष्टत्वात् ॥६५॥

65. On the other hand, it is a restrictive rule by reason of there being one object and by reason of its being specialised by the text.

विरोधित्वाच्च लोकवत् ॥६६॥

66. And by reason of there being contradictory as in the ordinary life.

क्रतोश्चतद्गुणत्वात् ॥६७॥

67. And of the sacrifice, by reason of its being of the same quality.

विरोधिनाञ्च तच्छ्रुतावशब्दत्वाद्विकल्पः स्यात् ॥६८॥

68. And of the contradictories being not mentioned, there is an option.

पृषदाज्ये समुच्चयाद्ग्रहणस्य गुणार्थत्वम् ॥६९॥

69. In *pṛṣadājya* by reason of the combination, because there the acceptance is for the object of the quality.

यद्यपिचतुरवत्तीति तु नियमे नोपपद्यते ॥७०॥

70. On the other hand, 'though *caturavattī*' does not arise in the view that it is a restrictive rule.

क्रत्वन्तरे वा तन्न्यायत्वात्कर्मभेदात् ॥७१॥

71. On the other hand, in another sacrifice by reason of its being proper; because it is a different act.

यथाश्रुतीति चेत् ॥७२॥

72. 'According to the text' if you say.

न चोदनैकत्वात् ॥७३॥

73. Not so, by reason of there being one injunction.

END OF PĀDA 7

***

PĀDA 8

प्रतिषेधः प्रदेशेऽनारभ्यविधाने च प्राप्तप्रतिषिद्धत्वाद्वि कल्पःस्यात् ॥१॥

1. The prohibition in the case of the scattered text and the transferred text is optional by reason of the transferred prohibition.

अर्थप्राप्तवदिति चेत् ॥२॥

2. "Like the attaining of the object" if you say.

न तुल्यहेतुत्वादुभयं शब्दलक्षणम् ॥३॥

3. Not so, by reason of the equal causes; both are based on the word.

अपि तु वाक्यशेषः स्यादन्याय्यत्वाद्विकल्पस्य विधीनामेकदेशः स्यात् ॥४॥

4. On the other hand, it is a supplementary sentence by reason of the impropriety of the option; the command is only partial.

अपूर्वे चार्थवादः स्यात् ॥५॥

5. In the case of *apūrva*, it is a recommendation.

शिष्ट्वा तु प्रतिषेधः स्यात् ॥६॥

6. On the other hand, after having laid down, there is prohibition.

न चेदन्यं प्रकल्पयेत्प्रक्लृप्तावर्थवादः स्यादानर्थक्यात्परसामर्थ्याच्च ॥७॥

7. If it lays down another, on so laying down, it is by way of *arthavāda* by reason of its being meaningless and dependent on the force of another.

पूर्वैश्च तुल्यकालत्वात् ॥८॥

8. And with the preceding ones, by reason of equal time.

उपवादश्च तद्वत् ॥९॥

9. And the calumny is like it.

प्रतिषेधादकर्मेति चेत् ॥१०॥

10. "By reason of the prohibition, it is non-act" if you say.

न शब्दपूर्वत्वात् ॥११॥

11. Not so, by reason of its being based on the word.

दीक्षितस्य दानहोमपाकप्रतिषेधोऽविशेषात्सर्वदानहोम पाकप्रतिषेधः स्यात् ॥१२॥

12. The prohibition relating to donation, the sacrifice, and cooking by an initiated is a prohibition of the entire donation, sacrifice and cooking by reason of there being nothing special.

अक्रतुयुक्तानां वा धर्मः स्यात्क्रतोः प्रत्यक्षशिष्टत्वात् ॥१३॥

13. On the other hand, it is of those that do not pertain to the sacrifice, because as to those of the sacrifice, it is directly laid down.

तस्य वाप्यानुमानिकमविशेषात् ॥१४॥

14. On the other hand, the inferential one, by reason of there being nothing special.

अपि तु वाक्यशेषत्वादितरपर्य्युदासः स्यात्प्रतिषेधे विकल्पः स्यात् ॥१५॥

15. On the other hand, by reason of being a supplementary text, it is a *paryudāsa*; of the other in a prohibition it is optional.

अविशेषेण यच्छास्त्रमन्याय्यत्वाद्विकल्पस्य तत्सन्दिग्ध माराद्विशेषशिष्ट स्यात् ॥१६॥

16. That which is generally laid down, by reason of the impropriety of the option, is doubtful and inapplicable; the special laid down applies.

अप्रकरणे तु यच्छास्त्रं विशेषे श्रूयमाणमविकृतमाज्य भागवत्प्राकृतप्रतिषेधार्थम् ॥१७॥

17. On the other hand, what is laid down with reference to no particular context and is heard in connection with any particular act, it is unmodified like the ghee offerings and is with a view to prohibit the subordination to the model sacrifice.

विकारे तु तदर्थं स्यात् ॥१८॥

18. On the other hand, in a modification with that object.

वाक्यशेषो वा क्रतुना ग्रहणात्स्यादनारभ्यविधानस्य ॥१९॥

19. On the other hand, it is a supplementary sentence by reason of its application in a sacrifice and by reason of the scattered injunction.

मन्त्रेष्ववाक्यशेषत्वं गुणोपदेशात्स्यात् ॥२०॥

20. On the other hand, in the mantras, there is no subordination of sentence by reason of laying down the quality.

आनाम्नाते च दर्शनात् ॥२१॥

21. And by seeing in those also which are not laid down.

प्रतिषेधाच्च ॥२२॥

22. And by reason of the prohibition.

अग्न्यतिग्राह्यस्य विकृतावुपदेशादप्रवृत्तिः स्यात् ॥२३॥

23. There is non-application of the fire and the cups in the modified sacrifice by reason of the direct injunction.

मासि ग्रहणञ्च तद्वत् ॥२४॥

24. And the practice every month is like it.

ग्रहणं वा तुल्यत्वात् ॥२५॥

25. On the other hand, borrowing by reason of the equality.

लिङ्गदर्शनाच्च ॥२६॥

26. And by seeing the force of the text.

ग्रहणं समानविधानं स्यात् ॥२७॥

27. And the borrowing is of an equal *vidhi.*

मासिग्रहणमभ्यासप्रतिषेधार्थम् ॥२८॥

28. And borrowing in a month is with the object of prohibiting the repetition.

उत्पत्तितादर्थ्याच्चातुरवत्तं प्रधानस्य होमसंयोगादधिकमाज्यमतुल्यत्वाल्लोकवदुत्पत्तेर्गुणभूतत्वात् ॥२९॥

29. The origin being for it, the quartering is of the principal because it is connected with the sacrifice. The ghee is in excess by reason of the unequality just as in ordinary life, their origin being subordinate.

तत्संस्कारश्रुतेश्च ॥३०॥

30. And by reason of hearing as to their being purificatory.

ताभ्यां वा सह स्विष्टकृतः सकृत्त्वे द्विरभिधारणेन तदाप्तिवचनात् ॥३१॥

31. On the other hand with them, in one of *svisṭakṛtaḥ* with sprinkling of ghee twice, by reason of the text for securing it.

तुल्यवच्चाभिधाय सर्वेषु भक्त्यनुक्रमणात् ॥३२॥

32. Having mentioned the equal division in all by reason of the enumeration of the portions.

साप्तदश्यवन्नियम्येत ॥३३॥

33. Like the 17, there is the rule.

हविषो वा गुणभूतत्वात्तथाभूतविवक्षा स्यात् ॥३४॥

34. On the other hand, the offering being subordinate, there is a desire of the application in that state.

पुरोडाशाभ्यामित्याधिकृतानां पुरोडाशयोरुपदेशस्तच्छ्रुतित्वाद्वैश्यस्तोमवत् ॥३५॥

35. To those who are entitled under a text with the "two *puroḍāśa* cakes" it is a direction about the two *puroḍāśa* cakes by reason of the text to that effect like the *vaiśyastoma.*

न त्वनित्याधिकारोऽस्ति विधौ नित्येनसम्बन्ध स्तस्मादवाक्यशेषत्वम् ॥३६॥

36. Not so, it is not a permanent right; in the injunction there is a permanent connection, therefore it is not a supplementary sentence.

सति च नैकदेशेन कर्तुः प्रधानभूतत्वात् ॥३७॥

37. And in the case of its being so, it is not so with a portion by reason of the agent being the principal.

कृत्स्नत्वात्तु तथा स्तोमे ॥३८॥

38. On the other hand, by reason of the entirety in a song.

कर्त्तुः स्यादिति चेत् ॥३९॥

39. "It is of the agent" if you say.

न गुणार्थत्वात्प्राप्ते न चोपदेशार्थः ॥४०॥

40. Not so, by reason of his being for the subordinate act; he is not for the purpose of direction.

कर्मणोस्तु प्रकरणे तन्नयायत्वाद्गुणानां लिङ्गेन कालशास्त्रं स्यात् ॥४१॥

41. On the other hand, of the two acts, in the context by reason of the propriety, with the mark of the subordinate act, it is ordaining of time.

यदि तु सान्नाय्यं सोमयाजिनो न ताभ्यां समवायोस्ति विभक्तकालत्वात् ॥४२॥

42. On the other hand, if the soma sacrificers offer milk then there is no connection with the two cakes by reason of the divided time.

अपि वा विहितत्वाद्गुणार्थायां पुनः श्रुतौ सन्देहे श्रुतिर्द्विदेवतार्था स्याद्यथानभिप्रेतस्तथाऽऽग्नेयो दर्शनादेकदेवते ॥४३॥

43. On the other hand, by reason of being ordained, on hearing it again for the object of the subordinate act, the text is for the object of two deities; though not applicable, yet Āgneya is seen in connection with one deity.

विधिं तु बादरायणः ॥४४॥

44. On the other hand, it is an injunction according to Bādarāyaṇa.

प्रतिषिद्धविज्ञानाद्वा ॥४५॥

45. By reason of knowing the prohibited.

तथा चान्यार्थदर्शनम् ॥४६॥

46. And similarly there is seen another proof.

उपांशुयाजमन्तरा यजतीति हविर्लिङ्गाश्रुतित्वाद्यथाकामी प्रतीयेत ॥४७॥

47. In the text "he makes an *upāṃśuyāga* in the interval", by reason of there being no indication of the offering, it appears that one may offer according to his own will.

ध्रौवाद्वा सर्वसंयोगात् ॥४८॥

48. On the other hand, from the *dhruvā* vessel by reason of its connection with all.

तद्वच्च देवतायां स्यात् ॥४९॥

49. And similarly in the deity.

तान्द्रीणां* प्रकरणात् ॥५०॥

50. By reason of the context of the slow metre.

धर्माद्वा स्यात्प्रजापतिः ॥५१॥

51. Prajāpati is the deity by reason of the characteristic.

देवतायास्त्वनिर्वचनं तत्र शब्दस्येह मृदुत्वं तस्मादिहाधिकारेण ॥५२॥

52. On the other hand, there being no mention of the deity, and there is the softness of the word, so he is to be determined by the right.

विष्णुर्वा स्याद्धौत्राम्नानादमावास्याहविश्च स्याद्धौत्रस्य तत्र दर्शनात् ॥५३॥

53. On the other hand, Viṣṇu is the deity by reason of his being laid down in connection with hotā; and new moon oblation is the offering by reason of seeing hotā there.

अपि वा पौर्णमास्यां स्यात्प्रधानशब्दसंयोगाद्गुणत्वान्मन्त्रो यथा प्रधान स्यात् ॥५४॥

54. On the other hand, on the full moon day by reason of the connection with the principal word, because the mantra is subordinate just as it may become principal.

आनन्तर्य्यञ्च सान्नाय्यस्य पुरोडाशेन दर्शयत्यमावास्या विकारे ॥५५॥

55. And the interval of *sānnāya* is shown by *puroḍāśa* cake in the modification of *amāvāsyā*.

अग्नीषोमविधानात्तु पौर्णमास्यामुभयत्र विधीयते ॥५६॥

---

*In some copies, there is 'तांत्रीणां' which is better; it means "of the context".

56. On the other hand, by reason of laying down *agnīṣoma* in the full moon sacrifice, it is laid down in both.

प्रतिषिद्ध्यविधानाद्वा विष्णुः समानदेशः स्यात् ॥५७॥

57. On the other hand, by laying down after prohibition, (the deity) Viṣṇu is of equal time.

तथा चान्यार्थदर्शनम् ॥५८॥

58. Similarly there is another proof visible.

न चानङ्ग सकृच्छ्रुतावुभयत्र विधीयेतासम्बन्धात् ॥५९॥

59. Nor again the principal once laid down, appertains to both by reason of want of connection.

गुणानां च परार्थत्वात्प्रवृतौ विधिलिङ्गानि दर्शयति ॥६०॥

60. And the subordinate acts being for the object of another, the marks of the injunction are shown in the application.

विकारे चाश्रुतित्वात् ॥६१॥

61. And in the modification, it is not heard.

द्विपुरोडाशायां स्यादन्तरार्थत्वात् ॥६२॥

62. There is in the offering of the two cakes by reason of their being for the interval.

अजामिकरणार्थत्वाच्च ॥६३॥

63. And by reason of its being for not doing the same.

तदर्थमिति चेन्नतत्प्रधानत्वात् ॥६४॥

64. 'It is for it' if you say; it is not so by reason of its being principal.

अशिष्ठेन च सम्बन्धात् ॥६५॥

65. And by reason of the connection with one that is not laid down.

उत्पत्तेस्तु निवेशः स्याद्गुणस्यानुपरोधेनार्थस्य विद्यमानत्वाद्विधानादन्तरार्थस्य नैमित्तिकत्वात्तदभावेऽश्रुतौ स्यात् ॥६६॥

66. On the other hand, by reason of the origin, it is introduced with the uninterrupted connection with the quality, because there exists the object, by reason of laying down the object of interval and by reason of its being causal. In its absence, it is not heard.

उभयोस्तु विधानात् ॥६७॥

67. On the other hand, by reason of laying down in both.

गुणानाञ्च परार्थत्वादुपवेषवद्यदेति स्यात् ॥६८॥

68. And the subordinate parts are for the purpose of others, like *upaveṣa*; when it is, it will happen.

अनपायश्च कालस्य लक्षणं हि पुरोडाशौ ॥६९॥

69. And permanence; two *puroḍāśa* cakes are the characteristics of time.

प्रशंसार्थमजामित्वम् ॥७०॥

70. The absence of similarity is for the purpose of praise.

END OF PĀDA 8

* * *

END OF ADHYĀYA X

ADHYĀYA XI

PĀDA 1

प्रयोजनाभिसम्बन्धात्पृथक् सतांततः स्यादैककर्म्यमेकशब्दाभिसंयोगात् ॥१॥

1. By reason of the connection with the purpose, of the separate individual, there is one fruit by reason of the connection with one sentence.

शेषवद्वा प्रयोजनं प्रतिकर्म विभज्येत ॥२॥

2. On the other hand, like the subordinate acts, the purpose divides each act.

अविधानात्तु नैवं स्यात् ॥३॥

3. On the other hand, it would not be so by reason of not being so ordained

शेषस्य हि परार्थत्वाद्विधानात्प्रतिप्रधानभावः स्यात् ॥४॥

4. The subordinate being for another, by reason of the injunction, there will be a separation of each principal.

अङ्गानान्तु शब्दभेदात्क्रतुवत्स्या *त्फलान्यत्वम् ॥५॥

5. On the other hand, of the parts by reason of the difference of word like a sacrifice, there is separate fruit.

अर्थभेदस्तु तत्राथेहैकार्थ्यदैककर्म्यम् ॥६॥

6. On the other hand, there is a difference of objects; here by reason of the unity of the object, there is unity of act.

शब्दभेदान्नेति चेत् ॥७॥

7. "Not so, by reason of the difference of the text" if you say.

कर्मार्थत्वात्प्रयोगे ताच्छब्द्यं स्यात्तदर्थत्वात् ॥८॥

8. By reason of its being for the act, in the application that word is used because it is for its object.

कर्तृविधेर्नानार्थत्वाद्गुणप्रधानेषु ॥९॥

9. In the subordinate and principal, by reason of the variety of the object of the injunction relating to the agent.

---

*The word 'स्यात्' does not find its place in the Chaukhambha edition.

आरम्भस्य शब्दपूर्वत्वात् ॥१०॥

10. Because any act commenced depends on the text.

एकेनापि समाप्येत कृतार्थत्वाद्यथा क्रत्वन्तरेषु प्राप्तेषुचोत्तरावत्स्यात् ॥११॥

11. With one also, it can be completed by reason of having accomplished the object just as in separate sacrifices and on obtaining like the additional (cows).

फलाभावान्नेति चेत् ॥१२॥

12. "Not so, by reason of the absence of the fruit" if you say.

न कर्मसंयोगात्प्रयोजनमशब्ददोषं स्यात् ॥१३॥

13. Not so, by reason of the connection with the act; the object is not deprived of the fault of the word.

एकशब्द्यादिति चेत् ॥१४॥

14. "By reason of being one word" if you say.

नार्थपृथक्त्वात्समत्वादगुणत्वम् ॥१५॥

15. Not so, by reason of the difference of the object; by reason of the equality, it will not be subsidiary.

विधेस्त्वेकश्रुतित्वादपर्यायविधानान्नित्यवच्छ्रुतभूता भिसंयोगादर्थेन युगपत्प्राप्तेर्यथाप्राप्तं स्वशब्दो निवीतवत्सर्वप्रयोगे प्रवृत्तिः स्यात् ॥१६॥

16. On the other hand, by reason of the injunction based on one text and by not prescribing them alternately and being connected, as they are permanently heard, with the *itikartavyatā* and by reason of securing the object simultaneously, just as obtained, the own text like *nivīta* applies in all proceedings.

तथा कर्मोपदेशत्वात् ॥१७॥

17. And similarly by the direction for the action.

क्रत्वन्तरेषु पुनर्वचनम् ॥१८॥

18. In the other sacrifice, there is another text.

उत्तरास्वश्रुतित्वाद्विशेषाणां कृतार्थत्वात्सं *दोहे यथाकामी प्रतीयेत ॥१९॥

19. In other cows by reason of those being not laid down and by reason of the special being utilised in milking, it appears that he can do according to his desire.

---

*In some editions, it is 'स्व' in place of 'सं'.

कर्मण्यारम्भभाव्यत्वात्कृषिवत्प्रत्यारम्भं फल स्युः ॥२०॥

20. In an act by reason of its commencement, like agriculture every repetition bears fruit.

अधिकारश्च सर्वेषां कार्य्यत्वादुपपद्यते विशेषः ॥२१॥

21. All are entitled; by reason of being an act, the special is obtained.

सकृत्तु स्यात्कृतार्थत्वादङ्गवत् ॥२२॥

22. On the other hand, once by reason of the accomplishment like the parts.

शब्दार्थश्च तथा लोके ॥२३॥

23. And the meaning of the word is also similar in the ordinary life.

अपि वा संप्रयोगे यथाकामी प्रतीयेताश्रुतित्वाद्विधिषु वचनानि स्युः ॥२४॥

24. On the other hand, in the application it appears that one is to act according to his wishes; there is no direction as to the performance once: in connection with the injunction there are texts both ways.

एकशब्द्यात्तथाङ्गेषु ॥२५॥

25. And similarly in the parts, by reason of one text.

लोके कर्माऽर्थलक्षणम् ॥२६॥

26. In the ordinary life, the act is characterised with the object.

क्रियाणामर्थशेषत्वात्प्रत्यक्षतस्तन्निर्वृत्त्याऽपवर्गः स्यात् ॥२७॥

27. Of the action being fully completed with its object, visibly its end is the accomplishment.

धर्ममात्रे त्वदर्शनाच्छब्दार्थेनापवर्गः स्यात् ॥२८॥

28. On the other hand, in the case of *dharma* by reason of the invisible effect, the accomplishment is by compliance with the object of the word.

क्रतुवच्चानुमानेनाभ्यासे फलभूमा स्यात् ॥२९॥

29. Like the sacrifice, by the inference there is excessive fruit in the repetition.

सकृद्वा कारणैकत्वात् ॥३०॥

30. On the other hand, once by reason of the unity of the cause.

परिमाणं चानियमेन स्यात् ॥३१॥

31. And the limit will be without any restrictive rule.

फलस्यारम्भनिर्वृत्तेः क्रतुषु स्यात्फलान्यत्वम् ॥३२॥

32. By reason of the achievement of the fruit; in the sacrifices there is a difference of fruit.

अर्थवांस्तुनैकत्वादभ्यासः स्यादनर्थको यथा भोजनमेकस्मिन्नर्थस्यापरिमाणत्वात्प्रधाने च क्रियार्थत्वादनियमः स्यात् ॥३३॥

33. The repetition is fruitful by reason of the variety of the action; in one (act) it is useless like the food by reason of the unlimited nature of the principal fruit; and by reason of the object of the action there is no restrictive rule.

पृथक्त्वाद्विधितः परिमाणं स्यात् ॥३४॥

34. By reason of the separation, there is a limit under an injunction.

अनभ्यासो वा प्रयोगवचनैकत्वात्सर्वम्ययुगपच्छास्त्रादफलत्वाच्च कर्मणः स्यात्क्रियार्थत्वात् ॥३५॥

35. On the other hand, there is no repetition by reason of the unity of the text for application; all are simulteneously laid down and by reason of the subordinate acts being fruitless, because they are for the principal act.

अभ्यासो वा छेदनसम्मार्गाऽवदानेषु वचनात्सकृत्त्वस्य ॥३६॥

36. On the other hand, there is a repetition by reason of the word 'once' in cutting, washing and offering.

अनभ्यास्तु वाच्यत्वात् ॥३७॥

37. On the other hand, there is no repetition by reason of being laid down.

बहुवचनेन सर्वप्राप्तेर्विकल्पः स्यात् ॥३८॥

38. With the plural number, taking of all is optional.

दृष्टः प्रयोग इति चेत् ॥३९॥

39. "The application is seen" if you say.

तथेह ॥

39. Similarly here.

भक्तयेति चेत् ॥४०॥

40. "By figure of speech" if you say.

तथेतरस्मिन् ॥४१॥

41. Similarly in the other.

प्रथमं वा नियम्येत कारणादतिक्रमः स्यात् ॥४२॥

42. On the other hand, the first is restricted; for a reason it is violated.

श्रुत्यर्थाविशेषात् ॥४३॥

43. By reason of there being nothing special in the purpose of the text.

तथा चान्यार्थदर्शनम् ॥४४॥

44. And similarly there is another object seen.

प्रकृत्याच पूर्ववत्तदासत्तेः ॥४५॥

45. And with the model sacrifice like the preceding by reason of its proximity.

उत्तरासु यावत्स्वमपूर्वत्वात् ॥४६॥

46. In *uttarā* cows, as many as one owns, by reason of the extraordinary principle.

यावत्स्वं वाऽन्यविधानेनानुवादः स्यात् ॥४७॥

47. On the other hand, "as many as one owns" is an *anuvāda* by reason of laying down another.

साकल्यविधानात् ॥४८॥

48. By reason of laying down the entirety.

बहूर्थत्वाच्च ॥४९॥

49. And by reason of the sense of 'all'.

अग्निहोत्रे चाशेषवद्यवागूनियमः प्रतिषेधःकुमाराणाम् ॥५०॥

50. And in an Agnihotra the rule about the entire gruel and the prohibition with respect to the youngsters.

सर्वप्रायिणापि लिङ्गेन संयुज्यते देवताभिसंयोगात् ॥५१॥

51. It fits in with the mark showing all, by reason of the connection with the deity.

प्रधानकर्मार्थत्वादङ्गानां तद्भेदात्कर्मभेदः प्रयोगे स्यात् ॥५२॥

52. Of the subordinate acts being for the object of the principal act, by reason of its difference, there will be a difference of acts in the application.

क्रमकोपश्च यौगपद्यात् स्यात्* ॥५३॥

53. And there will be a breach of order if performed simulteneously.

तुल्यानां तु यौगपद्यमेकशब्दोपदेशात्स्याद्विशेषाग्रहणात् ॥५४॥

54. On the other hand, there is simultaneous performance of the equals by reason of laying down one direction and by not taking anything special.

एकार्थ्यादध्यवायः स्यात् ॥५५॥

55. By reason of having one object, there is no breach of order.

तथाचान्यार्थदर्शनं कामुकायनः ॥५६॥

56. "Accordingly there is another proof says Kāmukāyana.

तन्यायत्वादशक्तेरानुपूर्व्यं स्यात्संस्कारस्य तदर्थत्वात् ॥५७॥

57. By reason of its propriety; by reason of the helplessness, there is performance one after the other because the purificatory rite is for it.

असंसृष्टोऽपि तादर्थ्यात् ॥५८॥

58. Even separated, they are for its object.

विभवाद्वा प्रदीपवत् ॥५९॥

59. On the other hand, on account of its richness, like a lamp.

अर्थात्तु लोके विधितः प्रतिप्रधानं स्यात् ॥६०॥

60. In the ordinary life, by reason of the object; by an injunction it is with each primary.

सकृदिज्यां कामुकायनः परिमाणविरोधात् ॥६१॥

61. "Once the offering" says Kāmukāyana by reason of its being contrary to the limit.

विधेस्त्वितरार्थत्वात्सकृदिज्याश्रुतिव्यतिक्रमः स्यात् ॥६२॥

62. Because the injunction (as regards the subordinate parts) is for the other (principal); there will be a breach of the text which lays down simultaneous performance.

विधिवत्प्रकरणाविभागे प्रयोगं बादरायणः ॥६३॥

63. "Like the injunction in the indivisibility of the context, there is the application" says Bādarāyaṇa.

---

*In other editions, there is 'यौगपद्ये' instead of 'यौगपद्यात्'.

अपि चैकेन सन्निधानमविशेषकोहेतुः ॥६४॥

64. And also though in proximity with one, it is not a special cause.

क्वचिद्विधानान्नेति चेत् ॥६५॥

65. "Somewhere by reason of the injunction, it is not so" if you say.

न विधेश्चोदितत्वात् ॥६६॥

66. Not so, by reason of the binding force of the injunction.

व्याख्यातं तुल्यानां यौगपद्यमगृह्यमाणविशेषाणाम् ॥६७॥

67. Those acts which are not specially taken and are of equal grade have been explained to be done simultaneously.

भेदस्तु कालभेदाच्चोदनाव्यवायात्स्याद्विशिष्टानां विधि प्रधानकालत्वात् ॥६८॥

68. On the other hand, separately by reason of the difference of time and by reason of the intervening injunction; there is a special command because time is principal.

तथा चान्यार्थदर्शनम् ॥६९॥

69. And similarly seeing other proof.

विधिरिति चेन्न वर्तमानापदेशात् ॥७०॥

70. If you say that it is not an injunction, by reason of the use of the present tense.

END OF PĀDA 1

***

PĀDA 2

एकदेशकालकर्त्तृत्वं मुख्यानामेकशब्दोपदेशात् ॥१॥

1. Unity of space, time and agent of the primaries by reason of one command.

अविधिश्चेत्कर्मणामभिसम्बन्धः प्रतीयेत तल्लक्षणार्थाभिसंयोगाद्विधित्वाच्चेतरेषां प्रतिप्रधानभावः स्यात् ॥२॥

2. If it is not an injunction, it appears to be connected with the action; by reason of the connection with its secondary sense and by reason of the injunctive nature, it is primary with every other of them.

अङ्गेषु च तदभावः प्रधानं प्रतिनिर्देशात् ॥३॥

3. And in the subsidiaries, it is absent by reason of pointing to the primary.

यदि तु कर्मणो विधिसम्बन्धः स्यादेकशब्द्यात्प्रधानार्थाभिधासंयोगात् ॥४॥

4. If on the other hand, the injunction is connected with the action by reason of one text and being connected with the name of the object of the primary.

तथा चान्यार्थदर्शनम् ॥५॥

5. And similarly there is another proof.

श्रुतिश्चैषां प्रधानवत्कर्मश्रुतेः परार्थत्वात् ॥६॥

6. And the text in connection with them is like the primary, by reason of the text as regards action being for the object of another.

कर्मणोऽश्रुतित्वाच्च ॥७॥

7. By reason of the action being not heard of.

अङ्गानि तु विधानत्वात्प्रधानेनोपदिश्येरंस्तस्मात्स्यादे कदेशत्वम् ॥८॥

8. On the other hand, the subsidiaries being prescribed, are governed by the text relating to the primary, therefore their subordinate nature.

द्रव्यदेवतं तथेति चेत् ॥९॥

9. If you say "similarly the deity and the material".

न चोदनाविधिशेषत्वान्नियमार्थो विशेषः ॥१०॥

10. Not so, by reason of the part of the injunctive sentence; the special is for the object of restriction.

तेषु समवेतानां समवायात्तन्त्रमङ्गानि भेदस्तु तद्भेदात्कर्मभेदः प्रयोगे स्यात्तेषां प्रधानशब्दत्वात्तथा चान्यार्थदर्शनम् ॥११॥

11. In them of the combined (parts), by reason of the combination; the subordinate parts are governed by *tantra* and on separation, there is separation. There will be a difference of procedure in the application by reason of their being the principal word; and there is another proof.

इष्टिराजसूयचातुर्मास्येष्वैककर्म्यादङ्गानां तंत्रभावः स्यात् ॥१२॥

12. In the *iṣṭi*, *rājasūya* and *cāturmāsya*, by reason of the unity of the act, the subsidiaries are to be performed once for all.

कालभेदान्नेति चेत् ॥१३॥

13. "Not so, by reason of the difference of time" if you say.

नैकदेशत्वात्पशुवत् ॥१४॥

14. Not so, by reason of its being a part like an animal sacrifice.

अपि वा कर्मपृथक्त्वात्तेषां तन्त्रविधानात्साङ्गानामुपदेशः स्यात् ॥१५॥

15. On the other hand, by reason of the difference of the action, they are laid down to be done collectively and so there is a direction for their performance with the subsidiaries.

तथा चान्यार्थदर्शनम् ॥१६॥

16. And similarly there is another proof.

तथा तदवयवेषु स्यात् ॥१७॥

17. Similarly in their parts.

पशौ तु चोदनैकत्वात्तन्त्रस्य विप्रकर्षः स्यात् ॥१८॥

18. On the other hand, in the animal sacrifice, by reason of one command of *tantra*, there is remotness.

तथा स्यादध्वरकल्पेष्टौ विशेषस्यैककालत्वात् ॥१९॥

19. Similarly in the *adhvarakalpeṣṭi* by reason of the unity of the time of the special offering.

इष्टिरिति चैकवच्छ्रुतिः ॥२०॥

20. "*Iṣṭi*" is what is laid down as one.

अपि वा वाकर्मपृथकत्वात्तेषां च तन्त्रविधानात्साङ्गानामुपदेशः स्यात् ॥२१॥

21. On the other hand, by reason of the difference of the action, they are laid down to be done collectively and so there is a direction for their performance with the subsidiaries.

प्रथमस्य वा कालवचनम् ॥२२॥

22. On the other hand, it is a text, as regards the time of the first offering.

फलेकत्वादिष्टिशब्दो यथान्यत्र ॥२३॥

23. By reason of the unity of result, the word *iṣṭi* is used just as in others.

वसाहोमस्तन्त्रमेकदेवतेषु स्यात्प्रदानस्यैककालत्वात् ॥२४॥

24. The offering of marrow is to be done collectively to one deity by reason of the unity of the time of the offering.

कालभेदात्वावृत्तिर्देवताभेदे ॥२५॥

25. On the other hand, by reason of the difference of time, there is repetition on the difference of the deity.

अन्ते यूपाहुतिस्तद्वत् ॥२६॥

26. In the end, the offering at the sacrificial post like it.

इतरप्रतिषेधो वा ॥२७॥

27. On the other hand, it is a prohibition of the other.

अशास्त्रत्वाच्च देशानाम् ॥२८॥

28. And by reason of the place being not capable to be ordained.

अवभृथे प्रधानेऽग्निविकारः स्यान्न हि तद्धेतुरग्निसंयोगः ॥२९॥

29. In the sacrtificial bath which is principal, there is the modification of fire; for this reason there is no connection with fire.

द्रव्यदेवतवत् ॥

साङ्गो वा प्रयोगवचनैकत्वात् ॥३०॥

30. On the other hand, with the subsidiaries, by reason of the unity of the text for application.

लिङ्गदर्शनाच्च ॥३१॥

31. And by seeing the *liṅga.*

शब्दविभागाच्च देवतानपनयः * ॥३२॥

32. By reason of the division of the word, the application of the deity.

दक्षिणेऽग्नौ वरुणप्रघासेषु देशभेदात्सर्वं क्रियते ॥३३॥

33. In the southern fire in a *varuṇapraghāsa*, by reason of the difference of the place all is done.

अचोदनेतिचेत् ॥३४॥

34. "No stimulating command" if you say.

स्यात्पौर्णमासीवत् ॥३५॥

35. It is just like the full moon sacrifice.

प्रयोगचोदनेति चेत् ॥३६॥

36. "There is the command as to the procedure".

---

*In the Chaukhambhā edition, the reading is नमः in place of अपनयः.

इहापिमारुत्याः प्रयोगश्चोद्यते ॥३७॥
37. Here also, the application of *mārutī* is directed.

आसादनमिति चेत् ॥३८॥
38. "Placing near" if you say.

नोत्तरेणैकवाक्यत्वात् ॥३९॥
39. Not so, by reason of being one with the text in connection with the northern hearth.

अवाच्यत्वात् ॥४०॥
40. By reason of its being not conveyed.

आम्नायवचनं तद्वत् ॥४१॥
41. The Vedic text is like it.

कर्तृभेदस्तथेति चेत् ॥४२॥
42. "Similarly the difference of the agent" if you say.

न समवायात् ॥४३॥
43. Not so, by reason of the affinity.

लिङ्गदर्शनाच्च ॥४४॥
44. And by seeing the *liṅga.*

वेदिसंयोगादिति चेत् ॥४५॥
45. "By reason of the connection with the altar" if you say.

न देशमात्रत्वात् ॥४६॥
46. Not so, by reason of the limit of the space.

एकवाक्यत्वात् ॥४७॥
47. By reason of the unity of the sentence.

एकाग्नित्वादपरेषु तन्त्रं स्यात् ॥४८॥
48. By reason of one fire, the principle of *tantra* applies to other fires.

नाना वा कर्तृभेदात् ॥४९॥
49. On the other hand, differently by reason of the difference of the agents.

पर्यग्निकृतानामुत्सर्गे प्राजापत्यानां कर्मोत्सर्गः श्रुतिसामान्यादारण्यवत्तस्माद्ब्रह्मसाम्नि चोदनापृथक्त्वं स्यात् ॥५०॥

50. In the relinquishment of the animals round whom fire has been carried and who are dedicated to *prajāpati*, there is the end of the act by reason of the common text like the wild animals; therefore in *brahmasāma*, there is a separate injunction.

संस्कारप्रतिषेधो वा वाक्यैकत्वे क्रतुसामान्यात् ॥५१॥

51. On the other hand, it is a prohibition of the subsidiary act by reason of the common nature of the sacrifice in one sentence.

वावयैकत्वे क्रतुसामान्यात् ॥५२॥

52. By reason of the common nature of the sacrifice in one sentence.

वपानां चानभिघारणस्य दर्शनात् ॥५३॥

53. And by seeing of the omentum being not sprinkled with ghee.

पञ्चशारदीयास्तथेति चेत् ॥५४॥

54. "*Pañcaśāradīya* similarly" if you say.

न चोदनैकवाक्यत्वात् ॥५५॥

55. Not so, by reason of one sentence of the injunction.

यातयामत्वाच्च ॥५६॥

56. And by reason of being stale.

संस्कारणां च तद्दर्शनात् ॥५७॥

57. And by seeing the subsidiary acts.

दशपेये क्रयप्रतिषात्प्रतिकर्षस्ततः प्राचां तत्समानं तन्त्रं स्यात् ॥५८॥

58. In a *daśapeya* by reason of the transferene backward of the sale, there is the transference of the preceding ones; they are of equal *tantra*.

समानवचनं तद्वत् ॥५९॥

59. Similarly the text as to equality.

अप्रतिकर्षो वाऽर्थहेतुत्वात् ॥६०॥

60. There is no transference by reason of the object being the cause.

पूर्वस्मिंश्चावभृथस्य दर्शनात् ॥६१॥

61. And in the preceding one by seeing the sacrificial bath.

दीक्षाणां चोत्तरस्य

And the initiation of the succeeding one.

समानः कालसामान्यात् ॥६२॥

62. Equal, by reason of the common time.

निष्कासस्यावभृथे तदेकदेशत्वात्पशुवत्प्रदानविप्रकर्षः स्यात् ॥६३॥

63. By reason of the partial nature of the remnants of the *āmikṣā* in a sacrificial bath, like the parts of the animal, there is a difference of offering.

अपनयो वा प्रसिद्धेनाभिसंयोगात् ॥६४॥

64. On the other hand, it is a separate act, by reason of the connection with the well-known.

प्रतिपत्तिरिति चेन्न कर्मसंयोगात् ॥६५॥

65. If you say "it is a mode of final disposal" it is not so, by reason of the connection with the action.

उदयनीये च तद्वत् ॥६६॥

66. And in *udayanīya* similarly.

प्रतिपत्तिर्वाऽकर्मसंयोगात् ॥६७॥

67. It is a final disposal by reason of its having no connection with the act.

अर्थकर्म वा शेषत्वाच्छ्रयणवत्तदर्थेनविधानात् ॥६८॥

68. On the other hand, it is an *arthakarma* (purificatory act) by reason of its being subordinate like boiling, because it is ordained to be for its object.

END OF PĀDA 2

***

PĀDA 3

अङ्गानां मुख्यकालत्वाद्वचनादन्यकालत्वम् ॥१॥

1. The time of the subsidiaries by reason of the time of the principal, is different under a text.

द्रव्यस्य कर्मकालनिष्पत्तेः प्रयोगः सर्वार्थः स्यात्स्वकालत्वात् ॥२॥

2. By reason of the material being produced at the time of the action, the application is for the object of all, because it has its own time.

यूपश्चाकर्मकालत्वात् ॥३॥

3. And the sacrificial post, by reason of the different time of action.

एकयूपं च दर्शयति ॥४॥

4. And one sacrificial post is seen.

संस्कारास्त्वावर्तेरन्नर्थकालत्वात् ॥५॥

5. On the other hand, the purificatory rites are repeated by reason of the time of the object.

तत्कालस्तु यूपकर्मत्वात्तस्य धर्मविधानात्सर्वार्थानां च वचनादन्यकाल-त्वम् ॥६॥

6. On the other hand, at the same time, by reason of their being the rite in connection with the sacrificial post and by reason of laying down the duties in connection with it; and there is another time under a text of all accomplishing objects.

सकृन्मानं च दर्शयति ॥७॥

7. And once measuring shows.

स्वरुस्तन्त्रापवर्गः स्यादस्वकालत्वात् ॥८॥

8. The completion by *tantra* in the case of *svarū* is by reason of its having no time.

साधारणे वाऽनुनिष्पत्तिस्तस्य साधारणत्वात् ॥९॥

9. On the other hand, in common it is got after by reason of its being common.

सोमान्ते च प्रतिपत्तिदर्शनात् ॥१०॥

10. And seeing the *pratipatti* (final disposal) at the end of soma sacrifice.

तत्कालो वा प्रस्तरवत् ॥

On the other hand, its time (is) like the grass.

न चोत्पत्तिवाक्यत्वात्प्रदेशात्प्रस्तरे तथा ॥११॥

11. Not so, by reason of the text as to its origin as it is in case of the grass by reason of the principle of *atideśa.*

अहर्गणे विषाणाप्रासनं धर्मविप्रतिषेधादन्ते प्रथमे वाहनि विकल्पः स्यात् ॥१२॥

12. In the sacrifices lasting for days, the throwing of a horn by reason of the difference of the duties, is optional; either it is on the first day or on the last day.

पाणेस्त्वश्रुतिभूतत्वाद्विषाणानियमः स्यात्प्रातः सवनमध्यत्वाच्छिष्टे चाभिप्रवृत्तत्वात् ॥१३॥

13. On the other hand, by reason of the scratching by hand being not heard of, the rule as to scratching by horn is prescribed because there are many *prātaḥsavanas* and because the commencement is made of that which is sanctioned.

शिष्टे चाभिप्रवृत्तत्वात् ॥१४॥

14. And by reason of having undertaken to perform what has been laid down.

वाग्विसर्गो हविष्कृता वीजभेदे तथा स्यात् ॥१५॥

15. Similarly is the breaking of silence by the offering-maker in the *nānāvījeṣṭi.*

यथाह्वानमपीतिचेत् ॥१६॥

16. "Just as calling also" if you say.

पशौ च पुरोडाशे समानतन्त्रं भवेत् ॥१७॥

17. And in the animal and the *puroḍāśa* sacrifices the same *tantra* applies.

अंगप्रधानार्थोयोगः सर्वापवर्गे विमोकः स्यात्* ॥१८॥

18. The joining of fire being for the object of the subsidiary and principal, the release is after the completion of the whole.

प्रधानापवर्गे वा तदर्थत्वात् ॥१९॥

19. On the other hand, on the completion of the primary by reason of its being for its object.

अवभृथे च तद्वत्प्रधानार्थस्य प्रतिषेधोऽपवृक्तार्थत्वात् ॥२०॥

20. And in a sacrificial bath similarly for the primary; there is a prohibition by reason of the completion.

अहर्गणे च प्रत्यहं स्यात्तदर्थत्वात् ॥२१॥

21. And in the *ahargaṇa*, it is every dayby reason of its being for it.

सुब्रह्मण्या तु तन्त्रं दीक्षावदन्यकालत्वात् ॥२२॥

---

*The सूत्र is differently read by other commentators with the exception of खंडदेव.

22. The call of *subrahmaṇya* is by *tantra* like the initiation by reason of the different time.

तत्कालात्त्वादावर्तेत प्रयोगतो विशेषसम्बन्धात् ॥२३॥

23. By reason of being of that time, it should be repeated in the application, because there is a connection with the special.

अप्रयोगाङ्गमिति चेत् ॥२४॥

24. "It is not a part of the application" if you say.

प्रयोगनिर्देशात्कर्तृभेदवत्* ॥२५॥

25. By reason of the direction of the application like the difference of the agent.

तद्भूतस्थानादग्निवदिति चेत्तदपवर्गस्तदर्थत्वात् ॥२६॥

26. "If you say that by reason of the deity of that invocation like fire"; (the reply is) that there is the end by reason of that being for it.

अग्निवदिति चेत् ॥२७॥

27. 'Like fire' if you say.

न प्रयोगसाधारण्यात् ॥२८॥

28. Not so by reason of the common nature of the application.

लिङ्गदर्शनाच्च ॥२९॥

29. And by seeing the *liṅga* also.

तद्धि तथेति चेत् ॥३०॥

30. 'That is similarly' if you say.

नाशिष्टत्वादितरन्यायत्वाच्च ॥३१॥

31. Not so, by reason of that being not laid down and by reason of another principle.

विध्येकत्वादिति चेत् ॥३२॥

32. "By reason of one injunction" if you say.

न कृत्स्नस्य पुनः प्रयोगात्प्रधानवत् ॥३३॥

33. Not so, by reason of the application of the whole again, like the principal.

---

*There is 'स्यात्' before 'प्रयोग' in other editions.

लौकिकेतु यथाकामी संस्कारानर्थलोपात् ॥३४॥

34. On the other hand, in the ordinary things just as one wishes by reason of the non-omission of the purificatory rite.

यज्ञायुधानि धार्येरन्प्रतिपत्तिविधानादृजीषवत् ॥३५॥

35. The sacrificial weapons should be maintained by reason of the injunction for their final disposal like the soma dregs.

यजमानसंस्कारो वा तदर्थः श्रूयते तत्र यथाकामी तदर्थत्वात् ॥३६॥

36. On the other hand, it is a purificatory rite of the sacrificer and they are for the object there; so one may use them according to his wishes, being for the object of the action.

मुख्यधारणं वा मरणस्यानियतत्वात् ॥३७॥

37. On the other hand, the vessels of the first sacrifice should be kept by reason of the death being uncertain.

यो वा यजनीयेहनि म्रियेत सोऽधिकृतः स्यादुपवेषवत् ॥३८॥

38. On the other hand, one who dies on the sacrificial day, he is entitled like the lower part of a branch.

न शास्त्रलक्षणत्वात् ॥३९॥

39. Not so, by reason of the definition as laid down.

उत्पत्तिर्वा प्रयोजकत्वादाशिरवत् ॥४०॥

40. On the other hand, new ones by reason of their being subsidiary like the milk.

शब्दासामञ्जस्यमिति चेत् ॥४१॥

41. "Meaninglessness of the word" if you say.

तथाऽऽशिरेऽपि ॥४२॥

42. Similarly in the milk also.

शास्त्रात्तु विप्रयोगस्तत्रैकद्रव्याचिकीर्षा प्रकृतावथेहापूर्वार्थ-वद्भूतोपदेशः ॥४३॥

43. On the other hand, there is the separation by reason of its being laid down; there is a desire of one substance. Here there is the statement of fact in order to achieve the extraordinary principle.

प्रकृत्यर्थत्वात्पौर्णमास्याः क्रियेरन् ॥४४॥

44. By reason of their being for the model sacrifice, they should be preserved from the full moon sacrifice.

अग्न्याधेये वाऽविप्रतिषेधात्तानि धारयेन्मरणस्यानिमित्तवात् ॥४५॥

45. On the other hand, in the establishment of fire by reason of the non-obstruction, they should be preserved because death is uncertain.

प्रतिपत्तिर्वा यथान्येषाम् ॥४६॥

46. On the other hand, the final disposal is like that of others.

उपरिष्टात्सोमानां प्राजापत्यैश्चरन्तीति ॥४७॥

47. Subsequent to soma, they commence with the *prājāpatya* animals.

अङ्गविपर्यासोविनावचनादिति चेत् ॥४८॥

48. "There will be confusion of the parts without any command" if you say.

उत्कर्षः संयोगात्कालमात्रमितरत्र ॥४९॥

49. There will be transference forward by reason of the connection with (the animal sacrifice): elsewhere it indicates only a time.

प्रकृतिकालासत्तेः शस्त्रवतामिति चेत् ॥५०॥

50. "By reason of getting the time of the model sacrifice, after the songs" if you say.

न श्रुतिप्रतिषेधात् ॥५१॥

51. Not so, by reason of the contravention of the text.

विकारस्थाने इति चेत् ॥५२॥

52. "After the order of the modification" if you say.

न चोदनापृथक्त्वात् ॥५३॥

53. Not so, by reason of the different command.

उत्कर्षे सूक्तवाकस्य न सोमदेवतानामुत्कर्षः पश्वनङ्गत्वाद्यथा निष्कर्षेनान्वयः ॥५४॥

54. When the *sūktavāka* is transferred forward, the soma dieties are not transferred forward, by reason of their being not parts of the animal sacrifice, just as in expulsion, there is separation.

वाक्यसंयोगाद्वोत्कर्षः समानतन्त्रत्वादर्थलोपादनन्वयः ॥५५॥

55. By reason of the connection with the *sūktavāka*, there is a transference forward by reason of their belonging to their same *tantra* and by reason of the omission of the object, there is a separation.

END OF PĀDA 3

***

PĀDA 4

चोदनैकत्वाद्राजसूयेऽनुक्तदेशकालानां समवायात्तन्त्रमङ्गानि ॥१॥

1. By reason of one command, in a *rājasūya* on account of the combination of those whose time and place have not been ordained, the principle of *tantra* applies to the subordinate parts.

प्रतिदक्षिणं वा कर्तृसम्बन्धादिष्टिवदङ्गभूतत्वात्समुदायो हि तन्निर्वृत्त्यातदेकत्वादेकशब्दोपदेशः स्यात् ॥२॥

2. On the other hand, there is a different fee by reason of the connection with the agent, just as in the *iṣṭis* by reason of the subordination there is a combination because when that is accomplished, there is one text on account of its unity.

तथा चान्यार्थदर्शनम् ॥३॥

3. Similarly there is another proof.

अनियमः स्यादिति चेत् ॥४॥

4. "There is no rule" if you say.

नोपदिष्टत्वात् ॥५॥

5. Not so, by reason of the direction.

लाघवापत्तिश्च ॥

And there is the defect of levity.

प्रयोजनैकत्वात ॥६॥

6. By reason of the object being one.

अविशेषार्था पुनः श्रुतिः* ॥७॥

7. The repetition of the text is for the object of the common.

अवेष्टौ चैकतन्त्र्यं स्याल्लिङ्गदर्शनाद्वचनात् काम संयोगेन ॥८॥

8. And in an *aveṣṭi* the principle of *tantra* applies by reason of seeing the *liṅga*, because of the text and of the connection with the desire.

क्रत्वर्थायामिति चेन्न वर्णसंयोगात् ॥९॥

9. If you say it is for the object of the sacrifice; not so, by reason of the connection with the caste.

पवमानहविःष्वैकतन्त्र्य प्रयोगवचनैकत्वात् ॥१०॥

*In some editions, there is विशेषार्था.

10. The principle of *tantra* applies to the *pavamāna* offerings by reason of the unity of the text of the application.

लिङ्गदर्शनाच्च ॥११॥

11. And by seeing the *liṅga*.

वर्तमानापदेशाद्वचनात्तु तन्त्रभेदः स्यात् ॥१२॥

12. On the other hand, by reason of the text having the present tense, there is the difference of Tantra.

सहत्वे नित्यानुवादः स्यात् ॥१३॥

13. In the simultaneity, there is a permanent statement.

द्वादशाहे तु प्रकृतित्वादेकैकमहरपवृज्येत कर्मपृथक्त्वात् ॥१४॥

14. On the other hand, in a *dvādaśāha* by reason of the model sacrifice, it should be completed everyday because the action is separate.

अह्नां वा श्रुतिभूतत्वात्तत्रसाङ्ग क्रियेत यथा माध्यन्दिने ॥१५॥

15. And by reason of the days being laid down, all should be performed there with the subsidiaries just as in the *mādhyandina*.

अपि वा फलकर्तृसम्बॅन्धात्सह प्रयोगः स्यादाग्नेयाग्नीषोमीयवत् ॥१६॥

16. On the other hand, by reason of the connection of the fruit and the agent, there is the joint application just as there is in *āgneya* and *agnīṣoma*.

साङ्गकालश्रुतित्वाद्वा स्वस्थानानां विकारः स्यात् ॥१७॥

17. On the other hand, by reason of the time of the subsidiary with the principal being laid down, there is the modification of those that are at their places.

दीक्षोपसदां च संख्या पृथक्पृथक् प्रत्यक्षसंयोगात् ॥१८॥

18. And the number of *dīkṣā* and *upasada* is separate by reason of the connection with the direct.

वसतीवरीपर्यंतानिपूर्वाणितंत्र मन्यकालत्वादवभृथादीन्युत्तराणिदीक्षाविसर्गार्थत्वात् ॥१९॥

19. The preceding ones up to the taking of water for soma are to be performed on the principle of *tantra* by reason of their different time and the following ones i.e. the sacrificial bath &c. by reason of their being for the completion of the *dīkṣā*.

तथा चान्यार्थदर्शनम् ॥२०॥

20. And similarly there is another proof.

चोदनापृथक्त्वे त्वैकतन्त्र्यं समवेतानां कालसंयोगात् ॥२१॥

21. On the other hand, on the *codanā* being separate, there is simultaneity of performance of the connected ones by reason of the relationship with the time.

भेदस्तु तद्भेदात्कर्मभेदः प्रयोगे स्यात्तेषां प्रधानशब्दत्वात् ॥२२॥

22. There is a separate performance by reason of the difference of time; there is difference of action in the application, they being connected with the term principal.

तथा चान्यार्थदर्शनम् ॥२३॥

23. And similarly there is another proof.

श्वासुत्यावचनं तद्वत् ॥२४॥

24. Similarly the call after morning extraction.

पश्वत्तिरेकश्च ॥२५॥

25. And the excess of animal.

सुत्याविवृद्धौ सुब्रह्मण्यायां सर्वेषामुपलक्षणं प्रकृत्यन्वयादावाहनवत् ॥२६॥

26. In the case of the increase of *sutyā*, in the call of *subrahmaṇyā*, there will be generalisation every where by reason of the relationship with the model sacrifice like the invocation formula.

अपि वेन्द्राभिधानत्वात्सकृत्स्यादुपलक्षणं कालस्यलक्षणार्थत्वात् ॥२७॥

27. On the other hand, by reason of naming Indra, it should be uttered once, by reason of the time being for the secondary sense.

अविभागाच्च ॥२८॥

28. And by reason of impartibility.

पशुगणे कुम्भीशूलवपाश्रपणीनां प्रभुत्वात्तन्त्रभावः स्यात् ॥२९॥

29. In the animal sacrifice, the pot, the rod and the cauldron by reason of their sufficiency are fit to be used for all.

भेदस्तु सन्देहाद्देवतान्तरे स्यात् ॥३०॥

30. On the other hand, they should be separate, by reason of the doubt for another deity.

अर्थाद्वा लिङ्गकर्म स्यात् ॥३१॥

31. For the purpose, the mark or symbol should be made.

प्रतिपाद्यत्वाद्वसानांभेदः स्यात्स्वयाज्याप्रदानत्वात् ॥३२॥

32. By reason of the disposal of the marrow, there is a separate vessel, because it is incapable of gift under its own *yājyā*.

अपि वा प्रतिपत्तित्वात्तन्त्रं स्यात्स्वत्वस्याश्रुतिभूतत्वात् ॥३३॥

33. On the other hand, by reason of its being for the final disposal, there will be only one vessel, because nowhere it is laid down that it should be offered with its own offering formula.

सकृदिति चेत् ॥३४॥

34. Once, if you say.

न कालभेदात् ॥३५॥

35. Not so, by reason of the difference of time.

पक्तिभेदात्कुम्भीशूलवपाश्रपणीनांभेदः स्यात् ॥३६॥

36. By reason of the difference of cooking, the pot, the rod and cauldron should be separate.

जात्यन्तरेषु भेदः पक्तिवैषम्यात् ॥३७॥

37. In the different species of animals there is a difference, by reason of the dissimilarity of cooking.

वृद्धिदर्शनाच्च ॥३८॥

38. And by seeing the increase.

कपालानि च कुम्भीवत्तुल्यसंख्यानाम् ॥३९॥

39. And the pans are of equal number like the pot.

प्रतिप्रधानं वा प्रकृतिवत् ॥४०॥

40. On the other hand, for each primary as in the model sacrifice.

सर्वेषां वाभिप्रथमं स्यात् ॥४१॥

41. On the other hand, there is the extension of all.

एकद्रव्ये संस्काराणां व्याख्यातमेककर्मत्वात् ॥४२॥

42. In one substance, the purificatory rite is explained by reason of its being one act.

द्रव्यान्तरे कृतार्थत्वात्तस्य पुनः प्रयोगान्मन्त्रस्य च तद्गुणत्वात्पुनः प्रयोगः स्यात्तदर्थेन विधानात् ॥४३॥

43. In the different substance, by reason of its accomplishing the object, by reason of the repetition of the *mantra* and by its being subordinate, it is to be repeated because it is laid down for it only.

निर्वपणलवनस्तरणाज्यग्रहणेषु चैकद्रव्यवत्प्रयोजनैकत्वात् ॥४४॥

44. In offering, cutting covering, and taking of ghee like one substance by reason of the unity of the object.

द्रव्यान्तरवद्वा स्यात्तत्संस्कारात् ॥४५॥

45. On the other hand, it will be like the different substances by reason of their being purified.

वेदिप्रोक्षणे मन्त्राभ्यासः कर्मणः पुनः प्रयोगात् ॥४६॥

46. In sprinkling water on the altar, the mantra is to be repeated by reason of the repetition of the act.

एकस्य वा गुणविधिर्द्रव्यैकत्वात्तस्मात्सकृत्प्रयोगः स्यात् ॥४७॥

47. On the other hand, it is laying of quality of one by reason of the unity of the substance; therefore there will be one application.

कंडूयने प्रत्यङ्गं कर्मभेदात्स्यात् ॥४८॥

48. In rubbing each part of the body, by reason of the difference of the act.

अपि वा चोदनैककालमैककर्म्यं स्यात् ॥४९॥

49. There is no *codanā*, it happens at one time and it is one act.

स्वप्नदीतरणाभिवर्षणामेध्यप्रतिमन्त्रणेषु चैवम् ॥५०॥

50. In the repetition of the *mantras* on the occasion of dream, crossing of the river, excessive rain and dung, the same principle applies.

प्रयाणे त्वार्थनिवृत्तेः ॥५१॥

51. On departure by reason of the completion of the object.

उपरवमन्त्रस्तन्त्रं स्याल्लोकवद्बहुवचनात् ॥५२॥

52. The *uparavamantra* is governed by the principle of *tantra*, as it is in ordinary life by reason of the plural number.

न सन्निपातित्वादसन्निपातिकर्मणां विशेषग्रहणे कालैकत्वात्सकृद्वचनम्* ॥५३॥

*Śabara and खंडदेव have omitted सकृद्वचनम् from the सूत्र.

53. Not so by reason of the association of ideas (of the acts to be performed); in taking the special acts in which there is no association of ideas, there is a recitation of the mantra once by reason of time being one.

हविष्कृदध्रिगुपुरोऽनुवाक्यामनोतस्यावृत्तिः कालभेदात् स्यात् ॥५४॥

54. (The mantras pertaining to) *haviṣkṛt, adhrigu, puronuvākyā* and *manotā* are to be repeated by reason of the difference of time.

अध्रिगोश्च विपर्यासात् ॥५५॥

55. And by reason of the transposition of the *adhirgu.*

करिष्यद्वचनात् ॥५६॥

56. By reason of the word "done".

END OF PĀDA 4

***

END OF ADHYĀYA XI

ADHYĀYA XII

PĀDA 1

तन्त्रिसमवाये चोदनातः समानानामेकतन्त्र्यमतुल्येषु तु भेदः स्याद्विधि-प्रक्रमतादर्थ्यात् श्रुतिकालनिर्देशात् ॥१॥

1. When there are many primaries, there is simultaneous performance, if they are governed by one command; but in unequal, there is difference because the commencement of the subordinate is for it and because the scripture has directed its time.

गुणकालविकाराच्च तन्त्रभेदः स्यात् ॥२॥

2. By reason of the modification of the quality and time, there will be a difference of Tantra.

तन्त्रमध्ये विधानाद्वा मुख्यतन्त्रेण सिद्धिःस्यात्तन्त्रार्थस्याविशिष्टत्वात् ॥३॥

3. On the other hand, by reason of its being laid in connection with the primary, the accomplishment will be by one primary, because the object of the primary is not special.

विकाराच्च न भेदः स्यादर्थस्याविकृतत्वात् ॥४॥

4. And there is no difference by reason of the modification, because the object is not changed.

एकेषां वाशक्यत्वात् ॥५॥

5. On the other hand, by reason of the capacity for one.

आहोपुरीषकं स्यात् ॥६॥

6. It may be a boasting of heroic exploit.

एकाग्निवच्च दर्शनम् ॥७॥

7. There is also proof like one fire.

जैमिनेः परतन्त्रत्वापत्तेः स्वतन्त्रप्रतिषेधः स्यात् ॥८॥

8. The view of Jaimini is that by reason of the application of the *tantra* one's own application of *tantra* is prohibited.

नानार्थत्वात्सोमे दर्शपूर्णमासप्रकृतीनां वेदिकर्म स्यात् ॥९॥

9. By reason of the variety of the objects, in a soma sacrifice, the construction of the altar is of the full and new moon sacrifices, as its models.

अकर्म वा कृतदूषा स्यत् ॥१०॥

10. On the other hand, it should not be constructed; if constructed, it is defective.

पात्रेषु च प्रसङ्गः स्याद्धोमार्थत्वात् ॥११॥

11. The principle of *prasaṅga* applies in the case of the vessels by reason of their being for the *homa.*

न्याय्यानि वा प्रयुक्तत्वादप्रयुक्ते प्रसङ्गः स्यात् ॥१२॥

12. On the other hand, they are proper, by reason of being used; when not used, the principle of *prasaṅga* applies.

शामित्रे च पशुपुरोडाशो न स्याद्रितरस्य प्रयुक्तत्वात् ॥१३॥

13. In the *śāmitra* fire, the animal *puroḍāśa* sacrifice should not be performed by reason of the other being used.

श्रपणं वाऽग्निहोत्रस्य शालामुखीये न स्यात्प्राजहितस्य विद्यमानत्वात् ॥१४॥

14. On the other hand, cooking in the *agnihotra* should not be in the *śālāmukhīya*, because of the presence of the *prājahita.*

हविर्द्धाने निर्वपणार्थं साधयेतां प्रयुक्तत्वात् ॥५॥

15. In a *havirdhāna* cart, the completion should be made for the purpose of the offering, by reason of the act being commenced.

असिद्धिर्वाऽन्यदेशत्वात्प्रधानवैगुण्यादवैगुण्ये प्रसङ्गः स्यात् ॥१६॥

16. On the other hand, there will be a failure by reason of the separate place and by reason of the principal being spoiled. On the principal being not spoiled, the principle of *prasaṅga* will apply.

अनसाञ्च दर्शनात् ॥१७॥

17. And by seeing the carts (in the plural number).

तद्युक्तत्वं च कालभेदात् ॥१८॥

18. And combination with it by reason of the difference of time.

मन्त्राश्च सन्निपातित्वात् ॥१९॥

19. And the *mantras* by reason of their distant benefit.

धारणार्थत्वात्सोमेमऽग्न्यन्वाधानं न विद्यते ॥२०॥

20. In soma by reason of its being for the maintenance, there is no re-establishment of fire.

तथा व्रतमपेतत्वात् ॥२१॥

21. Similarly the vows, by reason of their being already undertaken.

विप्रतिषेधाच्च ॥२२॥

22. And by reason of the prohibition.

स्त्यवदिति चेत् ॥२३॥

23. 'Like truth' if you say.

न संयोगपृथक्त्वात् ॥२०॥

24. Not so, by reason of the separate connection.

ग्रहार्थं च पूर्वमिष्टेस्तदर्थत्वात् ॥२५॥

25. And for the object of reception of gods by reason of being for the object before the *iṣṭi*.

शेषवदिति चेन्न वैश्वदेवो हि स्याद्व्यपदेशात् ॥२६॥

26. "If you say like the subordinate parts". not so, by reason of all the deities; it may be a designation.

न गुणार्थत्वात् ॥२७॥

27. Not so, by reason of its being for the praise.

सन्नहनञ्च वृत्तत्वात् ॥२८॥

28. And the equipment by reason of its being already undertaken.

अन्यविधानादारण्यभोजनं न स्यादुभयं हि वृत्त्यर्थम् ॥२९॥

29. By reason of laying down another, there is no forest food; both are for maintenance.

शेषभक्षास्तथेति चेन्नान्यार्थत्वात् ॥३०॥

30. If you say "remnants of the food similarly"; no, by reason of their being for another object.

भृतत्वाच्च परिक्रयः ॥३१॥

31. And by reason of maintenance, there is hiring of services.

शेषभक्षास्तथेति चेत् ॥३२॥

32. And eating of the remnants of food similarly, if you say.

न कर्मसंयोगात् ॥३३॥

33. Not so, by reason of the connection with the act.

प्रवृत्तवरणात्प्रति तंत्रवरणात्प्रतितन्त्रवरणं होतुः क्रियेत ॥३४॥

34. By reason of the commencement of the appointment and by reason of the appointment for each Tantra, there is appointment of the *hotā* for each part.

ब्रह्मापीति चेत् ॥३५॥

35. "Brahmā also" if you say.

न प्राङ्नियमात्तदर्थं हि ॥३६॥

36. Not so, by reason of the previous appointment, because it is for it.

निर्दिष्टस्येति चेत् ॥३७॥

37. "Of the directed" if you say.

न श्रुतत्वात् ॥३८॥

38. Not so, by reason of not being laid down.

होतुस्तथेति चेत् ॥३९॥

39. "The Hotā similarly" if you say.

न कर्मसंयोगात् ॥४०॥

40. Not so, by reason of the connection with the act.

यज्ञोत्पत्त्युपदेशे निष्ठितकर्मप्रयोगभेदात्प्रतितन्त्रं क्रियेत ॥४१॥

41. In the direction relating to the origin of the sacrifice by reason of the difference of the application of the fixed act, it is to be done separately.

न वा कृतत्वात्तदुपदेशो हि ॥

Not so by reason of having done it, because the direction is for it.

देशपृथक्त्वान्मन्त्रोव्यावर्तते ॥४२॥

42. By reason of the separation of the place, the mantra is repeated.

सन्नहनहरणे तथेति चेत् ॥४३॥

43. "In *sannahanaharaṇa* similarly" if you say.

नान्यार्थत्वात् ॥४४॥

44. Not so, by reason of the object being different.

END OF PĀDA 1

***

PĀDA 2

विहारो लौकिकानामर्थं साधयेत्प्रभुत्वात् ॥१॥

1. The three fires may accomplish the ordinary act by reason of the capacity.

मांसपाकप्रतिषेधश्च तद्वत् ॥२॥

2. The prohibition about the cooking of flesh is like it.

निर्देशाद्वा वैदिकानां स्यात् ॥३॥

3. On the other hand, by reason of the direction, it is for the Vedic acts.

सति चोपासनस्य दर्शनात् ॥४॥

4. And in its existence, there is seen *upāsana* fire.

अभावदर्शनाच्च ॥५॥

5. And by seeing the absence.

मांसपाको विहितप्रतिषेधः स्यादाहुतिसंयोगात् ॥६॥

6. The cooking of flesh is in the nature of the prohibition of that which is laid down by reason of the connection with the offering.

वाक्यशेषो वा दक्षिणस्मिन्ननारभ्यविधानस्य ॥७॥

7. On the other hand, it may be a supplementary sentence of the scattered text in the southern fire.

सवनीये छिद्रापिधानार्थत्वात्पशुपुरोडाशो न स्यादन्येषामेवमर्थत्वात् ॥८॥

8. In a *savanīya* by reason of the object for covering the hole, there is no animal to because others are for the purpose.

क्रिया वा देवतार्थत्वात् ॥९॥

9. On the other hand, it should be performed by reason of its being for the purpose of the deity.

लिङ्गदर्शनात् ॥१०॥

10. And by seeing the *liṅga.*

हविष्कृत्सवनीयेषु न स्यात्प्रकृतौ यदि सर्वार्था पशुं प्रत्याहूता सा कुर्याद्विद्यमानत्वात् ॥११॥

11. The call of *haviṣkṛt* is not in the *savanīyas*; if in the model sacrifice, it is for the accomplishment of all objects, and the call is made already for the animal sacrifice by reason of the existence.

पशौ तु संस्कृते विधानात् ॥१२॥

12. On the other hand, in the animal which has been purified there is, by reason of its being laid down.

योगाद्वा यज्ञाय तद्विमोके विसर्गः स्यात् ॥१३॥

13. On the other hand, by reason of being engaged for the sacrifice, the discharge is on its completion.

निशि यज्ञे प्रकृतस्याप्रवृत्तिः स्यात्प्रत्यक्षशिष्टत्वात् ॥१४॥

14. In the nocturaal sacrifice, the Tantra of the model sacrifice ends by reason of the direct injunction.

कालवाक्यभेदाच्च तन्त्रभेदः स्यात् ॥१५॥

15. And by reason of the difference of time and text, there is a difference of Tantra.

वेद्युद्धननव्रतंविप्रतिषेधात्तदेव स्यात् ॥१६॥

16. The fast, observed in connection with the digging of the altar by reason of the prohibition shall remain the same.

तंत्रमद्ये विधानाद्वा तत्तन्त्रा सवनीयवत् ॥१७॥

17. By reason of its being ordained in one particular Tantra, its tantra is governed like that of a *savanīya* animal sacrifice.

वेगुण्यादिध्मबर्हेर्नसाधयेदग्न्यन्वाधानं च यदि देवातार्थम् ॥१८॥

18. By reason of the failure the fuel and grass would not accomplish it; and the re-establishment of fire, if it is for the deity.

अग्न्यन्वाधानं च यदि देवतार्थम् ॥१९॥

19. And the re-establishment of fire, if done for the object of the deity.

आरम्भणीया विकृतौ न स्यात्प्रकृतिकालमध्यत्वात् कृता पुनस्तदर्थेन ॥२०॥

20. The *ārambhaṇīyā* should not be performed in the modified sacrifice by reason of falling within the time of the model sacrifice; if done again, it will be for its object.

सकृदाऽऽरम्भसंयोगात् ॥२१॥

21. By reason of the connection with the commencement at one time.

स्याद्वा कालस्याशेषभूतत्वात् ॥२२॥

22. On the other hand, it may be performed by reason of the time being subordinate.

आरंभविभागाच्च ॥२३॥

23. And by reason of the division of the commencement.

विप्रतिषिद्धधर्माणां समवाये भूयसां स्यात्सधर्म्मकत्वम् ॥२४॥

24. When there is a combination of the conflicting characteristics, those of the majority of one type will prevail.

मुख्यं वा पूर्वचोदनाल्लोकवत् ॥२५॥

25. On the other hand, the first by reason of the first command as in ordinary life.

तथा चान्यार्थदर्शनम् ॥२६॥

26. And similarly there is another proof.

अङ्गगुणविरोधे च तादर्थ्यात् ॥२७॥

27. And in a conflict between the subordinate part and the quality (of the principal) by reason of its being for the object of it.

परिधेर्द्व्यर्थत्वाद भयधर्मा स्यात् ॥२८॥

28. The *paridhi* being used for two objects, partakes the characteristics of both.

यौप्यस्तु विरोधे स्यान्मुख्यानन्तर्यात् ॥२९॥

29. On the other hand, the characteristics of the sacrificial post shall prevail, if there be conflict by reason of its being close to the chief (principal).

इतरो वा तस्य तत्र विधानादुभयोश्चांगसंयोगः ॥३०॥

30. On the other hand, the other by reason of its being laid down there; both are connected with the parts.

पशुसवनीयेषु विकल्पः स्याद्वैकृतश्चेदुभयोरश्रुतिभूतत्वात् ॥३१॥

31. There is option in the *savanīya* animal; if there are characteristics of the modified sacrifice, by reason of both being not laid down.

पाशुकं वा तस्य वैशेषिकाम्नानात्तदनर्थकं विकल्पे स्यात् ॥३२॥

32. On the other hand, the Tantra of the animal sacrifice governs it, by reason of the special being laid down; it will be meaningless, if it be optional.

पशोश्च विप्रकर्षस्तन्त्रमध्ये विधानात् ॥३३॥

33. And there is a separation of the animal sacrifice by reason of its being laid down in the middle.

अपूर्वं च प्रकृतौ समानतन्त्रा चेदनित्यत्वादनर्थकं हि स्यात् ॥३४॥

34. And in the model sacrifice there will be no precedence, if the modified sacrifice is of the same Tantra; by reason of its having no permanent character, it will be meaningless.

अदिकश्च गुणः साधारणेऽविरोधात्कांस्यभोजिवदमुख्येऽपि ॥३५॥

35. In the common, the one with greater quality by reason of no opposition like a pupil eating in a vessel made of bell metal, though not principal.

तत्प्रवृत्त्या तु तन्त्रस्य नियमः स्याद्यथा पाशुकं सूक्तवाकेन ॥३६॥

36. On the other hand, with the application of that, the Tantra is laid down, just as in the puroḍāśa cake pertaining to the animal sacrifice, by the *sūktavāka*.

न वाऽविरोधात् ॥३७॥

37. No so, by reason of there being no inconsistency.

*अशास्त्रलक्षणत्वाच्च ॥३८॥

38. By reason of the peculiarities not enjoined by the scripture.

END OF PĀDA 2

***

PĀDA 3

विश्ववजिति वत्सत्वङ्नामधेयादितर थातन्त्रभूय त्वादहतं स्यात् ॥१॥

1. In a *viśvajit*, the calf's skin by reason of the *nāmadheya*; otherwise by reason of the majority of Tantra, the lower garment.

अविरोधो वा उपरिवासो हि वत्सत्वक् ॥२॥

2. On the other hand, there is no inconsistency; the calf's skin is the upper garment.

अनुनिर्वाप्येषु भूयस्त्वेन तन्त्रनियमः स्यच्छिष्ठकृद्दर्श नाच्च ॥३॥

3. In the subsequent offerings, with the majority the Tantra should be governed and by seeing the *sviṣṭakṛt*.

आगन्तुकत्वाद्वा स्वधर्मा स्याच्छुतिविशेषादितरस्य च मुख्यत्वात् ॥४॥

---

*In Śabara and भाट्टदीपिका, it is शास्त्र; but I have preferred the reading of other commentators.

4. On the other hand, by reason of being incomers, they are governed by their own characteristics and by the special text, the other being the principal.

स्वस्थानत्वाच्च ॥५॥

5. And by reason of its own order.

स्विष्टकृच्छ्रपणान्नेतिचेद्विकारः पवमानवत् ॥६॥

6. "If you say no, by reason of the *sviṣṭakṛt* offering", (the reply is that), the modification is like *pavamāna.*

अविकारो वा प्रकृतिवच्चोदनां प्रति भावाच्च ॥७॥

7. On the other hand, without modification like the model sacrifice by reason of its being a statement of the command.

एक कर्मणिशिष्टत्वाद्गुणानां सर्वकर्म स्यात् ॥८॥

8. In one act by reason of their being laid down, the subsdiaries are all to be performed.

एकार्थास्तुविकल्पेरन्समुच्चये ह्यावृत्तिः स्यात्प्रधानस्य ॥९॥

9. On the other hand, those that have one object in view may be optionally used; in combination, there will be a repetition of the principal.

अभ्यस्येतार्थवत्त्वादिति चेत् ॥१०॥

10. 'It should be repeated by reason of its being for the purpose' if you say.

नाश्रुतत्वाद्धि विकल्पवच्चदर्शयति कालांतरेऽर्थवत्त्वं स्यात् ॥११॥

11. Not so, by reason of its being not laid down; the optional use is seen; and it may be of use in course of time.

सतिचाभ्यासशास्त्रत्वात् ॥

And where there is repetition, it should be done by reason of its being so laid down.

प्रायश्चित्तेशुचैकार्थ्यान्निष्पन्नेनाभिसंयोगस्तस्मात् सर्वस्य निर्घातः ॥१२॥

12. And in the expiatory rites by reason of the unity of the object, there is a connection with the accomplished (fault); therefore the whole (fault) is removed (by one).

समुच्चयस्तु दोषार्थः ॥१३॥

13. There is a combination for removal of fault (sin).

मंत्राणांकर्मसंयोगः स्वधर्मेण प्रयोगः स्यादधर्मस्य तन्निमित्तत्वात् ॥१४॥

14. The mantras are connected with the action; they are to be applied with their own characteristics, because the characteristics are for their object.

विद्यांप्रतिविधानाद्वा सर्वकारणं प्रयोगः स्यात् कर्मार्थत्वात् प्रयोगस्य ॥१५॥

15. On the other hand, by reason of being laid down for the object of knowledge, the application should be in all cases, because the application is for the object of the action.

भाषास्वरोपदेशेऐरवत् पपरायवचनपपरतिश्षेधः ॥१६॥

16. By reason of the direction of *bhāṣāsvara* like *er*, there is a prohibition of the original *svara*.

मंत्रोपदेशोवा न भाषिकस्य प्रायोपपत्तेर्भाषिकश्रुतिः ॥१७॥

17. On the other hand, it is a direction as regards mantra but not as regards modulation. The text as to *swar* is (based), by reason of the excellent development.

विकारः कारणाग्रहणे तन्यायत्वाद दृष्टेऽप्येवम् ॥१८॥

18. There is a modification on not accepting the reason; by reason of its propriety, it is so even in the seen.

तदुत्पत्तेर्वा प्रवचनलक्षणत्वात् ॥१९॥

19. On the other hand, by its origin by reason of the characteristics of being pronounced as directed.

मन्त्राणां करणार्थत्वान्मन्त्रान्तेन कर्मादिसन्निपातः स्यात्सर्वस्य वचनार्थत्वात् ॥२०॥

20. The mantras being for the act, the connection of the commencement of the action is with the end of the mantra; the whole of it is for the meaning of the text.

सन्ततवचनाद्धारायामादिसंयोगः ॥२१॥

21. By reason of the word 'immediate' in *dhārā*, the connection with the beginning will suffice.

कर्मसन्तानो वा नानाकर्मत्वादितरस्याशक्यत्वात् ॥२२॥

22. On the other hand, there is a series of acts, by reason of the variety of acts, because of the incapacity of the other.

आघारे च दीर्घधारत्वात् ॥२३॥

23. And in sprinkling with ghee by reason of long flow.

मन्त्राणां सन्निपातित्वादेकार्थानांविकल्पः स्यात् ॥२४॥

24. By reason of the mantras being associated with an act indirectly and having one object in view, there is an option.

संख्याविहितेषु समुच्चयोऽसन्निपातित्वात् ॥२५॥

25. In those acts where number is laid down, there is a combination by reason of there being no connection (with the act).

ब्राह्मणविहितेषु च संख्यावत्सर्वेषामुपदिष्ठत्वात् ॥२६॥

26. And in those *mantras* which have been laid down in the *brāhmaṇa*, there is a combination like the number, by reason of all being laid down.

याज्यावषट्कारयोश्च समुच्चयदर्शनं तद्वत् ॥२७॥

27. And there is seen combination of *yājyā* and *vaṣaṭkāra* similarly.

विकल्पो वा समुच्चयस्याश्रुतित्वात् ॥२८॥

28. On the other hand, there is an option because combination is no where laid down.

गुणार्थत्वादुपदेशस्य ॥२९॥

29. By reason of being the object of the quality, there is a direction.

वषट्कारे नानार्थत्वात्समुच्चयो हौत्रास्तु विकल्पेरन्नेकार्थत्वात् ॥३०॥

30. There is a combination in the *vaṣaṭkāra* by reason of its being for manifold objects; on the other hand, mantras pertaining to the *hotā* may be optionally used, by reason of their being for one object.

क्रियमाणानुवादित्वात् समुच्चयो वा हौत्राणाम् ॥३१॥

31. On the other hand, by reason of the statement of the acts to be done, the principle of combination to the mantras relating to the Hotā.

समुच्चयं च दर्शयति ॥३२॥

32. And it shows combination.

END OF PĀDA 3

***

PĀDA IV

जपाश्चाकर्मसंयुक्ताः स्तुत्याशीरभिधानाश्च याजमानेषु समुच्चयः स्यादाशीःपृथक्त्वात् ॥१॥

1. And the *japa mantras* are not connected with any act and are in praise, benediction and description; the principle of combination applies to the mantras pertaining to the sacrificer by reason of the separation of the benediction.

समुच्चयं च दर्शयति ॥२॥

2. And it shows combination.

याज्यानुवाक्यासु तु विकल्पः स्याद्देवतोपलक्षणार्थत्वात् ॥३॥

3. On the other hand, there is option in *yājyā* and *anuvākya* by reason of their being for pointing out the god.

लिङ्गदर्शनाच्च ॥४॥

4. And by seeing the *liṅga.*

क्रयेषु तु विकल्पः स्यादेकार्थत्वात् ॥५॥

5. On the other hand, there is option in the purchase by reason of its being for one object.

समुच्चयो वा प्रयोगद्रव्यसमवायात् ॥६॥

6. On the other hand, there is a combination by reason of the union of the commodities of purchase.

समुच्चयञ्चदर्शयति् ॥७॥

7. And it shows combination.

संस्कारे च तत्प्रधानत्वात् ॥८॥

8. And in the purificatory rite by reason of its being principal.

संख्यासु तु विकल्पः स्याच्छ्रुतिप्रतिषेधात् ॥९॥

9. On the other hand, there is option in the number by reason of the contradiction in the text.

द्रव्यविकारात्तु पूर्ववदर्थकर्म स्यात्तया विकल्पेन नियमप्रधानत्वात् ॥१०॥

10. By reason of the modification of the substance, it is an essential act; it is to be done at the option, because the rule is principal.

द्रव्यत्वेऽपि समुच्चयो द्रव्यस्य कर्मनिष्पत्तेः प्रतिपशु कर्मभेदादेवं सति यथाप्रकृति ॥११॥

11. Also in the nature of the substance, there is a combination by reason of the accomplishment of the act; there being difference of the acts with each animal, the procedure (is) just as (it is) in the model sacrifice.

कपालेऽपि तथेतिचेत् ॥१२॥

12. "In the pans also, similarly" if you say.

न कर्मणः परार्थत्वात् ॥१३॥

13. Not so, by reason of the act being for the object of another.

प्रतिपत्तिस्तु शेषत्वात् ॥१४॥

14. On the other hand, it is a final disposal by reason of its being a subordinate act.

शृतेऽपि पूर्ववत्स्यात् ॥१५॥

15. In the boiled milk also, as in the preceding.

विकल्पोऽन्वर्थकर्मनियमप्रधानत्वाच्छेपे च कर्मकार्यसमवायात्तस्मात्तेनार्थकर्म स्यात् ॥१६॥

16. It is optional, by reason of the rule of the essential act being principal; and in the subordinate, by reason of the act connected with the extraordinary principle, it is an essential act.

उखायां काम्यनित्यसमुच्चयो नियोगे कामदर्शनात् ॥१७॥

17. In an *ukhā* fire, there is a combination of the permanent and the desire-accomplishing acts, by seeing the connection of desire with the command.

असति चासंस्कृतेषु कर्म स्यात् ॥

And in the absence, the sacrifice will be in the non-consecrated fire.

तस्यच देवतार्थत्वात् ॥१८॥

18. And of its being for the deity.

विकारो वा नित्यस्याग्नेः काम्येन तदुक्तहेतुः ॥१९॥

19. On the other hand, it is a modification of the permanent fire, with the desire, the above said reason is connected.

वचनादसंस्कृतेषु कर्म स्यात्* ॥२०॥

*In Śabara and खंडदेव, there is 'स्यादिति'.

20. Under a text, there can be a sacrifice in an unconsecrated fire.

संसर्गे चापि दोषः स्यात् ॥२१॥

21. And in contact also, there is wrong.

वचनादिति चेदथेतरस्मिन्नुत्सर्गापरिग्रहः कर्मणःकृतत्वात् ॥२२॥

22. 'Under a text' if you say; so also in the other case, there is offering without acceptance of the deity, by reason of the act having been done.

स आहवनीयः स्यादाहुतिसंयोगात् ॥२३॥

23. It is the *āhavanīya* fire, by reason of the connection with the offering.

अन्यो वोद्धृत्याहरणात् तस्मिन्त्संस्कारकर्म शिष्टत्वात् ॥२४॥

24. On the other hand, it is other than the *āhavanīya* fire, by reason of getting it from elsewhere; in it there is purificatory rite by reason of its being laid down.

स्थानात्तु परिलुप्येरन् ॥२५॥

25. By reason of the place, they are omitted.

नित्यधारणे विकल्पो न ह्यकस्मात्प्रतिषेधः स्यात् ॥२६॥

26. There is option in tying it always; there is no prohibition for no reason.

नित्यधारणाद्वा प्रतिषेधो गतश्रियः ॥२७॥

27. On the other hand, by reason of tying it always, there is a prohibition for one who has lost fortune.

परार्थान्येकः प्रतियंतिवत् सत्राहीनयो यजमानगणेऽनियमोऽविशेषात ॥२८॥

28. Those that are for the purpose of another like the one going to every side, in an assembly of sacrificers in connection with the *satra* and *ahīna*; there is no rule, by reason of there being nothing special.

मुख्यो वाऽविप्रतिषेधात् ॥२९॥

29. On the other hand, the master of the sacrifice should do it, by reason of the prohibition.

सत्रे गृहपतिरसंयोगाद्धौत्रवदाम्नायवचनाच्च ॥३०॥

30. In a *satra* the master of the house by reason of there being no connection; and like the act pertaining to a *hotā*, by reason of the word of the scripture.

सर्वैः वा तदर्थत्वात् ॥३१॥

31. On the other hand by all, by reason of that being for them.

विप्रतिषेधे परम् ॥३२॥

32. When there is a conflict, the other (prevails).

हौत्रे परार्थत्वात् ॥३३॥

33. In the ceremonies pertaining to a hotā priest, by reason of his being for another.

वचनं परम् ॥३४॥

34. The text is other.

प्रभुत्वादार्त्विज्यं सर्ववर्णानां स्यात् ॥३५॥

35. By reason of being able, all castes are entitled to officiate as priests.

स्मृतेर्वा स्याद्ब्राह्मणानाम् ॥३६॥

36. On the other hand, the Brāhmaṇas by reason of the tradition.

फलचमसविधानाच्चेतरेषाम् ॥३७॥

37. By reason of *phalacamasa* being ordained in the case of others.

सान्नाय्येप्येवं प्रतिषेधः सौमपीयहेतुत्वात् ॥३८॥

38. So there is also a prohibition in *sannāya*, by reason of the soma drink.

चतुर्धाकरणे च निर्देशात् ॥३९॥

39. And by direction, in dividing into 4 parts.

अन्वाहार्य्ये च दर्शनात् ॥४०॥

40. And by seeing in the monthly wages.

END OF PĀDA 4

***

END OF ADHYĀYA XII

End of the Pūrva Mīmāṃsā Sūtras of Jaiminī